The Three Rs

Renewing the Spirit
Restoring the Soul
Reconstructing the Body

Amy Sever

Published by Three Rs Publishing

Published in association with Amazon Books.

Except where otherwise indicated, Scripture quotations are taken from THE HOLY BIBLE, NEW INTERNATIONAL VERSION® (NIV®), Copyright 1973, 1978, 1984 by International Bible Society. Used by permission of Zondervan Bible Publishers.

[1]Dedication quote taken from *Love You Forever* by Robert Munsch.

All other references are noted when they are used in the book.

Cover Design: Steve Sever with oversight by Nicole Campbell, www.NicoleCampbellCreative.com

Cover Photo: Robert Suddarth Photography

Logo Design & Interior Design: Steve Sever

Editing: Steve Sever, Dana Ballard, Glenn Polk

For more information about the author and her ministry, visit www.AmySever.com

ISBN-13: 978-1496134561

ISBN-10: 1496134567

Dedication

This book is dedicated to my beautiful daughter Savannah.
You will always be my greatest accomplishment!
"I will love you forever. I'll like you for always.
As long as I'm living, my baby you'll be."

Contents

Part Two: Restoring the Soul – continued

Part Three: Reconstructing the Body

Renewing the Spirit,

Restoring the Soul,

Reconstructing the Body

Prologue

As I walked along the path back to my cabin that night, I reflected on the last several days of my special trip. My long black dress stuck to my legs in the hot, humid air of the Dominican Republic. I could smell the sea air, mixed with the hibiscus flowers that lined the path. The full moon was casting a soft white glow on the palm trees and rocks along the trail back from the resort pub and dance floor. The place of my dream vacation was an all-inclusive resort, and my family was at the end of our week in paradise. This trip was my reward for graduating from high school with honors and the first real vacation we had taken as a family since the sudden and tragic death of my twin brother six years earlier.

On October 7th, 1984, I watched in horror as my twin brother fell 48 feet onto a concrete floor directly in front of me. It was two weeks before our 13th birthday. Time stood still as I watched the life ebb from my beloved brother, lying there on the floor. Jeff's death had almost ripped apart our family. It had altered each of our lives dramatically. We would never have survived that tragedy as a family, had we not leaned heavily on God. We all knew Jeff believed in Jesus as Savior and Lord, and he was in Heaven. Even though I knew I would see him again someday, Jeff's death had profoundly affected me. At first, I was extremely suicidal. Jeff was my twin. He and I had an incredible relationship. I can't remember us ever having a cross word. He was my very best friend and my confidant. He was *my other half!* As I saw his life slipping away that day, I felt like *half of me* was dying. I could think of nothing else but that I wanted to be with him...

As the hours turned to days, weeks and months, I forced the suicidal thoughts aside, and grew close to the Lord instead. I became a spiritual rock for my family. I held my family together in that first year, and every Sunday I was the first one up and dressed. I had my Bible in my hand and waited for my parents to take me to church. Eventually, the healing hands of time had gently begun to allow us to live again. Through the years, my family became more stable. I had been a good daughter to my parents. I had never wanted to see them hurt again. I made sure that I would always contribute positively in every way. I had always been a great student and never gave them any trouble.

...On this night though, I was a bit ashamed at how what I thought was innocent flirting with Julius had seemed to become more sexual. The dark dance floor was full of people as Julius pulled me into his strong body. And although I was taken aback, I allowed it. As a tingle went up my spine, I was surprised that I even enjoyed the "almost dangerous" attention. I was 18, and beginning to realize that older men were attracted to me.

Five days earlier, on the afternoon of our arrival, Julius was giving the orientation to the resort. As he spoke to the new group of travelers, I noticed that he was eyeing me intently. He seemed fixated, and I felt flattered. He was obviously someone in charge and it made me feel special.

He and I had been flirting all week. He was much older than I was, and I was definitely intrigued. There was something about him that fascinated me. He seemed a bit reckless. As I moved with him on the dance floor this final night, he pulled me into his hips and kissed me hard. At that moment, I realized I was glad it would be the last time I was in proximity to this dark stranger with newly aggressive lips and hands. I was embarrassed at the thought of my dad or older brother walking into that little dance pub and seeing me acting so out of character. I left the club that night feeling a little cheap.

Suddenly, I was grabbed from behind. An arm reached around my throat. As I choked, I heard Julius' low, growling voice, "You've been teasing me all week sweetheart. Now it is time to pay up!" I couldn't move. I tasted the salt of his sweaty palm as he clasped my mouth to keep me from screaming, and felt the cold blade of the knife at my throat. Fear gripped me as I looked around desperately trying to see someone, anyone! No one was near. The beautiful moonlit path full of flowers and trees was completely empty. They would be the only witnesses of my silent pleas for help...

Introduction

I wrote *The Three Rs* seminar workbook 12 years ago. As I began speaking and ministering, I knew this was the desire of my heart. God planted this message in my spirit, and gave me a taste of what it feels like to watch Him set people free through the effective use of Biblically sound knowledge.

At the time, I also realized that I had more to "work through" in my own life. In the last 12 years, the message has been strengthened and enhanced by the natural progression of growth, along with the experiences of building a business, raising a child, and walking through many new seasons.

I am thankful for the anonymity of these 12 years. During this prolonged season of waiting, I now understand the value of the structure and character building seasons of delay. In what seemed like a 12 year pause in a ministry that I know God gave me, and a necessary message to the Body of Christ, God was allowing me a protected, undisturbed, and sacred space to finish healing emotionally, as well as time to mature into this ministry.

As I combined the previous information together with the wisdom of another decade with the Lord, I realized that so many are still bound by the same strongholds they were years ago. I realized that I needed to revisit the past and publish this book.

However, in order for you to truly benefit from this book, there are some premises you need to know. My prayer is that you allow me the privilege of sharing my story, and that you will take these truths at face value, at least during your journey with me through these pages.

Growing up in the buckle of the Bible Belt in West Texas has been very beneficial to me when it comes to my knowledge of the Holy Scriptures. It has afforded me some foundational belief systems and core values that are immoveable.

As I have traveled around the world and had the pleasure of meeting wonderful people from other countries and other cultures, I have come to understand there are so many different levels of Biblical understanding. Growing up with the Word of God in my hands has shaped my belief systems. It has allowed me the opportunity to share my heart and experiences from a Biblical World View. If you are already familiar with the Bible, then the scripture will be familiar.

If you are not familiar with the Bible, this book is still for you! It will definitely be a learning experience. It will not only give you a foundational working knowledge of the scriptures, but also a deep and inexhaustible love for the Word of God.

I have inserted blank pages every few chapters, so you can have a place to write notes and reflections. You may have particular scriptures that stand out for you, and you need an easy reference to go back and find them to memorize them. Or a particular chapter may bring the names of people to mind, for any number of reasons... and you may want to write them down. Journal your thoughts. My prayer is for this book to become a tool for you – a "spiritual handbook" if you will. So feel free to mark it up and utilize these blank pages. That's what they are there for!

The Premises

If you can allow me these 7 foundational truths, then regardless of your previous background, this book will hold more meaning for you. It is full of scripture. So many people read the Bible and it makes no sense to them. Hopefully we can tie some things together for you and make it relevant to your life. If you are familiar with the Bible, then please let it continue to challenge and transform you.

Premise 1) The Bible is the actual Word of God - The Creator of the Universe. The Bible is 66 books, written across 1600 years, through the hands of 40 men. There are no discrepancies and it is completely seamless. It is indeed, the one book to which we must all pay close attention. If I'm wrong and it is "just another good book", then I have lived a better life for following its guidelines and principles. But If I am right, then my eternal salvation depends on it. I am not willing to bet against the oldest and most read book on earth. I hope you feel the same way!

Premise 2) According to the Bible, there are two forces at work in each of our lives; Good and Evil. And those two forces have real entities controlling them; God and Satan.

Premise 3) God is a triune being; God the Father, Jesus the Son, and the Holy Spirit. For our purposes I will give you some additional names for each:

- **God**: The Father, Jehovah, Yahweh, The Lord, The Most High.

- **Jesus**: Yeshua, Son of God, Son of man, Messiah, Prince of Peace, Redeemer, High Priest, King of Kings and the Word. He is currently our Intercessor, meaning He sits at the right hand of the Father and petitions Him on our behalf.

- **Holy Spirit**: The Comforter, The Counselor, Holy Ghost, The Spirit of Truth.

Premise 4) There is a cosmic battle for the souls of mankind, and *you* are at the center of that battle! *You* are on the mind of God ...even as you are reading at this very moment!

Premise 5) Unfortunately, you also have an enemy. The devil is real. And he *really does* want to destroy you. I will spend more time on this premise because Satan's primary tactic is to try and make *YOU* believe he does not exist. He does. And I want to make sure you know it. Here are a few other names and descriptions of the devil:

- **Lucifer**: This was his original name when he was created with the other angels and was still the most beautiful angelic being ever created. He is also known as the dragon, the beast, father of lies, the prince of the power of the air, the god of this world, the angel of light, your enemy, the enemy of your soul and obviously, Satan.

> The kingdom of darkness is absolutely real, and is made up of a hierarchy just like any government.

Throughout this book you will see me refer to Satan by all of his names, but most often I just use the name "Satan". Here's what I want you to know. When I say "Satan is trying *this* with you..." or "Satan is doing *that to you*...", I am not actually referring to the created being, Lucifer. The general reference to "Satan" in the book is a simplified way of referring to the kingdom of darkness.

There are angels and there are demons. The kingdom of darkness is absolutely real, and is made up of a hierarchy just like any government. Earth is divided into kingdoms spiritually just like it is divided into physical nations.

The book of Daniel makes reference to "the prince of the Persian kingdom" (see Daniel 10:13). There are principalities controlled by princes. And there are 16 strongmen that control an army of lesser demons.   These names of the strongmen have specific names and purposes. I cover all of that in my seminars.

All in all, Satan's army on earth is made up of one-third of the angels that rebelled along with Satan. You'll find various references to the story of the rebellion in Genesis 1:31, Isaiah 14:12, Luke 10:18 and Revelation 9:1. And evidence clearly points to a third of the angels falling with Satan in Hebrews 12:22 and Revelation 12:3-9.   So, anytime I speak of Satan in the book, mostly I'm using his name as a catch-all for the havoc being perpetrated on the earth by the demons in his army.   And if I'm freaking you out, just know that the other *two-thirds* of the angels remained with God and are here for our service and protection! All *we* have to do is *know how to utilize them* to protect ourselves. And *THAT* is what this book is about!

Incidentally, this one foundational premise explains why so many people wonder "*why a loving God would allow bad things to happen to good people*". He doesn't. He *never* has. What happens to any of us is at the center of our own free will – which I elaborate on in the book. God created the heavens and the earth. And right now, Satan controls the earth.   Until the return of Christ, the earth is in the grasp and control of this fallen angel;   the god of this world.

...not only is the devil very real, but remember, he is a liar. ...one of his principle tactics is to try and convince you that *he does not exist!*

You see, not only is the devil very real, but remember, he is a liar. His plans and schemes to ensnare us do not change. As I said already, one of his principle tactics is to try and convince you that *he does not exist!*   I hope you understand how huge that one statement is. He wants us to think we are dealing with genetic or emotional problems. If he can move us to medicate ourselves through prescription drugs and psychologists, then we may not ever seek THE TRUTH that will set us free!

 I am continually stunned at how many Christians are addicted to anti-depressants, sleep aids and more.   I realize there are circumstances where those things are needed. However, when I look at the vast overuse of prescription drugs, it's clearly one of the indicators that we as Christians have "missed the mark." We seek *our* doctors and *our* counselors more than we seek *THE* Counselor, *THE* Comforter, and *THE* Healer.

When Christ comes back, all things change. But for now, the devil is in charge. Christ came the first time to bridge the gap between Heaven and earth, thus allowing us a way to create relationship with the Father, our Creator. I will give you more on this later.

Premise 6) The Bible is a celestial handbook. It is a love letter from the Creator of the Universe to each of us. It was supernaturally written, and it contains everything we need to live abundant lives on the earth now, and afterward as we step into eternity. We are not human beings having a "spiritual experience." We are spiritual beings, having a "human experience."

Premise 7) You and I will spend eternity in one of two places; Heaven or hell. And God loves us *so* much that he gave us the power to choose. He gave us *free will*. He also made a way for us to choose to spend eternity with Him by sending His Son Jesus to die for the sins of mankind.

> *For God so loved the world that He gave His only begotten son, that whosoever believeth in Him should not perish, but have everlasting life.* ~ John 3:16.

Renewing the Spirit, **Restoring the Soul**, and **Reconstructing the Body** – *The Three Rs* – is a book about my journey from bondage to freedom. The Lord used another ministry at the time, to expose me to some of these concepts and initiate my freedom. Some of the information in the following chapters comes from what I began learning there. I would like to personally thank Joe and Sydna Hamilton and Toni Ridley for their roles in that experience. I would also like to thank my husband, Steve, for the extraordinary and supernatural wisdom and leadership he exhibited on a very dark night in my life. It was a deliverance from demons that would rival a movie scene. Later in the book, I will go into depth about not only my deliverance, but also the particular strongholds that plagued my soul, and how they had a legal right to occupy my body.

Right now though, I would like to thank my Lord and Savior Jesus Christ for seeing me through that deliverance, for His boundless grace and mercy, and for the blood He shed to set me free. Hallelujah!

I would also like to thank my parents, Glenn and Twila Polk for always believing in me and praying this book – and thus my ministry – into existence. I love you!

Mostly, I want to thank YOU for taking this journey with me. I thank you for being willing to follow me into my past. And hopefully – through my story – allow the enemy's plans against you to, *not only* be exposed, but completely thwarted in your life! I would like to thank you in advance for the courage it will take to make it through this *whole book.* I realize it is a large undertaking. But I do believe it can be life-changing. And *please*, if you have made it this far, keep reading until you finish the last "Amen."

I must tell you that Satan *does not* want you to read this book! He would just as soon keep you blind to knowledge that will unlock your destiny of freedom in Christ.

I believe the keys to your health, as well as your spiritual well-being, and even your financial prosperity are hidden in the following pages. But, you *must* understand that you need to stay in prayer for yourself ...and possibly find an intercessor while you journey through the following chapters. As a matter of fact, let me pray for you now...

> ...the keys to your health, as well as your spiritual well-being, and even your financial prosperity are hidden in the following pages.

"Father, I come to you in the matchless name of my Lord and Savior Jesus Christ. I come not in my own righteousness, but in the righteousness purchased by your Son's death on the cross for me. I pray for the one who is reading this right now. I ask for a spirit of wisdom and revelation to rest on them as they read your words of truth. I claim Isaiah 61 over my life right now. *'The Spirit of the Sovereign Lord is on me, because the Lord has anointed me to preach good news to the poor. He has sent me to bind up the brokenhearted, to proclaim freedom for the captives and release from darkness for the prisoners, to proclaim the year of the Lord's favor and the day of vengeance of our God, to comfort all who mourn, and provide for those who grieve in Zion - to bestow on them a crown of beauty instead of ashes, the oil of gladness instead of mourning, and a garment of praise instead of a spirit of despair."* Your Word says that you *"have given me the keys to the kingdom of Heaven; whatever I bind on earth will be bound in Heaven, and whatever I loose on earth will be loosed in Heaven...'* So I bind every evil spirit in the name of Jesus. And I loose a heavenly knowledge. As those who are reading this book work through these pages, I ask that the grace and mercy of Jesus reign in their hearts and minds. I pray for release of all things that are keeping them bound in any way. I break every chain and demand release for every captive. I thank you that you have given me '...*authority to tread over serpents and scorpions'.* I thank you for your Word that is *'living and active. Sharper than any double edged sword, it penetrates even to dividing soul and spirit, joints and marrow; it judges the thoughts and attitudes of the heart. Nothing in all creation is hidden from [your] sight. Everything is uncovered and laid bare before [your] eyes...'* I thank You that every scheme of the enemy will indeed be uncovered and laid bare before You. This knowledge has set me free, and I pray for that same freedom to encompass this precious life now. In Jesus' mighty name I pray, Amen."

I realize you may be thinking, *"Wow! That was weird! And more than a little heavy!"* Well, yes ...it is. And I can't apologize for it. I am asking you to permit me to get weird and heavy at times. I will share a lot of my journey with you. Most people would never be so transparent, but I believe this transparency through testimony is necessary to help you understand how it all works together. And *nothing* sets up victory and freedom more than raw, authentic truth. Jesus said it.

You shall know the truth, and the truth shall set you free.
~ John 8:32

My prayer is that this information frees you up in such a powerful and comprehensive way that He is all you will *ever* need. I believe that is the way Jesus intended it.

My journey – while so painful and ugly at times - has been a blessing from God. I remember the Lord speaking to me very clearly saying, *"Amy, when you walk through these things ...and you actually make it to the other side, you gain keys. And I say to you, congratulations beloved daughter. Now go take those keys and unlock other people's prisons. You have authority to collapse time frames. The years it took you to walk through your journey into freedom will only take days or weeks for those coming after you."*

Sometimes I feel like a janitor. The janitor in my elementary school had a whole batch of keys that jingled at his side. He was confident that he could open any door of the school if necessary. Well that is exactly how I feel. Praise God for His healing power! My trip represented in these pages was arduous, but I'm thankful for it. And I know now that His constant presence makes my trip easier.

During your time with me, I am going to ask you to take the seven premises you read earlier and relax into them as being Truths. I believe the Lord will do the exact same thing for you as He did for me. I believe you too can begin to enjoy your own life journey into freedom.

And I hope you take comfort knowing that someone is walking in front of you with a handful of keys to unlock the doors looming ahead...

Notes and Reflections

Part One
Renewing the Spirit

Chapter
1   ...The Spirit

The theme scripture for this book is from Thessalonians:

> *May God himself, the God of peace, sanctify you through and through. May your whole spirit, soul and body be kept blameless at the coming of our Lord Jesus Christ. The one who calls you is faithful and He will do it.*
> ~ 1 Thessalonians 5:23-24

There are also some other key scriptures for the book:

> *The thief comes to steal, kill and destroy. But I have come that they might have life and that more abundantly.*
> ~ John 10:10.

> *He whom the Son sets free is free indeed. ~ John 8:36*

Unfortunately, the Biblical information that allows this extraordinary freedom and access to the promises of God is not taught in schools, families, or even most churches. Even though I grew up in church, sang in the choir, taught Sunday School, went on mission trips, and was Spirit-filled... I didn't learn this life-changing, life-giving information until I was 30 ...after years of damage to my soul.

I thought I was going to be "broken" forever. I was continuously falling into patterns of iniquity and then quietly, desperately living with guilt and shame. That was a familiar cycle that characterized my life. I was overweight, depressed, lethargic, and I couldn't sleep. When I *did* fall asleep I was plagued by nightmares. I was miserable, even though I was all-the-while going through the motions of everyday life. I had a wonderful husband and a beautiful daughter. I went to church twice a week. Yet I had absolutely no joy.

The crazy thing is that I was saved at age 10! I *knew* Jesus. I was filled with the Holy Spirit at age 17. I could *"speak with the tongues of angels,"* but I had no love. I loved God, but I did not love myself.

In fact, quite the opposite was true. I was filled with self-hate. I felt like I was living a lie. I was the ultimate religious hypocrite. Anytime I would begin to try to reach out to God, guilt would slam at my conscience with such force that it left me crumpled at the throne and immediately backing away from His loving, outstretched arms. Whenever I read John 10:10 and my eyes floated across *"life more abundantly,"* I winced with internal pain. My heart literally *ached*. Physically. It actually *ached*.

> I did not realize I was living out the plans and schemes of Lucifer ...the father of lies. I knew of Satan, but had no idea the role he was playing in my own life.

I did not realize I was living out the plans and schemes of Lucifer ...the father of lies. I knew of Satan, but had no idea the role he was playing in my own life. I never realized how *real* spiritual warfare really is. The scriptures regarding deliverance were never taught in our small church in my little hometown. I had no idea that there was demonic influence working behind the spiritual scenes in order to keep me completely bound up and useless in the Body of Christ. It never occurred to me that a third of Jesus' ministry was delivering people who were *"harassed and helpless"* against an unseen enemy.

Most people are in that category. They are locked in the same cycles of sin, guilt, and shame that I was. That enemy still exists. And he is more aggressive now than ever before.

> Be self-controlled and alert. Your enemy the devil prowls around like a roaring lion looking for someone to devour.
> ~ 1 Peter 5:8

> ...he is filled with fury, because he knows that his time is short. ~ Revelation 12:12.

The thief comes to steal, kill and destroy. But I have come that they might have life and that more abundantly. ~ John 10:10

You see, this scripture sums it up perfectly. We have an enemy. And we also have a Savior that came to give us abundant life.

If Christ's promise was life more abundantly, then the problem is not on His end. The Bible states that:

All His promises are yes and amen. ~ 2 Corinthians 1:20

...The Lord is faithful to all his promises and loving toward all he has made. ~ Psalm 145:13

There are well over 300 promises in Scripture. However, when I observed my own life, I came to the conclusion that the problem was that I *knew* those promises, but did not have the *revelation knowledge* or the *spiritual wisdom* to access them...

My people perish for lack of knowledge. ~ Hosea 4:6

Most people are doing just that. We perish emotionally, spiritually, psychologically, and financially. We are perishing physically as well. I have a strong sense that most people have let their dreams of abundance die inside of them far too early in life. It has often been said that unfulfilled dreams are the primary occupants of any cemetery.

Even though this is the exact plight of most people, it certainly doesn't have to be. We can change that! We do not have to live in lack. We are children of the Most High! We are sons and daughters of God! We *can choose* to live that abundant life. We can live in spiritual, emotional, physical and financial health and abundance. It is our God-given right and inheritance. God wants us to live abundantly!

He who began a good work in you will be faithful to complete it. ~ Philippians 1:6

This passage means that we can have confidence that God *will finish* the work He started in us. This is good news! I pray the chapters of this book will assist in that work.

So please permit me to start you on that same journey that began in my life so many years ago, as I learned some very basic, but crucial information about how we are created. I want to take you back to this passage:

> *May God himself, the God of peace, sanctify you through and through. May your whole* **spirit, soul** *and* **body** *be kept blameless at the coming of our Lord Jesus Christ. The one who calls you is faithful and He will do it.*
> ~ 1 Thessalonians 5:13

The Bible distinctly differentiates the spirit from the soul. It is pretty easy to understand that the body is different, but knowing it about the spirit and the soul is a little more difficult. I never received this teaching in all my years in church, so let's start there...

The first "R" in the title of this book is "Renewing the Spirit." The reason behind that is scriptural and we will get to that in a moment. But for now, let's explore what the spirit is.

The North American English Dictionary defines the spirit as "the vital life force that characterizes a human being as being alive." The spirit is that part of us that will continue to live eternally beyond the death of our physical bodies.

> *...and the dust returns to the ground it came from, and the spirit returns to God who gave it.* ~ Ecclesiastes 12:7

> When Christ was crucified, *Jesus called out with a loud voice, "Father, into your hands I commit my spirit." When He had said this, He breathed His last.* ~ Luke 23:46

The spirit is that part of man where God dwells. It is God's temple inside your body. It is a special place in the center of your being. Most people have never really thought about the fact that there is an actual space inside the human body where our spirit resides. However, the Bible is very clear on this subject.

As science constantly advances to catch up with scripture, it continues to validate God's Word. Two of the greatest scientific and physical discoveries are the roles of the solar plexus and the pineal gland inside our bodies.

> The spirit is ...the highest element of man. It's the most powerful part of our being, capable of tapping into the very heart and mind of God.

The spirit has a purpose as the highest element of man. It's the most powerful part of our being, capable of tapping into the very heart and mind of God. It is our spirit that hears the voice of God!   It is by the spirit that we understand and comprehend spiritual truths. The Word says;

> *However, as it is written: "No eye has seen, no ear has heard, no mind has conceived what God has prepared for those who love him - but God has revealed it to us by His Spirit.   The Spirit searches all things, even the deep things of God.   For **who among men knows the thoughts of a man except the man's spirit within him?**   In the same way, no one knows the thoughts of God except the Spirit of God.   We have not received the spirit of the world but the Spirit who is from God, that we may understand what God has freely given us. This is what we speak, not in words taught us by human wisdom but in words taught by the Spirit, expressing spiritual truths in spiritual words.   The man without the Spirit does not accept the things that come from the Spirit of God, for they are foolishness to him, and he cannot understand them, because they are spiritually discerned...*
> ~ 1 Corinthians 2:9-16

Let's examine this beloved passage and look at all the "spirit" words. Notice that when the apostle Paul wrote this, he refers to the Spirit of God with a capital "**S**".   When he refers to *our* spirits, he refers to them with a small "**s**". Read this passage several times. Let it sink in. God is Spirit, and He speaks to us in our spirits ...not our minds. It comes from a different place altogether. The voice of God is more of an "impression." It is a still small voice that feels more like a "nudging" in the center of your body. Personally, I believe the solar plexus is the location of the spirit. When you research that mass of nerves, it lends itself to that possibility.

Chapter 2 ...Pitfalls

There are two pitfalls regarding hearing the voice of God.

The first is that people don't think God speaks. They can't hear Him at all. These people don't understand why they can't hear God and think others are crazy when they talk about God speaking to them. I talk to so many people who don't feel like God speaks to them. I tell them that God *is* speaking, but we may be listening with our ears instead of our spirits. In the earlier passage, the Bible makes it clear that in order to *"know the thoughts of God"* we have to listen with our spirits.

The second is that people are tapping into the pineal gland (known in some religions as the third eye) and the solar plexus and they are communicating with other dimensions (spirit guides), and what they *think* is God could actually be "the angel of light." You see, our bodies are designed to communicate spiritually. The pineal gland and the solar plexus are the "spiritual aspects of the brain and body." This little organ in the brain and the mass of nerves in the center of the body allow us to communicate physically with the spiritual realm.

So, when people without the Spirit are working to communicate with other dimensions, they are indeed hearing voices. Voices they believe are a higher consciousness, the universe, etc. ...and they can mistake those things for The Lord. Just because they hear a voice or communicate with a being from another dimension, it doesn't mean they are communicating with God the Father.

> *Dear friends, do not believe every spirit, but test the spirits to see whether they are from God, because many false prophets have gone out into the world. This is how you can recognize the Spirit of God: Every spirit that acknowledges that Jesus Christ has come in the flesh is from God, but every spirit that does not acknowledge Jesus is not from God. This is the*

spirit of the antichrist, which you have heard is coming and even now is already in the world. ~ 1 John 4:1-4

And no wonder, for Satan himself masquerades as an angel of light. ~ 2 Corinthians 11:14

You see, there is a requirement for us to be able to discern the thoughts of God. Can you see from this passage that hearing the voice of God is not automatic?

For who among men knows the thoughts of a man except the man's spirit within him? In the same way, no one knows the thoughts of God except the Spirit of God. We have not received the spirit of the world but the Spirit who is from God, that we may understand what God has freely given us... **The man without the Spirit does not accept the things that come from the Spirit of God, for they are foolishness to him, and he cannot understand them, because they are spiritually discerned...** ~ 2 Corinthians 2:11-12,14

Do you see how it says "The man without the Spirit..."?

We are not guaranteed the privilege of hearing God's voice and understanding the thoughts of God without first receiving *the Spirit* of God. We must be born again by asking Christ into our hearts and becoming saved. This is not a hard process. All we have to do is recognize that we need Jesus – and *ask.* More on this later.

When I was 10 years old, I was sitting in church like most children in my small town. I had grown up there. I was there on Sundays and Wednesday nights. On this particular Sunday morning, I had a tugging on my heart during the invitation. As the pastor asked if anyone wanted to receive Jesus as their personal Savior and as the choir sang "I Surrender All," I walked my little legs up to the altar and gave my heart to Jesus. Jeff and I became saved about the same time. We got baptized around the same time as well. It was sweet. I knew that I had innocently just accepted the Lord. Even though I was young, I *knew I was saved*, and I immediately started hearing God's voice.

Chapter 3   ...Adam's Story

In order to tie together the basic concept of the spirit, please allow me take you on a quick foundational tour through the life of Adam. To fully understand what has been *restored* through Jesus, we must first realize what we *lost* through Adam. *We lost life.*

We didn't lose our physical life on earth, but our eternal life in Heaven. Remember my earlier statement; "We are not human beings having a spiritual experience. We are spiritual beings having a human experience." We are spirits. We were created to live eternally with the Father. However, when Adam sinned, mankind lost the privilege of eternal life. We lost that eternal life through Adam's fall and can only gain it again through the sacrifice of Jesus Christ. He died so that we may live eternally.

> *For the wages of sin is death, but the gift of God is eternal life in Christ Jesus our Lord.* ~ Romans 6:23

In the following scriptures you will see that when God breathed life into Adam, he had communion with God. But, when Adam sinned, he lost his immortality and was cursed with death.

> *The Lord God formed the man from the dust of the ground and breathed into his nostrils the breath of life, and the man became a living being.* ~ Genesis 1:7

> *The Lord God took the man and put him in the Garden of Eden to work it and take care of it. And the Lord God commanded the man, "You are free to eat from any tree in the garden; but you must not eat from the tree of the knowledge of good and evil, **for when you eat of it you will surely die.**"* ~ Genesis 1:15-17

Notice that God said "*when*" you eat of it, not "*if*" you eat of it. He already knew that Adam would fall. He knew when He created Adam that man would need a Savior.   Jesus was already prepared to pay the ransom for mankind ...*before* mankind was even created.

God is Holy. He loves man dearly, but He cannot look upon sin. However, our loving Father already had a plan of redemption for mankind through the blood of His Son, Jesus Christ.

Adam sinned.   And because sin entered the world through him, mankind was condemned. But Jesus rescued us. He redeemed us from death.   Read the following passages.

> *Therefore, just as sin entered the world through one man, (Adam) and death through sin, and in this way **death came to all men**, because all sinned.* ~ Romans 4:12

> *Consequently, just as the result of one trespass was condemnation for all men, so also the result of one act of righteousness was justification that brings life for all men. For just as through the disobedience of the one man the many were made sinners, so also through the obedience of the one man the many will be made righteous.* ~ Romans 5:18-19

> *For since death came through a man the resurrection of the dead comes also through a man.   **For as in Adam all die, so in Christ all will be made alive**.* ~ 1 Corinthians 15:21-22

What does death really mean here?   I must tell you that these passages don't just refer to the death of the physical body. As a matter of fact, Adam lived hundreds of years. The death the Bible is referring to is *spiritual death* and an eternity separated from God.

Dear friend, there *really is* a Heaven and there *really is* a hell. Hell is a real place. Because of our sin, that is what we deserve. But Jesus took that punishment and nailed it to the cross! He took our penalty, so we don't have to!

> *As for you, you were dead in your transgressions and sins, in which you used to live when you followed the ruler of the kingdom of the air, the spirit who is now at work in those*

who are disobedient. All of us also lived among them at one time, gratifying the cravings of our sinful nature and following its desires and thoughts. Like the rest, we were by nature objects of wrath. But because of his great love for us, God, who is rich in mercy, made us alive with Christ even when we were dead in transgressions - it is by grace you have been saved. ~ Ephesians 2:1-5

When we accept Christ's sacrifice for our sins and receive Him as Lord, we are born again. Our spirits are "activated" and we once again have communion with the Father, as well as eternal life.

It is important to note that even though we "think" we may be a Christian, even if we have been raised in church all of our lives, even if we have been teaching Sunday school for 20 years, if we have not asked the Lord Jesus Christ into our hearts, He is *not* there. It's like receiving a present. God handed us the Gift, but we must decide to open it. Jesus explains this to Nicodemus...

I tell you the truth; **no one can see the kingdom of God unless he is born again**. *~ John 3:3*

How can a man be born when he is old? Nicodemus asked. Surely he cannot enter a second time into his mother's womb to be born! ~ John 3:4

I tell you the truth; no one can enter the kingdom of God unless he is born of water and the spirit. Flesh gives birth to flesh, but **the Spirit gives birth to spirit**. *~ John 3:5-6.*

Notice again the capital "**S**" and the little "**s**" in this last sentence. When we are born again, *our* spirits come to life. We are *alive* in Christ.

That may be where you are right now. You have prayed that prayer at some time in your life. You may be reading this and remember getting saved. I remember it like it was yesterday. I have had a wonderful relationship with Jesus since I walked down that aisle at church when I was 10. He has never left me. Even in my darkest hours - two of which I already shared with you - Jesus has always been there.

The most amazing thing takes place the minute you accept Christ - **you are saved!** Once and for all. No one can ever take that from you. In your worst moments and through your greatest failures, His grace is sufficient. So take comfort in this next passage...

> *If God is for us, who can be against us? He who did not spare His own Son, but gave Him up for us all - how will He not also, along with Him, graciously give us all things? Who will bring any charge against those whom God has chosen? It is God who justifies. Who is he that condemns? Christ Jesus, who died - more than that, who was raised to life - is at the right hand of God and is also interceding for us. Who shall separate us from the love of Christ? Shall trouble or hardship or persecution or famine or nakedness or danger or sword? ...No, in all these things we are more than conquerors through Him who loved us. For I am convinced that neither death nor life, neither angels nor demons, neither the present nor the future, nor any powers, neither height nor depth, nor anything else in all creation will be able to separate us from the love of God that is in Christ Jesus our Lord. ~ Romans 8:31-39*

Chapter 4 ...*Nurturing and Renewing*

Hopefully we have established the need for a Savior. Now let's keep working through this, because I know for a fact that just because we are saved doesn't mean we feel fantastic about life right now. I know that I grew up with Jesus as my Savior, but my life was full of tragedy and trauma. It started early. And it took *decades* to arrive at a point of spiritual, emotional and physical health. So let's continue. Let's talk about sin for a moment and how it affects our spirit.

The spirit must be renewed. We must constantly maintain our spiritual walk with God.

The definition of sin is "to miss the mark". When we sin, we automatically feel the separation of communion with our Father. There is no getting around it. Sin separates us from a Holy God. As long as we are on this side of eternity, we will mess up.

When we do sin, it is our responsibility to repent quickly and renew that relationship and communion with the Lord. This is when the title "Renewing the Spirit" starts making sense.

No matter how big the sin or how far we feel from God, it is imperative to understand that Jesus paid the price. All we need to do is turn around... And He is *right there*. The minute we decide to repent and come back to the Lord, we can just turn around and ask Him to renew our spirits. Miraculously, we are right back in communion with the Lord.

For over a decade, I have hesitated to write this book. Because in order to really help someone understand how it all works together, I must use examples from my own life. They are vivid and still painful to recall. However, the raw authenticity of my own story can help people in their own understanding. I will go into depth in the next section (Restoring the Soul) and bring you back to how the spirit and the soul work together regarding sin. Laying the groundwork is important though. So please walk through this information and know that the stories *are* coming.

Until then, here are two scriptural examples of the spirit being "Renewed"...

> *I will give them an undivided heart and put a **new spirit** in them; I will remove from them their heart of stone and give them a heart of flesh.* ~ Ezekiel 11:19

> *Create in me a pure heart, O God, and **renew a steadfast spirit** within me.* ~ Psalm 51:10

> *Therefore we do not lose heart. Though outwardly we are wasting away, yet inwardly we are being renewed day by day.* ~ 2 Corinthians 4:16

As you can see, the spirit needs maintenance. And we are capable of constantly renewing our spirits. As a matter of fact, if you have been a Christian for a while, but feel separated from your Heavenly Father, then I encourage you to pray this prayer...

> *"Dear God, I thank you that I am saved. I am alive in Christ. According to your Word, I am eternally saved. I also realize that I have missed the mark and sin separates us. So I repent for sins that I have committed knowingly or unknowingly. I turn from sin now and ask you to renew my spirit. Thank you for your grace. In Jesus name, Amen."*

Now, there is something else unique about our spirit. When we nurture our spirit, it grows in strength. When we don't, it won't.

When we are born again, that's exactly what happens. We are born. Our spirits are brand new. We are babes in Christ. It is our job to begin to nurture that relationship and mature. The difference between the physical body and the spirit is that our spirits do not grow automatically.

It is our responsibility to commune with our Heavenly Father. To learn how to pray. And more importantly, to listen. To discern the voice of God and develop a keen awareness of His Spirit.

It is in those precious hours spent alone with God that we discover His heart, His character, His personality, and His love for us. The time spent in worship and in the Word begins a deep and abiding friendship with the Creator of the Universe. As we become intimate with God, we discover His plan for our lives, as well as the many gifts that are available to His children.

Again, this intimate relationship is not automatic. It must be cultivated and nurtured. So many people are saved, but remain infants in their spirituality.

Unfortunately, sometimes tragic circumstances initiate that relationship. We don't cry out to the Lord when everything is wonderful. Often, it is in tragedy that we grow closest to our Father. This was the case with me, even at a very young age.

> As I saw his precious life slipping away in a deep, dark puddle on the floor, I knew that my own life would never be the same.

As I said in my prologue, when Jeff died, I went from suicidal to close to the Lord. When I was in 7th grade, I was forced to go through that horrific tragedy. I will never forget those first days and weeks after the accidental fall that caused his death. I had been saved for two years, but I was just doing what most Christians do their whole lives. I loved God, but wasn't really focused on getting to know Him or spending time with Him in relationship. I was just rocking along being a kid. But as Jeff lay on the floor that day – with blood coming from his eyes, ears, nose and mouth... As I saw his precious life slipping away in a deep, dark puddle on the floor, I knew that my own life would never be the same. My relationship with God changed drastically in an instant.

I went from shock, to crazy desperate thoughts of suicide, to clinging to God for dear life - a process that seemed like an eternity! It was as if time stood still in those first few weeks following his death. But in reality, it was only 24 days.

Jeff died two weeks before my 13th birthday, and I had to face that special teenage milestone alone, without my twin. My family was in complete emotional and spiritual lock down.

That day was the first time I ever experienced one of the gifts that we have in Christ: a supernatural peace. The Bible calls it "the peace that passes understanding." On the day of my birthday I had a quiet calm. I smiled. I didn't cry. I just ...was. My family was the same way. My parents, facing the death of their young son – and Jason, who was facing the death of his little brother – did not shed one tear on our birthday. It was surreal ...and such a needed respite in the onslaught of grief and shock. We still speak of it today. My 13th birthday was a day that God was very near my family. And He spoke supernatural peace to each of us in our spirits.

> *And the peace of God which transcends all understanding will guard your hearts and your minds in Christ Jesus... And the God of peace will be with you.* ~ Philippians 4:7, 9

> *Now may the Lord of peace Himself give you peace at all times and in every way.* ~ 2 Thessalonians 3:16

That supernatural peace is just one of the privileges of intimacy with the Lord. A relationship with God also brings countless other advantages.

However, most Christians never mature past salvation. We really never activate and utilize our rights and privileges as sons and daughters of the Most High. We never learn to hear that "still small voice." The more we act on those impressions, the more sensitive we become to the Voice of God and the stronger our spirits grow. Again, this is not automatic. It takes diligence and time spent communing with Him. It takes reading and meditating on His Word and asking Him to illuminate it.

> We are too busy living our lives, and thus remain in ignorance and spiritual immaturity ...and the devil takes full advantage.

Most Christians never get to benefit from this type of loving, intimate, interactive and powerful relationship with our Heavenly Father. We are too busy living our lives, and thus remain in ignorance and spiritual immaturity ...and the devil takes full advantage.

He literally rips our souls apart. And we never even realize the true source of our problems! In the following chapters I will walk you through my own deliverance from many demons. It gets interesting ...stay tuned.

For now, let me encourage you to commit to the process of spiritual growth. In the following passage, the apostle Paul chastises believers for their immaturity. When he lists the things that should be *elementary teachings*, I am painfully aware that he is probably appalled at the modern church. We must be seen as a bunch of toddlers in playpens throwing rattles back and forth, arguing such basic foundations of the gospel. We have so far to go!

> *We have much to say about this, but it is hard to explain because you are slow to learn. In fact, though by this time you ought to be teachers, you need someone to teach you the elementary truths of God's word all over again. You need milk, not solid food! Anyone who lives on milk, being still an infant, is not acquainted with the teaching about righteousness. But solid food is for the mature, who by constant use have trained themselves to distinguish good from evil. Therefore let us leave the elementary teachings about Christ and go on to maturity, not laying again the foundation of repentance from acts that lead to death, and of faith in God, instruction about baptisms, the laying on of hands, the resurrection of the dead, and eternal judgment.*
> ~ Hebrews 5:11-6:3

In summary, we must realize that because of Adam's sin, we inherited our sin nature, and our spirits are dead. We must decide to activate them by accepting Christ as our personal savior and inviting Jesus into our lives. When we sin, we lose that communion. We must repent and ask the Lord to renew our spirit. Finally, *we* are responsible for growing spiritually. It is not automatic. Throughout our physical life, God delights in the growth of our spirits. That communion with Him allows us incredible access to all kinds of rights and privileges as His children.

Notes and Reflections

Chapter 5 ...*The Gift*

Here is my prayer for you:

> *I pray that out of His glorious riches He may strengthen you with power through His Spirit in your inner being, so that Christ may dwell in your hearts through faith. And I pray that you, being rooted and established in love, may have power, together with all the saints, to grasp how wide and long and high and deep is the love of Christ, and to know this love that surpasses knowledge - that you may be filled to the measure of all the fullness of God. Now to Him who is able to do immeasurably more than all we ask or imagine, according to His power that is at work within us, to Him be glory in the church and in Christ Jesus throughout all generations, forever and ever!* ~ Ephesians 3:16-21

Now let's look at that last scripture. One of its key phrases is *"that you may be filled to the measure of all the fullness of God."*

What does that mean? In all my years of walking with the Lord, it has been my experience that most people do not exhibit characteristics of the passage above. And they certainly don't seem to be filled to the measure of the fullness of God. What I know now is that to be filled to the measure of the fullness of God means that one has to not only be born again, but also be baptized in the Holy Spirit. Now, if you are not Spirit-filled, please keep reading. I promise this book will challenge you to a deeper walk in the Lord - in many more areas than you can even imagine.

Again, this is a subject that I never really heard much about growing up. But as I got older and began to study the New Testament, I realized the Holy Spirit was an integral part of the Christian life. Jesus was very clear on the necessary function of the Holy Spirit after His ascension.

On the night before his crucifixion Jesus begins to prepare his disciples for his death and informs them of the promised Holy Spirit. This passage is a beautiful picture of what we have.

> *I tell you the truth, anyone who has faith in me will do what I have been doing. He will do even greater things than these, because I am going to the Father. And I will do whatever you ask in my name, so that the Son may bring glory to the Father. You may ask me for anything in my name, and I will do it... And I will ask the Father, and He will give you another Counselor to be with you **forever** - The Spirit of truth. The world cannot accept Him, because it neither sees Him nor knows Him. But you know Him, for He lives with you and **will be in you**... the Counselor, the Holy Spirit, whom the Father will send in my name, will teach you all things and will remind you of everything I have said to you...*
> ~ John 14:12-14, 16-17, 26

Jesus continues comforting them by reminding them of the promised Holy Spirit in John 16.

> *Because I have said these things, you are filled with grief. But I tell you the truth: It is for your good that I am going away. Unless I go away, the Counselor will not come to you; but if I go, I will send Him to you... When He, the Spirit of truth comes, He will guide you into all truth. He will not speak on His own; He will speak only what He hears, and He will tell you what is yet to come. He will bring glory to me by taking from what is mine and making it known to you. All that belongs to the Father is mine. That is why I said the Spirit will take from what is mine and make it known to you.*
> ~ John 16:6-7, 13-15

After Jesus was crucified and resurrected, on the day of His ascension our Savior's last words gave final instructions regarding the Holy Spirit.

*Do not leave Jerusalem, but wait for **the gift** my Father promised, which you have heard me speak about. For John baptized with water, but in a few days you will be baptized with the Holy Spirit... You will receive power when the Holy Spirit comes on you; and you will be my witnesses in Jerusalem, and in all Judea and Samaria, and to the ends of the earth.* ~ Acts1:4-5

I want to pause here for a second. Do you see how Jesus calls the Holy Spirit "the gift"?

I believe many churches don't see the Holy Spirit as a "gift," but a threat. As a matter of fact, some churches actually believe that the Holy Spirit is not on the earth today. This is just not true.

I got saved at 10 years old, but did not get introduced to the Holy Spirit until I was 17. And it was because I sought Him out. The summer of my junior year in high school I went on a mission trip to Guatemala. I remember it like it was yesterday. I was reading every scripture I could find on the Holy Spirit. The scriptures had me perplexed and frustrated.

Like I said, I grew up in a church where the Holy Spirit was never mentioned. However, after my sophomore year in high school, I moved from my hometown and started attending a Spirit-filled church. It wasn't until then I discovered that I apparently had been missing out on something other believers had.

"Amy, the Lord told me to come over here and talk to you about the Holy Spirit. He said you were asking to know about Him..."

The memory is still perfectly intact, even after all these years. I can still hear the laughter of the children in the orphanage as they played on the swings beside the area where I was. There were several birds in the tree beside the playground. The bench was metal and blistering hot, so I sat on the ground that summer day with my Bible in my lap, pouring over 1 Corinthians 12, 13, and 14. I had a deep hunger for God and if He was offering a Gift, *then I wanted it!*

At that very moment, a lady walked up to me and said, "Amy, the Lord told me to come over here and talk to you about the Holy Spirit. He said you were asking to know about Him and that you are ready to ask for the baptism of the Holy Spirit and receive a prayer language."

That freaked me out! It was about a minute after I prayed, "Lord, I want to know about the Holy Spirit. I want the baptism of the Holy Spirit. I want a prayer language." Wow! She had just repeated verbatim the exact prayer I had just prayed!

See, that's how the Holy Spirit works. He is the Counselor. And He knows what you and I need at all times. And He gave that lady a word of knowledge and let her know exactly what I was thinking. One of the nine gifts of the Spirit is "a message or word of knowledge". The gift of prophecy is amazing. That is when the Holy Spirit reveals to a believer the thoughts of another person. It allows you to speak accurately what that person is thinking. (See 1 Corinthians 14:25)

That night, I prayed and invited the Holy Spirit to come and fill me with power. He is a gentleman. He never forces himself on anyone. Just like Jesus. We have to choose to invite Him into our lives. I invited Christ into my heart at age 10, and seven years later I invited the Holy Spirit. And just like the disciples, when I did that, He flooded my mind and my body... and I physically felt an incredible surge of love wash through my entire being! It was the most incredible experience! One of the highlights of my life! As I felt the warmth of the Holy Spirit envelope me, I also received a prayer language. As the heavenly dialect poured from my lips, I was keenly aware of the fact that I would never be the same.

Chapter 6 ...Three Categories

Now, that story of my personal experience has placed you in one of three categories. The first category is that you have experienced something similar and you are keenly familiar. You know exactly what I am talking about. You have had a similar experience.

I'll take a few minutes on the second category. This is the one where you have asked for the baptism of the Holy Spirit, and you feel like you didn't receive it because you don't have a prayer language. I speak with many people in this category. And the bottom line is that if you've asked for the Holy Spirit, He *is* there! God gives *freely to all* who ask. He doesn't pick and choose. So the challenge is just accepting it. There are many precious believers that have a strong and abiding relationship with Christ and have asked for the Holy Spirit. They *have indeed* been Spirit-filled, but aren't sure of that fact because they don't pray in tongues. I want to encourage you!

Let me explain the gift of tongues as I understand it. Hopefully, this will shed some light on the subject. There are two kinds of "tongues." The first kind is for everyone who is Spirit-filled. We all have it, even though we may not know it, understand it, or utilize it.

It is the intercession of the Holy Spirit. It has nothing to do with us. It is *Him* speaking directly to the Father on our behalf. So many people get caught up in trying to form our own words and it doesn't work like that. It is a heavenly language, spoken *by the Holy Spirit* directly to the Father; it doesn't make sense to the human mind. It is a spiritual "frequency".

> *In the same way, the Spirit helps us in our weakness. We do not know what we ought to pray for, but **the Spirit himself intercedes for us** with groans that words cannot express. And he who searches our hearts knows the mind of the Spirit, because the Spirit intercedes for the saints in accordance with God's will.* ~ Romans 8:26-27

That constant intercession never ceases. When I force my mind to be quiet and still and I listen, I can hear the Holy Spirit interceding for me. It happens 24/7. The most amazing thing about a prayer language is that at any moment, I can choose to "dial into that frequency" and hear it with my spirit. Or I can choose to open my mouth and let it come out in a heavenly prayer language. It's called "praying in the spirit" and it fortifies your inner being. It strengthens you. It builds a spiritual scaffold around your life. It is the tongue of angels. The beautiful thing about this heavenly dialect is that the enemy can't decipher it, so he can't come against it. Satan hates this supernatural communication between us and our Father. That's why he goes to such great lengths to keep believers from utilizing it!

> Satan hates this supernatural communication between us and our Father. That's why he goes to such great lengths to keep believers from utilizing it!

When I don't know what to pray, I pray in the spirit. When I am troubled. Or scared. Or frustrated. When I want to worship, I pray in the spirit and I sing in the spirit. It's like tethering myself to the Holy Spirit and *His* line of communication to the Father on my behalf.

However, this intercession is happening, with or without my personal participation. The same goes for you. So even if you haven't "dialed in" and listened or spoken it, this does *not* mean that you aren't baptized with the Holy Spirit. Be encouraged. Nevertheless, you should eagerly desire this aspect of your rights as a Spirit-filled believer. Don't reject it. Yearn for it. My advice is to turn off all the secular noise in your life for a while. Only listen to worship music. Turn it up really loud, so you can't hear yourself speaking and just open your mouth and quietly sing or speak the syllables forming on your tongue. They may be just a few at first. Don't worry about it. It may just be the word "Hallelujah." Or it can be a soft clicking. There is no right or wrong. Just worship. Don't think about feeling silly. I promise, as you let the intercession of the Holy Spirit come out of your own mouth, it will empower you in ways you can't even imagine!

Now, there is a second kind of tongues. This is one of the nine gifts spoken of by the Apostle Paul in 1 Corinthians 12. I have never experienced this. This gift comes on you in times when the Holy Spirit needs you to speak another language, as with the apostles in Acts Chapter 2. I suspect missionaries working in countries with foreign languages get to experience this gift quite often...

> *When the day of Pentecost came, they were all together in one place. Suddenly a sound like the blowing of a violent wind came from Heaven and filled the whole house where they were sitting. They saw what seemed to be tongues of fire that separated and came to rest on each of them. All of them were filled with the Holy Spirit and began to speak in other tongues as the Spirit enabled them. Now there were staying in Jerusalem God-fearing Jews from every nation under Heaven. When they heard this sound a crowd came tighter in bewilderment, because each one heard them speaking in his own language. Utterly amazed, they asked' "Are not all these men who are speaking Galileans? Then how is it that each of us hears them in his own native language? Parthians, Medes and Elamites; residents of Mesopotamia, Judea and Cappodocia, Pontus and Asia, Phrygia and Pamphylia, Egypt and the parts of Libya near Cyrene; visitors from Rome (both Jews and converts to Judaism); Cretans and Arabs - we hear them declaring the wonders of God in our own tongues! ~ Acts 2:1-11*

I hope I get a chance to experience this kind of tongue one day. The Holy Spirit speaks all languages, and if He has willing vessels in men and women, He can use us to bring the gospel to every nation!

Now, back to my three categories...

The third category is that you know you have never asked for the baptism of the Holy Spirit. You know you have never experienced it, and either you want it desperately (like I did) or the whole thing is striking you as crazy and weird and you aren't sure you believe any of it. And right now you are thinking, "*Okay, Amy, you just went off the deep end.*"

Remember that I said one of Satan's main tactics is to convince you that he doesn't exist? Well, the same goes for the Holy Spirit! If Satan can make you believe any one of the number of myths surrounding the Holy Spirit, he can con you out of asking for this amazing and necessary aspect of our life in Christ. You are missing out on some great gifts from our Father! The Holy Spirit was sent to earth after Jesus' ascension to empower you. If you have no power, it is almost impossible to live a Christian life that truly attracts the hurting souls all around you.

> It was the miracles that preceded His teaching that caused them to sit and listen. It was what set Him apart from every other teacher.

What was it that made Jesus so attractive to those around him?   It was the miracles!   The healings, the deliverances, the resurrections. The blind seeing, the deaf hearing, the mute speaking. It was the miracles that preceded His teaching that caused them to sit and listen. It was what set Him apart from every other teacher. He actually *demonstrated the Truth* with evidence of the Kingdom! The words of Jesus:

> *Believe me when I say that I am in the Father and the Father is in me; or at least believe on the evidence of the miracles themselves.* ~ John 14:11

Remember that Jesus did not start His ministry or perform one miracle until He received the Holy Spirit Himself. In order to save us, Jesus, who created the universe, laid down His deity and became a man. Because He was fully man, even Jesus needed the Holy Spirit's power to help Him walk out His three-year ministry.

> *When all the people were being baptized, Jesus was baptized too. And as He was praying, Heaven was opened and the Holy Spirit descended on Him in bodily form like a dove. And a voice came from Heaven: You are my Son, whom I love; with you I am well pleased.* ~ Luke 3:21-22

Now let me ask you. How many people around you are "doing what Jesus did? Even greater things than Jesus did"? The disciples did. After the Holy Spirit came on them, not only did they speak in other languages, but they also performed the exact same miracles Jesus performed. They healed people, cast demons out, and even raised people from the dead!

We can do the exact same thing! As a matter of fact, we are *commanded* to.

The purpose of this book is to help you understand what you have your hands on. So, please allow me the privilege of putting it together for you. This is one of my favorite things to do as a believer ...to show others what is available to them with the Holy Spirit. You would be amazed at how many people who absolutely adore the Lord have never been baptized with power from on high!

> So many have a borrowed opinion of the Holy Spirit based on the views of their parents, or their church, or people that have distorted the whole beautiful picture.

So many have a borrowed opinion of the Holy Spirit based on the views of their parents, or their church, or people that have distorted the whole beautiful picture. We never really get alone with God, like I did in Guatemala, and "seek" Him. We just accept that it is something we don't need or want, based on outside judgments. That is such a shame! God calls the Holy Spirit "The Gift" for a reason...

Remember though, this is *not* a salvation issue. The disciples were saved. They all believed in Jesus. However, there is a huge distinction in Acts 2. If you have never really read this for yourself - or even if you have but have been taught through religion that it only happened back then, read this with a new set of eyes.

Everyone was filled with awe and disbelief that day, because these simple, uneducated men were doing the impossible. Some accused them of being drunk. That's when Peter spoke up.

> *...Fellow Jews and all of you who live in Jerusalem, let me explain this to you; listen carefully to what I say. These men are not drunk, as you suppose. It's only nine in the morning! No, this is what was spoken by the prophet Joel: In the last*

*days, God says, I will pour out my Spirit on **all people**. Your sons and daughters will prophesy, your young men will see visions, your old men will dream dreams. Even on my servants, both men and women, I will pour out my Spirit in those days, and they will prophesy. I will show wonders in the Heaven above and signs on the earth below, blood and fire and billows of smoke. The sun will be turned to darkness and the moon to blood before the coming of the great and glorious day of the Lord. And everyone who calls on the name of the Lord will be saved. ~ Acts 2:1-6, 14-21*

Chapter 7   ...Myths Surrounding the Gift

When people asked Peter what they must do, here was his answer. Notice what he says when he talks about the Holy Spirit...

> *Repent and be baptized, every one of you, in the name of Jesus Christ for the forgiveness of your sins. And you will receive the gift of the Holy Spirit.* **The promise is for you and your children and for all who are far off - for ALL whom the Lord our God will call.**
> ~ Acts 2:38-39

It also is one of the most misunderstood aspects of the New Testament. So many people have been taught that the Holy Spirit was only for that time. Let me ask you a simple question...

The disciples had just spent three years in the presence of Jesus. They had witnessed the miracles. They had listened to years of personal instruction and teaching. And *they* needed the Holy Spirit. How much *more* do we need Him 2000 years later? Why would God give *them* the gift of the Comforter and Counselor to infuse *them* with power, and not us? No. That is not the God I serve. He is the same yesterday, today, and forever. The Holy Spirit is *just as available to me and to you* as He was to the original disciples. And He just as necessary now, if not more so. If Jesus Himself needed the Holy Spirit's power, and He specifically told the disciples to wait for the Holy Spirit, then wouldn't it make sense that we would need to follow that same pattern?

That is one myth surrounding the Holy Spirit. The second myth is that Jesus and the Holy Spirit are the same... That when you accept Christ, you also have the baptism of the Holy Spirit. This is just not correct. I can understand the confusion, because in some texts, the Bible isn't clear. Even the above scripture makes it look like they are the same ...in this translation. Other translations are worded slightly different and allow you to see the distinction. Here is a passage that makes it crystal clear...

While Apollos was at Corinth, Paul took the road through the interior and arrived at Ephesus.   There he found some disciples and asked them, "Did you receive the Holy Spirit when you believed?" They answered, "No, we have not even heard that there is a Holy Spirit." So Paul asked, "Then what baptism did you receive?" "John's baptism," they replied. Paul said, "John's baptism was a baptism of repentance.   He told the people to believe in the one coming after him, that is, in Jesus." On hearing this, they were baptized into the name of the Lord Jesus. **When Paul placed his hands on them, the Holy Spirit came on them,** *and they spoke in tongues and prophesied.* ~ Acts 19:1-6*

There are more examples like above where normal believers just like me loved the Lord, believed in Jesus, but did not receive the Holy Spirit until later.

By the way, you *can* receive both at the same time. You can receive Christ as your personal Savior and be baptized with the Holy Spirit simultaneously. You just have to ask for both. As a matter of fact, that is preferable! However, most of the time, they come separately, as people gain more knowledge and understanding.

Another myth is that the "fruit of the Spirit" and the "gifts of the Spirit" are the same. They are not. When we receive Christ, we do receive the Spirit of God. We have Jesus living inside of us. And as we commune with the Spirit of God it produces fruit in our lives. That is what the first chapter of this book was all about.

The fruit of the Spirit is love, joy, peace, patience, kindness, goodness, faithfulness, gentleness, and self-control... ~ Galatians 5:22-23

In Chapter 1, I spoke of our spirits maturing as we spend time with the Lord, in His presence. This fruit is the natural result.

Although these character traits are necessary and wonderful, Jesus promised the disciples they would be clothed with *power* when the Holy Spirit came on them. Not *in* them, *on* them.

The baptism of the Holy Spirit is different. It is supernatural power that comes on you. It envelopes you and anoints you to be able to do the miraculous things Jesus did.

That power attracts. Like a magnet. It astonishes. And people want it. That's what I love about the Holy Spirit. How many people do you know that are fascinated by astrology and psychics? How many kids play with witchcraft trying to find *something* supernatural? Look at the popularity of the Harry Potter movies. Witchcraft is "in." Why? Because it has power. Things happen. Things that are different from our average, everyday, boring lives. And trust me, Satan obliges. He is more than willing to create a fascination with sorcery, while perpetuating the lie that the opposite side of evil power – the gifts of the Holy Ghost – are not real.

Notes and Reflections

Notes and Reflections

Chapter
8
...*Simon's Story*

That's why I love Acts Chapter 8. Let's read about Simon the Sorcerer...

> *Now for some time a man named Simon had practiced sorcery in the city and amazed all the people of Samaria. He boasted that he was someone great, and all the people, both high and low, gave him their attention and exclaimed, "This man is the divine power known as the Great Power." They followed him because he had amazed them for a long time with his magic.* ~ Acts 8:9

You see? People love the supernatural. We are drawn to it. That's why we *need* the Holy Spirit. Keep reading...

> *But when they believed Philip as he preached the good news of the Kingdom of God and the name of Jesus Christ, they were baptized, both men and women. Simon himself believed and was baptized. And he followed Philip everywhere, astonished by the great signs and miracles he saw.* ~ Acts 8:12-13

Okay. This is cool. The sorcerer got saved. Why? Because he recognized a power greater than his own. He was drawn to Philip, not because of the message, but because of the miracles.

Keep reading, because this text again distinguishes the difference between Jesus' baptism and the Holy Spirit's baptism.

> *When the apostles in Jerusalem heard that Samaria had accepted the Word of God, they sent Peter and John to them. When they arrived, **they prayed for them that they might receive the Holy Spirit, because the Holy Spirit had not yet come upon any of them; they had simply been baptized into the Name of the Lord Jesus.** Then Peter and John placed their hands on them, and they received the Holy Spirit."* ~ Acts 8:14-17

Again, do you see the difference? Just like the believers in Ephesus, these Samaritans were saved, but they didn't have the power yet. Now, check out what our friend Simon does next...

> *When Simon saw that the Spirit was given at the laying on of the apostles' hands, he offered them money and said, "Give me also this ability so that everyone on whom I lay my hands may receive the Holy Spirit." ~ Acts 8:18-19*

Peter gets angry and rebukes him mightily! Look how protective he is of the Holy Spirit.

> *Peter answered: "May your money perish with you, because you thought you could buy the gift of God with money! You have no part or share in this ministry, because your heart is not right before God. Repent of this wickedness and pray to the Lord. Perhaps he will forgive you for having such a thought in your heart! For I see that you are full of bitterness and captive to sin." ~ Acts 8:20-23*

Now, I want you to remember this passage, because I will bring it back to your attention later in the book. For now, notice that Simon the sorcerer saw the power the apostles had. He had been moving in evil, supernatural power, but these believers were doing greater things than he could do. And Simon was willing to pay money to get it!

> That is exactly what the Holy Spirit is – *A gift* from God. Sadly, just like with Jesus, not everyone opens the present.

Again, when the raw, authentic power of God moves in your midst, you want some of it! And if you do not have it, then - just like the believers in Ephesus and Samaria - you can receive it. You see, Peter calls the Holy Spirit *"the gift"* just like Jesus did. That is exactly what the Holy Spirit is – *A gift* from God. Sadly, just like with Jesus, not everyone opens the present. You must want it. And just like I did, you have to ask for it.

The Holy Spirit is the Comforter, the Counselor, and a guide into all truth. He is also supernatural, and He is the power behind, not only the miracles of Jesus, but also those of the disciples. The Holy Spirit is also the power behind any miracle in the body of Christ today. These miracles take place with the utilization of the gifts of the Holy Spirit. He gives them to us as we need them.

Earlier, we talked about the *fruit* of the Spirit. There are nine.   Now, here are the nine *gifts* of the Spirit.

> *Now to each one the manifestation of the Spirit is given for the common good. To one there is given through the Spirit the message of wisdom, to another the message of knowledge by the means of the same Spirit, to another faith by the same Spirit, to another gifts of healing by that one Spirit, to another miraculous powers, to another prophesy, to another distinguishing between spirits, to another speaking in different kinds of tongues, and to still another the interpretation of tongues. All these are the work of one and the same Spirit, and He gives them to each one just as He determines.* ~ 1 Corinthians 12:1-11

I have seen some of these gifts firsthand in my own life. Once, I actually took a class on the gifts of the Spirit. I earnestly wanted to learn about each one, and how they operate. In 1 Corinthians, Paul encourages believers to...

> *Follow the way of love and eagerly desire spiritual gifts, especially the gift of prophecy.* ~ 1 Corinthians 14:1

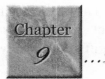

Chapter 9
...Darla's Story

That's exactly what I was doing. I was learning about the Holy Spirit and studying the gifts. It was a wonderful class. I was a massage therapist at the time. I realized that I was in a perfect setting to be able to really minister to my clients both physically and spiritually. As I worked on each client, I silently prayed for the Holy Spirit to empower my hands. And if He wanted to say something to them, then please give me a prophetic word that would speak directly to their circumstances and encourage them deeply. I was focused on the gifts of healing and prophecy.

I remember praying for the gift of prophecy for several weeks. Do you remember how I said that if we are obedient to the "impressions" of our spirit, then the more we will be "impressed"? That is exactly how it began to happen. As the soft worship music played and they relaxed there quietly, I used my prayer language to intercede for them (under my breath so they couldn't hear me). I would ask the Lord to give to give me a special word for that person, that they might be encouraged. Something that would be so specific that they would *know* it was from Him.

I began to have pictures form in my mind. Specific pictures or a specific sentence or two would burst into my mind from the center of my being. At first, I was nervous to break the silence and say something to my client like, *"You know, I was just praying for you, and I feel like there is something the Lord wants you to know. I am seeing a picture of..."* Or I would say, *"As I was praying for you, I feel like God is saying...."*

In most cases, the person was astounded! Just like me on that day in Guatemala, when the lady came over and told me exactly what I had just prayed, they too were fascinated and excited. It was usually something they were praying about, troubled by, or a question they had been privately asking the Lord. I was humbled that God was using me to minister to people on a deep and personal level.

As I became more familiar with the "impressions", I asked the Holy Spirit to please use me with the gift of healing as well.

One day I got a phone call from a local chiropractor. He asked if I could see a lady right then, as she was in intense pain and couldn't move. He was afraid to work on her himself, because she was so acute. I immediately began to pray in the spirit for her and asked the Holy Spirit to use my hands as His instruments of healing.

When she arrived at my office, her face was twisted with pain. Her back was completely locked down and she had to have help getting up onto my massage table. I felt *so* sorry for her, because her muscle spasms wouldn't allow her to sit or lie down. We finally got her up on the table and onto her side. She couldn't lie on her stomach, her back, or sit up.

As I put my hands on her, I discovered that she was in great emotional pain as well. She was gritting her teeth and her whole body jerked with each spasm. As tears rolled down her flushed cheeks, she said, *"I am the keynote speaker for a women's conference tonight! What am I going to do?"*

"Holy Spirit, I pray for this woman. I ask that you use my hands to heal her back right now in Jesus' name!"

I told her that I was going to pray for her. I wasn't sure what would happen, but I was confident that the Holy Spirit could heal her. As the spasms were coming just seconds apart, I could see that she was completely open to my prayer. I gently placed my hands on her back. It felt like stone! I prayed this simple prayer, *"Holy Spirit, I pray for this woman. I ask that you use my hands to heal her back right now in Jesus' name!"*

Immediately, an electric current came from the center of my being through my shoulders, down my arms and into my hands. I literally felt that same electricity I had felt in Guatemala. As it traveled into my hands and touched her, she jumped in surprise. Then she immediately relaxed. I just kept my hands motionless on her back, and it began to soften. Her back muscles completely responded to the electric love that flowed from the Holy Spirit, as He ministered to her through my palms. I was amazed as her whole body began to respond. We just stayed in that position, as the pulse continued to course through my arms and hands. After a few minutes, I could no longer feel the supernatural healing current. As I removed my hands from her back, I asked her how she felt. She moved gingerly at first, then a little more. Then she began to test it by slowly twisting and bending. She finally jumped up off the table and began to really move. She and I both started smiling, and then laughing. Her tears of pain had disappeared and a beautiful smile of astonishment lit up her face.

*"How did you **do** that?!"* she exclaimed.
"I didn't! The Holy Spirit did it!" I said. *"I asked the Holy Spirit to heal you."*
"Who? What? I have no idea what you are talking about!" she responded. That statement led to a great conversation and a great friendship. This lady went from being an absolute stranger to a sister in five minutes. As a token of that day, she bought me a Bible.

As a matter of fact, even though that was years ago, I still use the Bible she gave me, to this very day. I cherish that Bible, because it is a symbol of the first time the Holy Spirit's healing power flowed through my hands.

> Now, here is the other side of that story. She had been a Christian for years, but just like me... she had not yet received the baptism of the Holy Spirit.

Now, here is the other side of that story. She had been a Christian for years, but just like me and the Biblical believers in Ephesus and Samaria, she had not yet received the baptism of the Holy Spirit. As our friendship continued, and I pointed out some of the scriptures you have been reading just now, she became Spirit-filled and received her prayer language. She was as hungry for the Holy Spirit as I had been, because she had *felt* the Holy Spirit heal her.

The challenge was that she belonged to a church, like I mentioned earlier, that does not believe the Holy Spirit is on the earth today. This particular denomination actually teaches against the Holy Spirit.

And when she began to move in the Holy Spirit's power, it caused all kinds of upheaval in her life. When she told them that she had been healed and that she had received the baptism of the Holy Spirit, it really freaked some people out and they thought she had lost her mind. Unfortunately, she went through some very intense personal challenges immediately following that incredible experience.

You see, people are either threatened or frightened by what they don't understand ...and the Holy Spirit is a mystery. Our human tendency is to either disregard or reject Him, because we can't *see* Him.

> ...people are either threatened or frightened by what they don't understand ...and the Holy Spirit is a mystery. ...because we can't *see* Him.

> *The man without the Spirit does not accept the things that come from the Spirit of God, for they are foolishness to him, and he cannot understand them, because they are spiritually discerned.* ~ 2 Corinthians 2:14

And yet, the sad reality is most people are completely desensitized to the demonic power displayed all around them. Satan has been hard at work creating a culture easily fascinated by ghosts, aliens, and demons. We seek out these three demonic displays in movies, video games, books, and art. We don't think twice when we walk into a movie theater and see these things, but when we walk into a church and see people being healed or hear a heavenly language, we think people are crazy and we are frightened by what we see. Tell me ...what is wrong with this picture?

You see, I rest in the fact that I have the same supernatural power that Jesus used to perform all of the miracles in the gospels. I have the Comforter, the Counselor, and the Intercessor as a constant companion in my life. He is the Spirit of Truth, the Healer, and He is my friend!

... Connie's Story

One Wednesday night at church, I was standing there visiting with some people before it started. A woman came up to me and asked my name. She said she had seen me at a Bible study once. I couldn't remember her, so I asked her name. As she reminded me of her name, she suddenly said, *"Do you believe God answers prayers?"*
"Absolutely! Of course He does!" I answered.
"Good. Because I just prayed and asked Him to tell you what I was praying about. I told Him that if He could tell you what I was praying about, then I would believe He was for real." I was taken by surprise at her matter of fact statement. She continued, *"I told God that I was going to come back over here at the end of the church service and if you knew what I have been praying for, then I would believe in Him."*
What?! Did I just hear that right? I began to backtrack. *"Well, uh, sometimes we have to wait for God to answer..."*
"Nope!" she said adamantly, her monotone voice matter of fact. *"I told God that if He was real, then He could tell you what I was praying about! I will see you after service."*

As she walked off, I panicked. Nothing like that had ever happened before. She was there one minute and gone the next. And I suddenly had a huge weight on my shoulders. *"What if I am wrong? Lord, what am I going to do?"*

As the music started and the worship started, I began to sing in the spirit with my prayer language. Throughout the whole music service I didn't sing one word in English. I don't think I heard any of the sermon. I was praying in the spirit under my breath. Urgently! This woman's face was on my mind, as I allowed the Holy Spirit to intercede for me.

About 30 minutes in, that "impression" that I had become so familiar with in the massage clinic hit my spirit and filtered up through my mind. Here is the one sentence that I heard... *"I want her to stop smoking."*

"What?! Oh, no! That CAN'T be it! She could be praying about a million things, but how do I even know if she IS a smoker? Lord, what if I'm wrong? Here she is, placing her belief in You on my response to her request, and the ONE sentence I get is, 'I want her to stop smoking'?! No way!" I continued to pray in the spirit, even more urgently this time. As the service was winding down, I never got anything else. Just that one sentence. Finally I relented and agreed to tell her that one sentence. I prayed and said, *"Lord, I may make a fool of myself here, and she may be extremely offended if she isn't a smoker... but I will tell her that you want her to stop smoking. Is there anything else you want to say?"*

Suddenly a whole "Word of Knowledge" flooded my spirit. Because I had finally agreed to be obedient to tell her the one sentence – even if I felt like a fool – the Holy Spirit revealed her thoughts in vivid detail. *"She got saved five months ago. She has been praying and asking for me to help her stop smoking. As she has struggled, it has begun to erode her faith. She is wavering in her belief because she feels like if I can't help her stop smoking, then how am I powerful enough to forgive her sins and save her? But I am going to show myself strong on her behalf tonight. She will never have to worry about her addiction again."*

Wow! The impression was so *clear.* I had no more doubt. I was confident that this was indeed what she had been praying about. So I excitedly said, *"Okay, Lord. I am thrilled that you are going to help her stop smoking. Is there anything else you want me to tell her?"* *"Yes,"* He said. *"Tell her, 'As her lungs clear, so will her vision.'"* I had no idea what that meant, but I agreed that I would relay it to her just as I had received it.

After the church service was over, she walked up to me, looked me directly in the eyes, and said, *"Well, did you hear anything?"*

I was hoping her facial expression would give me confirmation that what I had spoken was accurate. Nothing. Her face was completely blank as she just stared at me.

"Yes." I said. *"I feel like the Lord did speak to me concerning you. If this isn't what was on your mind, I can assure you that it IS on His mind. He said to tell you that He wants you to stop smoking."*

As I said that, I was hoping her facial expression would give me confirmation that what I had spoken was accurate. Nothing. Her face was completely blank as she just stared at me. I began to feel awkward as we both just stood there silently for a few seconds.

I figured I had already gone down the "stop smoking" path... I didn't have anything to lose. So I dived in and clumsily blurted out, *"The Lord told me that you got saved five months ago. You have been praying and asking for Him to help you stop smoking. As you have struggled, it has begun to erode your faith. You are wavering in your belief because you feel like if He can't help you stop smoking, then how is He powerful enough to forgive your sins and save you? But He is going to show Himself strong on your behalf tonight. You will never have to worry about your addiction again. And ...as your lungs clear, so will your vision."*

The silence seemed like an eternity. I was staring at her, and she was staring at me. – This stranger who had interrupted "church as usual" for me that night. Suddenly, Connie blurted, *"Tell me the truth, did you smell smoke on me?!"*
"Are you a smoker? No! I didn't smell smoke on you!" I said.
She burst into tears and exclaimed, *"I can't believe it! That's EXACTLY what I have been praying about! God heard my prayer! God heard my prayer!"*
"Well let's go to the front and have someone pray for you!" I said, as I gently took her by the hand and headed for the altar. When we walked down to the front of the church and relayed the story to one of the pastors standing there, he handed me a small bottle of anointing oil and said, *"Amy, the Holy Spirit gave you the Word of Knowledge. You should pray for her."* So, I dabbed a tiny bit of oil on my forefinger and touched her forehead, like I had observed so many people do. I was planning on saying a short, sweet prayer asking the Lord to help her stop smoking.

What happened next took me by such surprise that it instantly and completely changed many of my spiritual paradigms. Well, that's putting it mildly... Really, it blew my mind.

The second my finger barely touched her forehead, it felt like a bolt of lightning went through my arm. It hit her and knocked her backward into the pastor standing there behind her.

> ...it felt like a bolt of lightning went through my arm. It hit her and knocked her backward into the pastor standing there behind her.

She instantly went completely "out" and would have landed flat on her back if the pastor hadn't caught her and kept her standing upright. He stayed right behind her holding her up, even though she was completely unconscious. I was so glad he was there, because it would have made a scene at the altar if she had fallen flat on her back!

You must understand I didn't push her. I softly touched one finger to her forehead, and she was completely incapacitated! As I quietly prayed in the Spirit, with my finger gently on her forehead, she began to tremble violently from head to toe. Her whole body was quaking as if she was being electrocuted. It didn't hurt, however. It wasn't painful to me at all. So I assumed she wasn't in pain either.

I remembered the time with my friend in excruciating back pain. She had felt better after the electric current stopped. So, even though this was much stronger, I knew it had to be similar. We stayed that way for several minutes, until I didn't feel the current coming through my arm anymore. I released my finger. After another couple of minutes, she began to stir, and her eyes slowly fluttered open.
"Are you alright?" I asked. The pastor and I helped her find a chair a few feet away. I sat down beside her and just let her breathe deeply for a few minutes.
Finally, she jumped up and began to laugh. She exclaimed, *"I've been healed! I've been set free! I've been delivered! Praise God! Hallelujah!"* Tears of joy streamed down her cheeks because she was convinced that she had been healed. What an incredible experience!

As I drove home from church that night, I thanked God for the Holy Spirit and for His intervention in this woman's life, and for the fact that He had allowed me to participate in a small way. You see, when we are empty and willing, the Holy Spirit can use us in amazing ways that bless us just as much as the people He is ministering to through us!

Chapter
11   ...The Rest of Her Story

A couple of weeks later, another young woman came up to me at church. She introduced herself and said she was this lady's daughter. *"It is so nice to meet you! How is your mom doing?"* I asked.
"She is amazing! She hasn't smoked one cigarette since that night." I was impressed but not surprised.
"Did she ever tell you how much she smoked?" I told her no, and that we had barely established that she *was* a smoker when I had taken her hand and led her down front.
"She smoked three packs a day... for 30 years!" she said, with a huge smile on her face. *"The addiction is completely gone! And not only that, but this morning she was reading the cereal box ...with her glasses on top of her head!"*

The Lord's words immediately resurfaced in my mind, *"As her lungs clear, so will her vision."* It had never crossed my mind that God meant actual "physical" vision!

That word of prophesy had come to pass! In the days and weeks following that Wednesday night service, God had healed her eyesight just as He had said He would.

As I pondered that conversation and the life of this precious lady and how it had changed so dramatically in an instant, I was saddened by the fact that so many believers have never had supernatural moments like that. They are just going through the motions of the Christian life. They love Jesus and on their way to Heaven... but have never had the privilege of personally participating in the miraculous ministry of the Holy Spirit. They have not experienced His incredible power in their own lives, much less in the lives of others.

There are too many precious believers who have just been baptized in the name of the Lord Jesus Christ, but have not yet received the baptism of the Holy Spirit. They don't have this exciting and powerful aspect of the Christian life. They don't see miracles or hear prophesy. They don't have the constant beautiful clicking in their spirits of a heavenly language – as the Holy Spirit continually intercedes for them. I can't imagine my life without this precious GIFT!

If that is you, please ask the Lord to give you the gift of the Holy Spirit. You can pray with someone that has the Holy Spirit and have them lay hands on you. You can also just ask the Lord yourself. You just need to *earnestly* seek Him.

There are many books on the Holy Spirit. I encourage you to read and study. I promise you will find Him! It is absolutely imperative for you to live an exciting Christian life. Like I said before, you can be saved and going to Heaven and not be Spirit-filled. But as long as we are on this side of eternity, why in the world would you cheat yourself out of the best part?

Now, these are just two of my personal examples of the Holy Spirit using me as an instrument in someone's life. And they are great. It is a wonderful feeling to be used to minister to others on behalf of the Lord.

However, I want to backtrack a few years.

You see, even though I had been Spirit-filled since I was 17, it wasn't until God restored my soul that I was really able to walk in my own personal healing and deliverance, and thus allow the Lord to effectively use me in the lives of others.

As I mentioned in my introduction, I was saved. I was Spirit-filled... and I was miserable. I was enslaved, confined in a prison of self-hate and shame. It is that sad reality that leads me to the second part of this book. I want to share a very personal story of how God set me free and Restored My Soul.

Notes and Reflections

Notes and Reflections

Part Two

Restoring the Soul

Chapter

12 ...*Trying to Get Started*

...He leads me beside quiet waters. He restores my soul.
~ Psalm 23:2

It has been several days since I finished the first section on the Spirit. I thought I could just continue writing into this next one on the Soul. It requires me to venture back into the painful aspects of my past.   I have been stuck at an uncomfortable, and yet very familiar place. It is the same place in my book when I put the manuscript down for an entire decade.   Writing this section is still proving to be just as difficult as it was back then. Because, even though there are no longer gaping wounds in my life, the scars are still very real.

Honestly, this section has had me perplexed for years. How do I tell my story, and not *"tell my story"*?   How do I help you understand without painting a graphic display? It benefits no one. So after much thought and many tears in the last couple of days, I have decided to press on. I have intentionally left several things unsaid. However, if you ever do attend one of my seminars, you will indeed hear the whole story. I love personal time with people. Because it is then that the authentic truth can't be misconstrued.

I will, however, share several "situations". These situations *are* real. Some are mine, and some belong to people I have counseled through the years. I have obviously changed the names and places. I will also use a couple of great Biblical examples. The objective is to help *you*. So as you read the different stories and scenarios, you can decide if they apply to your life. If they do, then hopefully you can allow them to aid in initiating *your freedom*.

The first section on Renewing the Spirit was easy. This one is much more difficult, because of the nature of the material.   The Soul is a different story. These next several chapters will be challenging for me to write... and probably challenging for you, as you read them.

You can't restore something that is not broken or damaged. Just like restoring a priceless piece of art, our souls need the touch of the Master's hand to properly reinstate them to their original beauty. They are indeed a "Masterpiece." And they desperately need and require the "Master's Peace."

Why are you downcast, O my soul? Why so disturbed within me? ~ Psalm 42:11

Come to me all you who are weary and burdened, and I will give you rest. Take my yoke upon you and learn from me, for I am gentle and humble in heart, and you will find rest for your souls. ~ Matthew 11:28-29

In my twenties, both of these words were perfect descriptions of me. I was carrying a tremendous amount of unnecessary weight and emotional baggage.

These two passages reveal that the soul can be "downcast" and it can be "weary and burdened." I can certainly attest to that. In my twenties, both of these words were perfect descriptions of me. I was carrying a tremendous amount of unnecessary weight and emotional baggage. But I am *free* now! Praise God!

So let's lay the foundation here, and embark on a journey that will take you through all the different aspects of the soul. My goal through the next several chapters, is for us to construct an easy to read, relevant handbook for spiritual freedom.

Chapter 13 ...What is the Soul?

According to the North American English Dictionary, the definition of the soul is "The nonphysical aspect of a person. The complex of human attributes that manifests as consciousness, thought, feeling and will. It is regarded as distinct from the physical body."

I stated earlier that I believe the Solar Plexus is the physical location of the human spirit.

According to my research, I also believe the pineal gland in the brain is the physical location of the soul. Of course, the internet allows all kinds of research. Here are just a couple of interesting paragraphs.

There are many research studies I've found dedicated to the pineal gland in the brain. It has been called by some, "the principal seat of the soul." And it is believed to be the point of connection between the intellect and the body. There is a great deal of significance attached to the gland because it is understood to be the only section of the brain to exist as a single part rather than one-half of a pair.

The pineal gland works much like our eyes, but also serves to send information to our brains from the spiritual dimension. Known as the organ that anchors the soul to the body, this pea- sized organ is shaped much like a pine cone and yet is *not part of the brain,* but entirely separate from it. To me, without a doubt, the pineal gland is the "God Organ."

The soul is the part of our being that comprises:

1) How we think (the mind)
2) What we desire (the will)
3) How we feel (the emotions)

Again, according to our dictionary, the mind is "the center of consciousness that generates thoughts, feelings, ideas and perceptions, and stores knowledge and memories."

The will is "the part of the soul that makes decisions. When we choose to act, we use our will."

The emotions are "an affective state of consciousness in which joy, sorrow, fear, hate, guilt or the like, is experienced, as distinguished from cognitive and volitional states of consciousness."

> By creating the soul, God gave His children the *right to choose*. What a chance our Father has taken by giving us that ability!

The soul is one of God's most exquisite and complex creations. By creating the soul, God gave His children the *right to choose*. What a chance our Father has taken by giving us that ability! Because of choice, God must let his creation decide to *choose* life or death, sickness or health, freedom or bondage.

It is with our "soul" that we choose to renew our *spirit* and be born again. It is with the "soul" that we choose to develop an intimate relationship with our Creator and we experience abundant, fulfilling life as He intended.

Or we can choose to go through life without even knowing Him. This opens the doors of chaos, confusion, and deceit. It also ultimately leads to an eternity in hell, in complete and utter separation from our Creator.

Not only is the soul the most complex, but it is undoubtedly the most vulnerable part of our being. It is entirely capable of being deceived – just as Adam and Eve were. We can choose to believe anything, act any way we desire, and live by the motto *"if it 'feels good' do it."* This can be deadly! This may sound intense, but we all know people who have died because of bad choices they made. Drug and alcohol addiction are just two examples of this sad fact.

Knowing we would listen to the lies of the deceiver and fall into temptation and sin, God *still* created the soul. Why? Because He is not a dictator demanding our devotion. He is a loving Father who adores His children and wants His children to love Him back. God desires relationship with His beloved creation.   He created us for fellowship and communion.

Chapter 14 ...David's Story

A great Biblical character to study, regarding that kind of fellowship and communion with his Creator, is King David. He was extremely intimate with God. David is also a great example of understanding the many aspects of the soul. Even though he was known for being a "man after God's own heart," David was intensely human. He constantly struggled with his soul, just as we do.

David was a leader. He was a warrior. This is the guy who, as a teenager, actually ran straight into the fight with Goliath. Even though Goliath is believed to have been over 14 feet tall, David had no fear. He was offended that this Philistine would insult the God of Abraham, Isaac, and Jacob. This young man took the head off of the leader of the Philistine army and initiated the victory of the Israelites that day. The Lord had anointed David to battle on behalf of Israel.

David was obviously an anointed lyricist and musician as well. He wrote most of the Psalms we enjoy today. I love the Psalms because David displays every aspect of the human soul through his lyrics. From the beloved passages of scripture concerning this man, we learn that David was extremely passionate... about everything. He was passionate about his relationship with God. About justice. About music. About war. About love and friendship. David was tender, and yet he was a killer. He was fun loving, and yet he thought nothing of slaying hundreds of men. He spent his mornings with his Creator in intimate, uninhibited worship and his afternoons conquering cities. David lived with passion. He lived "in the moment" every day, even though some of those moments got him into a *lot* of trouble.

> David was tender, and yet he was a killer. He was fun loving, and yet he thought nothing of slaying hundreds of men.

You see, emotion and passion are the jurisdiction of the soul. And that's when "passion" creates all kinds of interesting scenarios –

because passion begets passion. David was also a lover. He was obviously very in touch with his sexuality. Most passionate people are...

> *One evening David got up from his bed and walked around on the roof of the palace. From the roof he saw a woman bathing. The woman was very beautiful, and David sent someone to find out about her. The man said, "Isn't this Bathsheba, the daughter of Eliam and the wife of Uriah the Hittite?" Then David sent messengers to get her. She came to him and he slept with her... Then she went back home. The woman conceived and sent word to David, saying, "I am pregnant."* ~ 2 Samuel 11:2-5

Let me summarize this story for you. King David sees a married woman and sends for her. He sleeps with her, gets her pregnant, and then hatches a plan to bring her husband home from the war so he would have sex with his wife to make it look like the baby was his. The problem escalated when the husband didn't cooperate as planned. So David conceived another plan to have Uriah killed on the front lines. When he dies, David marries the guy's wife.

What?! *This* is a man after God's own heart? Those are God's words (See 1 Samuel 13:14). This guy was an adulterer and a murderer! And yet God loved him dearly. However, the consequences of David's sin were extreme. It devastated aspects of his life and his family.

> What?! *This* is a man after God's own heart? Those are God's words. This guy was an adulterer and a murderer! And yet God loved him dearly.

At times David was completely devoted to the Lord. Other times he fell flat on his face. Although he loved the Lord, he sinned greatly. King David struggled with his passion. He wrestled with the desires of his soul.

Let's talk about the soul. We've already discussed the fact that the soul is made up of the mind, the will, and the emotions. It is with the *mind* that we entertain temptation to sin. It is with the *will* that we choose to sin. And it is the *emotions* that suffer the devastating consequences of sin. Can you see this? David's story is a prime example.

When we let our soul (our mind, will, and emotions) dictate our thoughts, feelings, and actions, we are headed for disaster! Because these three areas are where sin is contemplated, birthed, and lived out. The soul is, therefore, our "sinful nature" or "flesh nature" as described in the passages below.

Think about it. David blew it and sinned big. It started with a *thought* that hit his mind when he saw Bathsheba bathing. He entertained that thought. "Wouldn't it be nice to..." He *knew* he shouldn't do it. He was warned against it, "She is another man's wife!" ...But the thought just kept persisting. Then he began to justify and get comfortable with the immediate gratification that it would bring.

Then, there was a point when he decided to *act* on the thought (temptation). During the action, he felt great ...for a short time. Must have been one heck of an evening on the roof in the moonlight. Must have been amazing. I can imagine the exhilaration of two people with just the right combination of atmosphere, intrigue, passion, and raw desire. Makes for an explosive few minutes. Maybe even a few hours. An incredibly electric, illicit evening at the palace...

> I can imagine the exhilaration of two people with just the right combination of atmosphere, intrigue, passion, and raw desire.

And then, almost immediately, the consequences set in. Right on the heels of all that fun, the drama started. Pregnancy. Now a cover up. *"No one must know! We have to figure this out!"* **Fear, guilt, shame**. I'm sure there was a sick feeling in the pit of his stomach when he was confronted and rebuked by the Lord through the prophet Nathan. Even though David immediately repented, the child they bore became ill. David wept. He fasted. He prayed. But he still lost his son. Imagine the emotional onslaught of guilt he must have felt.

You should go read the whole story. It really is a fascinating portrait of how our sin nature works. It is also a picture of how, even as much as the Father loves us, there are always devastating consequences to sin. But if we stay close to the Lord, even through His loving discipline, He will work all things together for our good. Even though David and Bathsheba's illegitimate son died, they eventually had Solomon, the wisest man who ever lived.

Though not to this degree, I have experienced this very same "sin cycle" so many times in my own life. Being a Christian doesn't make us immune to temptation and sin. It just makes us feel terrible when we follow through. It is amazing how many Christians love the Lord with all their heart, yet stay locked in the same cycle; temptation... sin... guilt... shame...

Even the Apostle Paul, who wrote two- thirds of the New Testament, struggled with sin...

> *I do not understand what I do. For what I want to do I do not do, but what I hate I do... I know that nothing good lives in me, that is, in my sinful nature. For I have the desire to do what is good, but I cannot carry it out. For what I do is not the good I want to do; no, the evil I do not want to do - this I keep on doing. ...When I want to do good, evil is right there with me. For in my **inner being** I delight in God's law; but I see another law at work in the members of my **body**, waging war against the law of my **mind** and making me a prisoner of the law of sin at work within my members. What a wretched man I am! Who will rescue me from this body of death? Thanks be to God through Jesus Christ our Lord!* ~ Romans 7:15-25*

Have you ever heard that "an idle mind is the devil's workshop"? That is a true statement!

Notice how Paul talks about delighting in God's law in his **inner being** (his spirit)... but the law of sin wages war against his **mind** and the members of his **body**. He calls it his "sinful nature."

That's what I want to discuss here. As I stated earlier, the sinful nature is located in the soul. Have you ever heard that "an idle mind is the devil's workshop"? That is a true statement! The temptation to sin always starts with a thought that hits your **mind.** It is acted out by the **will**, and guilt is an **emotion**. This is the sinful nature Paul is referring to here.

The Bible has much to say about the sinful nature, and how it is completely different from the spirit! I love this passage because it creates a distinct picture of that difference.

> *So I say, live by the Spirit, and you will not gratify the desires of the sinful nature. For the sinful nature desires what is contrary to the Spirit, and the Spirit what is contrary to the sinful nature. They are in conflict with each other, so that you do not do what you want... The acts of the sinful nature are obvious: sexual immorality, impurity and debauchery; idolatry and witchcraft; hatred, discord, jealousy, fits of rage, selfish ambition, dissensions, factions and envy; drunkenness, orgies, and the like. I warn you, as I did before, that those who live like this will not inherit the Kingdom of God. But the fruit of the Spirit is love, joy, peace, patience, kindness, goodness, faithfulness, gentleness and self-control... Those who belong to Christ Jesus have crucified the sinful nature with its passions and desires. Since we live by the Spirit, let us keep in step with the Spirit.*
> ~ Galatians 5:16-25

> *Those who live according to the sinful nature have their minds set on what that nature desires; but those who live in accordance with the Spirit have their minds set on what the Spirit desires. The mind of sinful man is death, but the mind controlled by the Spirit is life and peace; the sinful mind is hostile to God. It does not submit to God's law, nor can it do so. Those controlled by the sinful nature cannot please God.*
> ~ Romans 8:5-8

From these two passages it is easy to see that we, as Christians, have two opposite forces working in us. There is the Spirit, and there is the sinful nature. When we accept Jesus Christ as our personal Savior and invite Him into our hearts, we are born again and receive His Spirit. The Spirit of Jesus resides in us. We have established where He resides. He resides in our human spirit.

We are *born with* our sin nature. We inherited it from Adam. Until Christ comes back we will *always* have our sinful nature. Each of us carries our very own unique sin nature (See Psalm 51:5).

Now, you may be thinking *"I would NEVER do the things King David did! I would NEVER cheat on my wife or my husband. I would NEVER have another man murdered!"*

Well, you may be right. Your sin nature may not be the same as David's. You may not be into debauchery and orgies and witchcraft as in the above scripture. You may be more prone to other aspects of the sin nature – perhaps according to your astrological sign. Keep reading...

Chapter 15   ...*King David's Flesh Nature*

My husband Steve and I talk about this all the time. He got saved on his 40th birthday. He had believed he was a Christian all of his life because he grew up in church. Not so. It wasn't until he was sitting alone on the floor of his apartment, with a cardboard box for a table, after his 4th failed marriage, that he hit rock bottom.

It was that night that he realized he had made a serious mess of his life and had left several broken relationships in his wake. Steve finally understood there was nothing he could do to save himself from ...himself. He desperately needed a Savior. That night he asked Christ to come into his life. He invited Jesus into his heart, received forgiveness from his sin, and he also asked for wisdom. Jesus became extremely real to Steve that night. He not only received forgiveness and grace, but also supernatural revelation and wisdom on several different levels.

> ...he was sitting alone on the floor of his apartment, with a cardboard box for a table, after his 4th failed marriage...

One of them was astrology. He believes that the Lord shed some light on that whole subject. Now, this is not one of my premises for the book. It is strictly conjecture. However, I do believe Steve is accurate in his thinking here. He had spent years being fascinated by how he could be around someone for long enough to see their personality emerge and he could tell them their "sign." He could even sometimes tell them their exact birthday, based on their personality.

I had never studied astrology, horoscopes, etc. But after being married to Steve for 18 years, I have noticed the same thing. We have four children between us and their personalities are right in line with their astrological signs. You see, we believe the Zodiac is *indeed accurate*. It plots your general nature, your personality and how you naturally act and react to those around you.

That isn't all bad. Your nature is ...your nature. Some people are direct and decisive, take-charge leaders. Some are cautious and calculating, weighing everything before making a decision, because they are contemplators. Some are nurturers and very sensitive. They are listeners and team players. Others are the inspiring, motivational, life-of-the-party types that love to be around people. There are many aspects of your personality. As a matter of fact, I do trainings on the personality types in my seminars. Your flesh nature is not all bad; it is your personality.

Your birth date determines the general make-up of your soul's natural tendencies. In addition, your flesh nature also determines the sins you would be prone to fall to, given your particular personality type. Let's use King David as an example.

It wouldn't surprise me one bit to find out that he was probably a Scorpio. He was probably born from *October 24 - November 22*. If you are familiar with the Biblical account of David, you will identify these traits through many aspects of his story.

"Scorpio is the astrology sign of extremes and intensity. Scorpios are very deep, intense people; there is always more than meets the eye. They present a cool, detached and unemotional air to the world, yet lying underneath is tremendous power, extreme strength, intense passion and a strong will and a persistent drive.

"Scorpios are very emotional. Their emotions are intensified, both good emotions and bad. Negative emotions of jealousy and resentment are hallmarks of this turbulent astrological sign. On the other side, Scorpios are well known for their forceful and powerful drive to succeed and their amazing dedication."

"Do not ever expect them to fess up or share their tale with anyone however because this shows signs of weakness and Scorpio always wins, they are always the self-proclaimed best! One of the reasons they seem like they always accomplish their goals is because they set tangible short-term goals they know they can accomplish. They know what they are capable of and this is what they go for. Most Scorpios are direct and forceful and they seem to be an expert at what they do."

"Sex with a Scorpio is a total emotional and physical experience with passion and intensity. They have amazing stamina. Scorpio is the zodiac sign that is the most likely to act out a sexual fantasy. Most people will talk about it but the Scorpio will do it. They will fully throw themselves into the role." (Reference: http://zodiac-signs astrology.com/zodiacsigns/scorpio.htm)

David's night of passionate sex on the roof in the moonlight and the subsequent cover-up and murder has "Scorpio" written all over it!

> You may not be prone to David's sins, but to God, worry, anxiety, addiction, gossip, anger, murder, et cetera, are all equal sins.

You may not be prone to David's sins, but to God, worry, anxiety, addiction, gossip, anger, murder, et cetera, are all equal sins. All sins are equal in God's eyes. None is more heinous than another.

Now, if you go to the different "astrological signs" and you read the one that *you* fall into, you will probably be amazed at how accurate *yours* is as well. It is good to understand your general make-up. Just don't follow your sign and get attached to horoscopes. Because of the accuracy, it can quickly draw you in. It is easy to become fascinated and addicted to the whole process.

As a matter of fact, I googled the "Zodiac" just to do some research for this chapter. I found myself pouring through and reading all kinds of information. When I clicked on images, I was surprised at some of the evil-looking pictures haunting my computer screen. All of a sudden, I had all kinds of websites popping up. I was asked if I wanted to look at my free physic reading, if I wanted a copy of my shocking 2014 horoscope, and if I wanted to learn how to use divination. (No thank you)!! But, *it is* easy to get lost in all of it... fascinating to say the least, and also a bit spooky.

I can see how someone without knowledge of Christ can get entangled in the maze of images and information. Many already are. They put more stock in their horoscope than the Word of God. This is when it can become idolatry. The Bible says *don't do it.*

...watch yourselves very carefully, so that you do not become corrupt and make for yourselves an idol, and image of any shape, whether formed like a man or a woman, or like any animal on earth or any bird that flies in the air, or like any creature that moves along the ground or any fish in the waters below. And when you look up to the sky and see the sun, the moon and the stars-all the heavenly array – do not be enticed into bowing down to them and worshiping things the Lord your God has apportioned to all the nations under Heaven. ~ Deuteronomy 4:15-19

They will be exposed to the sun and the moon and all the stars of the heavens, which they have loved and served and which they have followed and consulted and worshiped. ~ Jeremiah 8:2

When Steve received revelation on astrology, he asked the Lord, "If it is so accurate, then why does the Bible tell us not to use it?" Here was the Lord's response: *"Because it plots the flesh nature. When someone sees you, they should see Christ in you, not your flesh nature or sin nature."* In other words, we are supposed to live by the Spirit, not the flesh. If we live by the flesh, we risk finding ourselves entrapped in the snares of the soul.

By reading your basic genetic personality make-up, it may help you understand what you are prone to lean to so that you can recognize some of the arrows the enemy might throw your direction. Just don't become fascinated with it. Don't keep looking at it. And if you are a Christian who follows your horoscope, I encourage you to read the above scriptures again. Meditate on them, repent, and start looking to the Spirit instead.

Incidentally, if you "make excuses" for your behavior based on the fact that *"it's just the way you are,"* that's another area for repentance and growth. Just because we have a particular set of personality traits and natural tendencies according to our astrological sign, it doesn't mean we have to acquiesce to them!

As a matter of fact, as we become stronger and stronger, we can be controlled by the Spirit as in the above scriptures. As followers of Christ, it is our responsibility to mature into that relationship.

> *Put to death, therefore, whatever belongs to your earthly nature: sexual immorality, impurity, lust, evil desires and greed, which is idolatry... You used to walk in these ways, in the life you once lived. But now you must rid yourselves of all such things as these: anger, rage, malice, slander, and filthy language from your lips. Do not lie to each other, since you have taken off your old self with its practices and have put on the new self, which is being renewed in knowledge in the image of its Creator ...Therefore, as God's chosen people, holy and dearly loved, clothe yourselves with compassion, kindness humility, gentleness and patience.*
> ~ Colossians 3:5-12

Notes and Reflections

Chapter 16 ...*Follow Your Heart?*

I was not taught these basic principles of scripture. A lot of churches don't really get into the deeper aspects of the Word. I was taught that as long as I confessed Jesus as my Savior and Lord, I would go to Heaven and life on earth was supposed to be abundant.

While all of that is true, it just isn't all there is. I had no idea how to *"live by the Spirit,"* which would allow my spirit to grow and my soul to be protected.

As a matter of fact, the world teaches us to *"follow our hearts."* At least that is the lesson I learned, and it turned out to be the wrong lesson. Actually, following your heart is extremely dangerous! When we follow our hearts, we are in the realm of the soul. The Bible has a lot to say about the heart. It says the heart is deceitful and it can be drawn to what is evil. It can be hardened. It can be led astray, and it can condemn us...

> The **heart is deceitful** above all things and beyond cure. Who can understand it? ~ Jeremiah 17:9

> Set a guard over my mouth, O Lord; keep watch over the door of my lips. **Let not my heart be drawn to what is evil**, to take part in wicked deeds with men who are evildoers; let me not eat of their delicacies. ~ Psalm 141:3-4

> Today, if you hear His voice, do not **harden your hearts** as you did in the rebellion, during the time of testing... This is why I was angry with that generation, and I said, "Their **hearts are always going astray**, and they have not known my ways." ~ Hebrews 3:7-10

> This then is how we know that we belong to the truth, and how we set our hearts at rest in His presence whenever **our hearts condemn us**. For God is greater than our hearts, and He knows everything. ~ 1 John 3:19-20

Have you ever *"followed your heart"* – right off a cliff?

I have! How many times have I made a decision to do something that my heart was telling me to do, only to find out that it was a devastating mistake.

> **Have you ever *"followed your heart"* – right off a cliff?**

Often, I realized the snare immediately. Yet in many cases, it took years and even decades to recover from the emotional damage. Those mistakes usually involved a sin. And when I traced it back, that sin started with a thought that was followed by an action.

It took me years to break free of the cycle. However, most of us are still in the process of coping with the emotional devastation of *"following our hearts"* and giving in to the *"sinful nature."*

At some point in our lives, most of us started on this same cycle: sin, guilt, shame. It wreaked havoc on our souls. Well, I have good news! We don't have to continue to make devastating mistakes. That's why God gave us His Spirit! We can be guided by the Spirit and not the sinful nature. We can choose to live according to the Spirit – and trust me, it is so much easier!

> *You, however, are controlled not by the sinful nature but by the Spirit, if the Spirit of God lives in you. And if anyone does not have the Spirit of Christ, he does not belong to Christ. But if Christ is in you, your body is dead because of sin, yet your spirit is alive because of righteousness. And if the Spirit of Him who raised Jesus from the dead is living in you, He who raised Christ from the dead will also give life to your mortal bodies through His Spirit, who lives in you.*
> ~ Romans 8:9-11

It was obvious that King David understood this same process. He had a fascinating journey with the Lord while here on Earth. I love his passion! He was so human, yet so in love with his Heavenly Father. Even though David made massive mistakes, God used him mightily. His son Solomon would become the wisest man to ever live and would also build the Jewish temple. David's lineage brought forth our Messiah, Jesus Christ. God even swore an oath to David that his offspring would establish God's Kingdom and throne forever.

Maybe it was because he had an intimate relationship with God. Maybe it was because he understood that even though we may give in to the flesh nature and sin, we can always turn back to the Lord and ask him to "restore our soul!" Read this next passage. Take a breath, and be encouraged!

> *Praise the Lord, oh my* **soul***; all my inmost being, praise His holy name. Praise the Lord, O my* **soul***, and forget not all His benefits - who forgives all your sins and heals all your diseases, who redeems your life from the pit and crowns you with love and compassion, who satisfies your desires with good things so that your youth is renewed like the eagle's. The Lord works righteousness and justice for all the oppressed...*
>
> *The Lord is compassionate and gracious, slow to anger, abounding in love. He will not always accuse, nor will He harbor His anger forever; He does not treat us as our sins deserve or repay us according to our iniquities. For as high as the heavens are above the earth, so great is His love for those who fear Him; as far as the east is from the west, so far has He removed our transgressions from us. As a father has compassion on his children, so the Lord has compassion on those who fear Him; for He knows how we are formed, He remembers that we are dust. As for man, his days are like grass, he flourishes like a flower of the field; the wind blows over it and it is gone, and its place remembers it no more. But from everlasting to everlasting the Lord's love is with those who fear Him and His righteousness with their children's children - with those who keep His covenant and remember to obey His precepts.* ~ Psalm 103:1-6, 8-18*

I want to take a moment here and tell you that is one of my favorite passages of scripture. It is so comforting to me. When you dissect it and meditate on it, this passage gives you a clear understanding of how much our Father loves us. However, so many people get hung up on the words *"those who fear Him."*

According to the original Hebrew text, the word fear is *"אָרֵי yare' pronounced {yaw-ray'}"* And it means *reverent; to be morally reverent.* (Reference: Hebrew Word Study. Transliteration - Pronunciation Etymology & Grammar)

To be morally reverent means something altogether different from "fear." I have had the privilege of knowing and loving God all my life. I have never "feared" Him, but I do revere Him. I do respect Him. I do honor Him.

> God is a Father who loves you. Please don't fear Him in the sense that we use the term today. That would break His heart.

Even when I was in the middle of blowing it, I still had a "fear of the Lord." To fear Him doesn't mean you will never sin. We will all continue to *miss the mark,* which means He knows we will all continue to sin. However, God is a Father who loves you. Please don't fear Him in the sense that we use the term today. That would break His heart. The fear of the Lord brings protection for not only you, but for your children. I love these promises...

He who fears the Lord has a secure fortress, and for His children it will be a refuge. The fear of the Lord is a fountain of life, turning a man from the snares of death.
~ Proverbs 14:26-27

The fear of the Lord leads to life: Then one rests content, untouched by trouble. ~ Proverbs 18:23

The fear of the Lord adds length to life, but the years of the wicked are cut short. ~ Proverbs 10:27

But the eyes of the Lord are on those who fear Him, on those whose hope is in His unfailing love, to deliver them from death and keep them alive in famine. We wait in hope for the Lord; He is our help and our shield. In Him our hearts rejoice, for we trust in His holy name.
~ Psalm 33:18-21

The angel of the Lord encamps around those who fear Him,
and he delivers them. Taste and see that the Lord is good;
blessed is the man who takes refuge in Him. Fear the Lord,
you His saints, for those who fear Him lack nothing.
~ Psalm 34:7-9

Chapter 17 ...A Very Personal Story

Now, let's you and I go back to *"follow your heart"* for a few minutes. Because although this is a nice cliché, it is *not a good idea.* It goes right along with the saying, *"If it feels good, do it."* Also not a good idea. Any decision based on emotion is usually the wrong decision – especially if it is made in haste or in the heat of the moment. The soul is a tricky jurisdiction, and if your attitude is *"What the heck, just go with it."* ...it usually turns out to be a destructive mess.

There have been so many examples in my life when I followed my heart. I knew I was walking according to my sin nature – and right

> ...if your attitude is *"What the heck, just go with it."* ...it usually turns out to be a destructive mess.

into a trap.   However, when I look back, I realize that these experiences, although painful and costly, can be stepping stones for someone else to collapse a time frame in their own healing. Thus, the reason for this book.

God has been so faithful to me! Not only has He forgiven me and healed my heart, but He literally brought me back from the brink of suicide ...twice.

The first time was immediately following Jeff's death. I already told you that all I could think about was that I wanted to be with Jeff in Heaven. If my twin was there, I wanted to be there too!

The next time I contemplated suicide was when I was in my early twenties. And I was raped ...again.

In the prologue, I spoke of the first time I was raped. I will bring that story back around in a few more chapters, because it is a key for you. However, the second time was different. I wasn't held at knifepoint like before, so I felt like I deserved it. I felt like it was entirely my fault. I'm not even sure if he knew it *was* rape. It happened so fast. I was a massage therapist at the time and I worked in a busy clinic. He was a trusted family friend who had originally come to see me for a sports injury. Over the course of several months as we rehabilitated the injury, I saw him once a week. We both enjoyed that time together and would look forward to our standing appointment. You see, we were dear friends. He had earlier played a huge role in my life. And because I felt safe, I allowed my heart to get involved. During that one hour per week, we had developed a relationship that involved deep conversation about all kinds of things. Over time, our feelings for each other and the friendship had begun to grow. Mind you, we were both happily married.

> It is naïve to think that we can't fall in love with someone other than our spouse ...and still deeply love our spouse. God built us for relationship.

I want to dispel a myth here. You *can* love more than one person at once. Actually you can love multiple people at the same time. I have never stopped loving Steve for a moment of our marriage. But I am capable – and so are you – of loving someone else simultaneously. Think about it. We love our friends. We love our family. We love our children. We even love our pets. It is naïve to think that we can't fall in love with someone other than our spouse ...and still deeply love our spouse. God built us for relationship. And when you have relationship with someone – anyone – it is natural for the feelings to progress into love.

We are created in God's image. He is capable of loving all of us at once. We too are capable. It is a matter of proximity. We love those that are around us. Look at Abraham. He loved Sarah, but he must have loved Hagar to some degree. Isaac loved Rachel, but he had to have loved Leah as well. Maybe not in the same way, but there had to be a love there. And don't forget about the two maid servants Bilhah and Zilpah. (See Genesis 29:30). Jacob was actively sleeping with four women at once ...and siring children.

Regardless of who is the "favorite" or who has the "most special place" in one's heart, we are created with the capacity to love multiple people at different levels – all at once.

There are so many examples in the Old Testament of multiple wives and concubines. It was completely normal. Not ideal for the women in my opinion ...but it was certainly normal for the men. My goodness! Look at King Solomon. His world must have been crazy! Talk about a *player*!

> *King Solomon, however, loved many foreign women besides Pharaoh's daughter - Moabites, Amononites, Edomites, Sidonians and Hittites. They were from nations about which the Lord had told the Israelites, 'You must not intermarry with them, because they will surely turn your hearts after their gods. Nevertheless, Solomon held fast to them in love. He had seven hundred wives of royal birth and three hundred concubines...* ~ 1 Kings 11:1-3

Can you imagine that?! Seven hundred wives and three hundred concubines? And he *"held fast to them in love"*? Wow. I rest my case. Anyway, back to my point.

> Seven hundred wives and three hundred concubines? And he *"held fast to them in love"*? Wow. I rest my case.

Love of any kind, passion of any kind, emotion of any kind ...can absolutely turn sexual.

In my case, I learned that he would be moving across the country in a few months, so our wonderful friendship was coming to a close. Consequently, at the end of his appointments, quick fluttering good bye kisses became our protocol. I came from a "kissing" family. I was a bit immune to the possibility that many men see *all* kisses as sexual. As the next few weeks wore on and his leaving became closer, the small kisses began to last just a little longer. Still nothing major. Just small, friendship kisses. No big deal ...I assumed.

That was a slow process. It lasted for months. And my feelings for him grew incrementally. My heart was "leading me astray" – and I was justifying the whole process, because he was so close to my family... especially to Steve. This man was very involved in our lives. Steve and I both admired and respected him. I was enamored that he cared so much about me. The whole time I was following my heart as it said, *"This is a sweet friendship. It's not that bad to kiss someone goodbye. It would end nicely. This chapter was concluding and it would just ... come softly to a close."*

The last time I saw him before he moved, I was completely stunned when it turned very sexual. It happened so fast. Although I was not dressed provocatively, I did have a skirt on, and so had unwittingly made myself more accessible and more vulnerable. It never even occurred to me that morning when I dressed for work at the massage clinic that I would be in such a crazy circumstance three hours later.

> It never even occurred to me that morning when I dressed for work at the massage clinic that I would be in such a crazy circumstance three hours later.

This was our last day; then he would be moving. Before I left the room I leaned over for a final kiss goodbye. My eyes welled with tears. I knew I would miss him terribly. He was sitting up on the table and was still under the massage sheet. It was a small kiss, but a strong, "safe" embrace. As the embrace ended and I began to pull away, he started breathing hard. He pulled me to him and whispered, *"I just can't resist you anymore!"*

One minute I was standing beside my table, the next I was being pushed down. In an instant he was on top of me. I was fully clothed, but because of the massage – he wasn't. In a matter of seconds, he pulled my skirt up, pushed my underwear aside, and he was inside me. Just like that. I never saw it coming. The whole thing lasted seconds. I didn't even have time to fight him off. It wasn't like that. There was no huge struggle. I was caught completely off guard. The clinic was full of people. I couldn't have fought and wouldn't have screamed. I was just too stunned. It was over as fast as it had begun. As he got up off of me, pulling the sheet around him, I barely heard him say something to the effect of *"I'm sorry, Amy. You were just too irresistible."*

I pulled my skirt back down and ran out of my massage studio into the clinic restroom right across the hall. I washed my face and hands, took several deep breaths and tried to pull myself together. My next client was already waiting for me in the lobby.

As he emerged from my room fully dressed, I stared at him in disbelief. *"What just happened?!"* I stammered under my breath. As he handed me a wad of money, he shrugged his shoulders, *"I'm sorry Amy. Like I said, I just couldn't resist you anymore.   But it will be ok... there is no condemnation for those that are in Christ Jesus."* The money fell from my hand to the floor.

And ...he left.

Chapter 18 ...The Scarlet Letter

As I watched him saunter out of the clinic that day, I was confronted with the cold hard fact that I had just committed adultery. And the feelings I had for this man immediately disappeared. I was completely overwhelmed as the steel hook of shame was instantly and firmly implanted deep in the recesses of my soul. Amy Sever: Adulteress. It felt as if the invisible Scarlet Letter bled through my shirt and appeared for the world to see.

And there it would remain.

He had moved off to another life and I was left to process the guilt, shame, and anger alone. Over the next days, weeks, and months, that anger began to take root. First at him and then at myself. Eventually that anger became hate... self-hate.

His last words, *"There is no condemnation for those that are in Christ Jesus"* haunted me. Every time I went to church, sang a worship song, or tried to pray, the *opposite* occurred. Even though I had begged for forgiveness over and over, all I could hear in my head and heart was condemnation. The voices never stopped. I was literally sick with guilt. I began to deteriorate emotionally. The shame was like a cancer in my bones.

> ...the invisible Scarlet Letter bled through my shirt and appeared for the world to see.

You see, this man was a strong Christian. A brother in Christ. And he had used scripture that day to justify sin. *My* sin was following my heart into an emotional affair. *His* sin was rape. They were both the same in God's eyes... one no worse than the other.

I actually think a lot of men *wouldn't* consider that scenario rape. Some men would justify it and say that I must have been "wanting it." Julius thought I deserved it, because I had been "a tease." I can only guess this "friend" thought I must have needed it because I had started to cry. Or worse, he just wanted it and nothing else mattered.

Here is some simple clarity: unwanted sex of any kind is rape. If a man ever overpowers a woman – whether physically or through the use of alcohol or drugs of any kind – it is rape. Where there is no cognizant consent ...there is *only* rape.

Steve has always said, any time there is a physical situation between a man and woman and that situation goes badly, it is always the fault of the man. He says sometimes men tend to cast the blame, but the responsibility to stop "always and forever belongs to the man." I can't tell you how many times I've heard him say it and prove it in conversations with others. You will see how he proved it to me "always and forever" in Chapter 42.

You see, it wasn't until years later that I really understood it wasn't me. The first time, of course the knife was at my throat. But, this had been different. There were

> How could this much emotional damage take place in only seconds?

feelings involved. It happened so fast. It didn't actually hurt physically. As a matter of fact, the actual intercourse lasted only seconds, so it must not have been that bad, right? How could this much emotional damage take place in only seconds?

In society, if a rape is physically traumatic, then it gets labeled as rape. If it isn't, it usually gets swept under the rug of the heart and left there to fester and create gaping wounds. The fact of the matter is, that without spiritual and emotional healing, it actually opens the door to demonic torment. There will be more on that later.

For now, let me say that if you are female and you are reading this book... you or someone you know has been in a similar situation. Women all around you are struggling with this silent epidemic. Either you... or a lovely lady in your midst is wrestling with it right now.

It could be at the hand of a family member. For many it's an uncle or a cousin, or even a father or brother who committed the rape. It is so often someone that no one would ever suspect. Sometimes, it starts as child's play, with the children honestly having no idea the psychological damage being done. You must understand that *most women* have been in some kind of similar scenario that I just described. And they blame themselves, just like I did. Statistically, 7 out of 10 women have been a victim of unwanted sex – either at knife or gun point, or as a child being molested, or in a scene similar to what I just recounted. They may have been slipped a drug and can't remember anything. But deep down, there is an emptiness and a sick feeling... And they know they have been violated.

> Men... as you read this book, I want you to know two things.

Men... as you read this book, I want you to know two things. All around you, 7 out of 10 women are in deep emotional pain as a result of one or more sexual violations. If you have the gift of discernment, you can look into their eyes and see it right now. It can be your wife, girlfriend, sister, or a close friend. It can be a mom or an aunt. They are everywhere and most have lived in their invisible prison for years.

Please hear my heart – especially if it is your wife or girlfriend – finish this book to see what my husband ultimately did. Most men react exactly as the enemy would have them react. Consequently, they make the situation worse. This is why most women choose to remain in their silent pain.

The second thing is, I absolutely know some men who are reading this book have, *themselves* been violated sexually. It goes both ways. Satan doesn't just pick on women. I am not writing this book just for women. I have worked with many men who were molested as boys. Sexual molestation as a boy can envelop that man in the same silent prison, and it can open another door that is even more difficult to close. More on that later.

What I know for a fact is that sexual sin - big or small - is still sin. And it wreaks emotional havoc for both women and men.

In my case, it affected me immediately. I was terrified that if I told Steve, it would end our relationship. Every time we made love, it was all I could think about. He began to sense the distance and ask me what was wrong. *"Nothing..."* was my typical response. When he would press in and ask again, I would snap back and say it stronger. He knew he was losing me to an invisible opponent, but he had no idea what that foe was, or how to help me. Our marriage began to suffer, as I slowly drifted away from the vibrant, fun-loving wife he married and became quiet, withdrawn, shy about my body, and slow to engage physically.

As the months wore on, Steve continued to press in. Every time he asked me, the burden of my sin washed over me again. We were at church all the time. I was constantly surrounded with worship music, small groups, sermons, etc. I was presented with an altar call at least two times per week, so it was constantly in my face. No matter how many times I asked forgiveness, I never felt free. I was buckling under the emotionally agonizing weight of guilt and shame.

> He knew he was losing me to an invisible opponent, but he had no idea what that foe was, or how to help me.

I began to consider the option of actually telling Steve what had happened.   And every time, I immediately dismissed it. I remembered how he had reacted when I told him about Julius and that night in the Dominican Republic.

This guy was Steve's friend. He was a friend of my entire family. He and my dad were friends. He and my brother were friends. I feared that Steve would probably blame me and it would end my marriage, or he would confront the guy and my whole family would find out. This man was popular in our community and for this to get out would be devastating, not just for my family, but also for his. I couldn't imagine that picture either. I was stuck in an impossible scenario.

I began to hate my beauty. Every time I looked in the mirror, both rapes came rushing back; I would hear these words; *"If you were ugly, this wouldn't have happened."* Subconsciously, I reasoned that to become fat would make me less attractive. I began to change my eating habits and gain weight – intentionally.

Chapter 19 ... One Night in the Rain

I remember it like it was yesterday. The thunder rolled and cracked. Streaks of splintered lightning split the sky that night. I had been at a weekend seminar in Wichita Falls, Texas. As I drove down the unfamiliar two-lane highway, I could barely see through the pounding rain battering my windshield. The steady, rapid rhythm of the wipers allowed about 50 feet of vision in front of my car.

Steve would be expecting me in about 3 hours. I knew he would want to make love when I got home... My thoughts drifted. I recalled that afternoon several months earlier ...with someone other than my husband. The sick, familiar onslaught of guilt and shame came rushing back. I thought about Julius; how I had teased him that week in paradise, and remembered that I felt like I deserved his response. I began to recall other instances in my life after Julius ...and how they all played a role in the woman I had become.

I thought of Jeff. He was my best friend. I could have told him. He would have listened and understood. He wouldn't have judged me... but it had been years since I had spoken with my beloved brother. I still missed him so much! Every day, I longed to hear his voice, to see his smile. My heart grew heavier as a deep, dark sadness enveloped me. I was just... so... tired...

> Headlights! My thoughts were abruptly interrupted as I was startled by an oncoming vehicle...

Several different scenes flashed onto the screen of my mind. Things no one knew about. Things that had shaped the young woman driving that vehicle. I did not like her. I hated her. I was ashamed of her. She was supposed to be a Spirit-filled Christian. She went to church every Sunday. She was a wife and a mother. She was...

Headlights! My thoughts were abruptly interrupted as I was startled by an oncoming vehicle that suddenly appeared right beside me on the two-lane highway. I had not even seen that car coming! The rain was driving so hard and the visibility was extremely low. To top it off, fog had begun to move in. I had been lost in thought. Lost in my life. The past... ever present.

*"You know Amy, when the next car comes, you could 'accidently' drift over into the other lane, and end it all... It would be quick and painless if you drive fast... No one would ever know that it was intentional. You would be completely justified. It is dark. It is raining. The roads are wet. Why don't you just move to the left and speed up? Then you would be with Jeff right now. Then Steve would never know that you cheated on him... Your parents still have Jason ...Just ...**swerve to the left!!!**"*

The loud, accusing thought slammed into my consciousness with the same force as the lightning slammed into the ground all around me. It was sudden and it was real. Almost audible. I literally began to fight my steering wheel and my gas pedal simultaneously. It was like an unseen driver had suddenly taken over my Ford Explorer.

As I sped down the highway that night, I began to tremble with fear. An eerie presence was in the car with me. I *felt* it. I knew something evil had invaded my vehicle. The hair on the back of my neck stood up. I was nauseated. As the headlights of an 18-wheeler came into view, I gripped my steering wheel and forced my foot off the gas.

Suddenly from out of nowhere, a goat jumped in the lane right in front of me. I had no time to react. I knew that if I hit my brakes my car would start sliding on the wet road. I had no other choice but to brace and hit the goat. To swerve meant a certain head-on collision.

A second later, the impact of the goat on a wet highway knocked me directly into the other lane just as the driver of the 18-wheeler slammed on his brakes and blasted the horn.

I screamed *"Jesus! Help me!!!"* and burst into my prayer language as my car skidded directly into the blasting horn and the oncoming headlights! The head-on collision happened anyway...

I will never be able to understand what happened next – this side of Heaven – and I will never forget it. I literally *felt my car pass right through that truck*! It is so hard to describe. Something weird and inter-dimensional? I don't know. I only know there are indeed miracles that take place! It was like something I've seen in the movies. One of those special effects where things are warped as they are going through another dimension. This is the most supernatural thing I have ever witnessed. *I most certainly had a head-on collision with an 18-wheeler in the rain that night.*

I steadied my steering wheel as I continued to brake and my car gently slowed to a stop on the shoulder of the highway. Trembling, I got out of my car just as the trucker came running toward me. He was crying uncontrollably. *"I KNOW I hit you! I KNOW I hit you!! How could this be?! My God! I KNOW I hit you!"* He was shaking from head to toe. I could see him in the lightning. This stranger grabbed me and hugged me in the rain. *"I just KNOW I hit you. I FELT myself hit you! ...God was here tonight. I know he was!"*

It was just the two of us on a lonely highway, late that night. We were the only witnesses to an incredible miracle. In a moment of stunned silence, we both stood there in the pounding rain and looked at each other, then at the goat on the highway. The only damage to either of our

> In a moment of stunned silence, we both stood there in the pounding rain and looked at each other, then at the goat on the highway.

vehicles was my front license plate lying on the glistening pavement beside the dead animal. After a few minutes, the man helped me drag the goat off the road and into the ditch. As he picked up my license plate and ceremoniously handed it to me, he said, *"You need to keep this – To help you remember that you had angels watching over you tonight... Don't ever forget that! Angels were watching over you!"* After several minutes of making sure I was okay, he reluctantly got back up into his rig and slowly drove off.

Still trembling I walked back to my car, opened the door and climbed back into the driver's seat. I was soaking wet. I just sat there. I didn't start the vehicle. I just stared at the license plate lying in the passenger seat beside me. Softly I began to pray in the spirit again. As the intercession of the Holy Spirit flowed from my lips once more, the paralyzing fear eventually began to dissipate. The gripping thoughts of suicide retreated. The trembling subsided.

I knew beyond a shadow of a doubt that my life had just been supernaturally spared. I also knew that I was not wrestling with flesh and blood that night. I had been wrestling with demonic forces that had tried to take my life. Hot tears spilled down my cheeks as I began to cry. Then I began to sob. As I sat there alone in my car, one deep guttural sob turned into another. An unending stream of tears slid down my face and blended in with the rain water that soaked my lap. Sobbing uncontrollably, I rested my forehead on the same steering wheel I had just wrestled.

I thanked God for sparing my life. I begged God to guide me back to Him. I asked Him to show me a way out of the never-ending waves of guilt and shame.   I asked Him to protect me from the constant, bloody nightmares that had been occurring since I was 18, and the ever-present voices that accompanied me.

I was sick of living a spiritual lie. I longed for the sweet relationship that I had enjoyed with Jesus as a young girl. I yearned for communion with the Holy Spirit that I had experienced in Guatemala at age 17. But since my rape at 18, my life had been a roller coaster of emotion. I had made so many mistakes...

> I hadn't considered that it might be rape. I had taken full responsibility, and the weight was crushing me.

I had been married and divorced. Six months after my divorce, the day before my daughter's second birthday, my first husband was killed in a car wreck. I had not even gotten over our divorce when I was forced to bury him.

He had cheated on me with so many women. In my pain I had sworn I would never do that to Steve. Yet in the weeks and months following that fateful afternoon, I felt like I had. I hadn't considered that it might be rape. I had taken full responsibility, and the weight was crushing me. I had been lying to Steve about it for months.

"Jesus! I need you so desperately! I'm tired. I am so tired. I'm tired of living a lie! I'm tired of pretending I'm happy. I'm tired of hating myself!"

I had gained 40 pounds since the incident at work that day. I hated how I looked. I hated ...everything. I had been listening to the voice that said *"If you were ugly, men wouldn't be attracted to you and this stuff wouldn't happen..."*

I hated that voice. It had become my constant companion. Just like the nightmares. Constant companions. That night on the highway, that voice manifested inside my car and had tried two separate ways to kill me.

I had finally come to the end of myself and I asked God for a way out. I asked God to heal my heart and bring me back to Him. I needed His grace. I needed His mercy. I needed Jesus. Desperately.

Chapter
20 *... Coming Back*

Even though I walk through the valley of the shadow of death, I will fear no evil, for you are with me; your rod and your staff, they comfort me. ~ Psalm 23:4

As I look back in retrospect at that stormy night, I know firsthand that I was, by angelic intervention, supernaturally spared from death.

I also realize I was in the presence of something wicked that night. I shudder to think how close I came to attempting to end my life. Then, in the next moment, a supernatural attempt from evil tried to end it for me.

I realize that our enemy *is real*, and he does indeed desire to "steal, kill, and destroy," in every way he can. He will do it through our ignorance and our sin,

> I also realize I was in the presence of something wicked that night. I shudder to think how close I came to attempting to end my life.

or even the sins of others perpetrated upon us. The devil wants to kill everything we hold dear. He can even attempt to kill us if we leave ourselves unprotected. Even though he likes it best when we are executed by our own hand, he will go to great lengths himself.

Now, I realize how some are reacting after reading that last chapter. I know it seems so unbelievable. I almost didn't put it in the book. However, it was so instrumental in my spiritual journey that I couldn't leave it out. I had to remind myself that I am not writing this book to further your faith in Amy Sever. I am writing this book to further your faith in the Lord of Hosts. I pray that He quickens your spirit to *know that truth.*

The challenge with my head-on collision story is that interrupts our "normal" religion. It doesn't fit our current spiritual paradigms. Believe me, I know! I have said many times now, that the church I grew up in did not address the supernatural side of Christianity – good or evil. Angels, demons, the Holy Spirit, and Satan were never mentioned.   Personally going through these things *forced* my paradigm shift from "those kinds of things only happened to the early Biblical characters; they don't happen today... to *God is the same yesterday, today and forever.*"

We still have interaction with the spiritual realm, both good and evil. Not only do we still have an enemy, but more importantly, we still have guardian angels that protect us from all kinds of harm.

However, I feel the need to give you some scriptural examples of supernatural miracles that took place to rescue God's children.   We read these examples in the Bible, but somehow we don't readily believe they actually *still happen* for us today. Trust me. *They do!*

The logical question we have to ask ourselves is, "Did God change? Did the devil change?   Would the devil give up on this generation? Certainly not!   So why would God forfeit the angelic protection of Biblical days?"   He *does not change.*   And the angels are still here, guiding and protecting God's beloved children.   Just as they have since the beginning.

I encourage you to read these scriptures and then go read the referenced stories on your own, and pray for the Lord to strengthen your spirit. Let faith build in your heart as you become readily aware of the angelic host sent to guard you, protect you, and keep you from the evil one...

> *Be self-controlled and alert. Your enemy, the devil prowls around like a roaring lion looking for someone to devour.* ~ 1 Peter 5:8

> *The angel of the Lord encamps around those who fear him, and he delivers them.* ~ Psalm 34:7

> *If you make the Most High your dwelling – even the Lord, who is my refuge – then no harm will befall you, no disaster will come near your tent. For He will command His angels concerning you to guard you in all your ways; they will lift you up in their hands, so that you will not strike your foot against a stone.* ~ Psalm 91:9-12

Are not angels ministering spirits sent to serve those who will inherit salvation? ~Hebrews 1:14

A few Biblical accounts of supernatural intervention and angelic activity on behalf of the children of God:

- The parting of the Red Sea. ~ Exodus 14:19-22

- An angel drives out entire nations to prepare the way for the Israelites. ~ Exodus 23:20-23

- The Israelites cross the Jordan River (another dry ground experience). ~ Joshua 3:14-17

- (This will test your belief!) The sun stands still for a day. ~ Joshua 10:12-14

- Ezekiel watches a valley of dry bones become a living army. ~ Ezekiel 37:1-10

- Shadrach, Meshach and Abednego thrown into a fiery furnace and not burned. ~ Daniel 4:19-27

- Daniel is supernaturally protected in the lion's den. ~ Daniel 6:19-23

- Philip is supernaturally transported from one place to another. ~ Acts 8:26-40

- Peter's miraculous escape from prison. ~ Acts:12:5-11

- An angel spares Paul and his crew. ~ Acts 27:23-25

Now is a good time for a coffee break. Grab something to drink. Get a snack. Take a breath. I'm doing the same thing right now as I write. Chapters 17-19 were difficult to write! You can see now why I hesitated to put this all down on paper. It really is hard for me to relive these aspects of my life in such vivid detail.

I have cried a lot this week while writing this. Today (Chapter 19) was particularly hard, as you can imagine. I thank God for my family! Steve has been so patient and loving. My parents are so supportive and encouraging, as well as my brother Jason, sister-in-law Tracy, and my two precious nieces Kynnzie and Jaslynn. They all know at least some of my story, and are all in favor of me publishing it. Savannah, my amazing daughter, and I had this text conversation just last night...

> **Me**: This book is hard for me to write.
>
> **Savannah**: I'm sure. Lots of forces that don't want that book published. Fight through it.
>
> **Me**: I haven't cried this much in years.
>
> **Savannah**: They are tears that have probably been locked in for years and will probably be very healing for you. This whole process will.
>
> **Me**: You are wise beyond your years.
>
> **Savannah**: The devil knows your story and he knows the secrets that you're about to reveal -about a lot of his strategies. Keep writing, Mom. Persevere. It's not just about you. It's about the girls and women who need your courage.
>
> **Me**: I love you.
>
> **Savannah**: I love YOU. Keep fighting. I pray for you constantly. Stay covered. Have Daddy pray for you out loud. It wouldn't hurt for him to anoint you either.
>
> **Me**: Okay, I will.
>
> **Savannah**: I love you, Mom.
>
> **Me**: Thank you for your texts. I cherish you.
>
> **Savannah**: I'm always here. Thank you.

So, with my fresh cup of coffee sitting beside my computer, I press on. My goal is to walk us all the way through to 1 Thessalonians 5:23-24. If you are already enjoying that abundance of spiritual, emotional, and physical freedom, I rejoice with you. If you feel like you don't need this material and it doesn't apply to you, then I suspect it found its way into your hands because someone close to you – does.

So, let's get back to the Soul.

I walked through that aspect of my story to create a foundation on which to overlay the next several chapters. This section is on "Restoring the Soul." As I said earlier, you can't restore something that isn't damaged or broken... and my soul was definitely damaged. It was battered and bruised.

Our souls catch the brunt of devastation caused by sin. Consider my story. The **mind**: Throughout that whole time, I was thinking wrong thoughts. I was entertaining temptation to go deeper into a friendship with a man that wasn't my husband. The **will**: I chose to kiss him. I chose to put myself in wrong proximity, in a wrong situation. The **emotions**: My emotions were all over the place the minute the hook was set.

Can you see why I say that the soul is the devil's workshop? I encourage you to look into the window of your own life. Do that exercise. See if you can trace a traumatic situation back to the soul. Walk through it. Was an initial thought or temptation involved? Did you choose to act on it by following your heart, even knowing that it was wrong? How did your emotions hold up under the weight of your situation? If you are like me, it will prove to be an interesting path of reflection and self-evaluation.

So, how do we protect it? How do we defend our souls from the spiritual onslaught?

So, how do we protect it? How do we defend our souls from the spiritual onslaught? Obviously, some things are just going to happen because we live in a fallen world. Until we cross over into an eternity with Christ, we will always have trauma.

However, I am writing this book because I have been given some keys. We can indeed protect ourselves and our children from damage caused by sin. We do not have to walk according to the sinful nature (the mind, will, emotions). We *do* have a choice! **We live by the Spirit!**

I mentioned at the beginning of this book that I was introduced to another ministry several years ago. Not long after that crazy rainy night outside of Wichita Falls, TX, and my desperate prayer for help, I met Joe and Sydna Hamilton. Actually, they had been friends of the family from church, but I was reintroduced to them and to Toni Ridley and the ministry they led.

That ministry helped free people from addictions, etc. It was a course that lasted for several weeks with homework every night, culminating in a weekend retreat, where one could experience freedom from bondage.

It sounded easy enough, and I was certainly quietly desperate. Steve and I started attending the class one night a week. As the different chapters were introduced, I began to grasp some of the concepts. The difference between the spirit and the soul, and how to walk in alignment. This class and the concepts introduced there, along with the deliverance that followed, were indeed the answer to my plea for help. It has changed my life drastically.

Twelve years ago I felt the Lord nudge me to document what I learned, intertwined with my personal story. (Sigh), so I sit here and write, determined to finally follow through in obedience. I pray now that if you are reading this, it will benefit you or someone you love.

Notes and Reflections

Chapter 21 ...*Benefits of Living by the Spirit*

"A spiritual man is not a man born again, but a man born again and walking in alignment." ~ Watchman Nee

So I say, live by the Spirit, and you will not gratify the desires of the sinful nature. ~ Galatians 5:16

Do not be deceived: God cannot be mocked. A man reaps what he sows. The one who sows to please his sinful nature, from that nature will reap destruction; the one who sows to please the Spirit, from the Spirit will reap eternal life. ~ Galatians 6:7-9

The definition of "Living by the Spirit" is simply choosing to live life with our spirit guiding our soul. Seems easy. Got it. *"Spirit, guide my soul,"* and I will be healed.

Well, yes, it *is* that simple. However, actually getting our souls to come under the jurisdiction of our spirits is another thing altogether. Believe me, it is a learned discipline and does *not* come naturally!

For the sinful nature desires what is contrary to the Spirit, and the Spirit what is contrary to the sinful nature. They are in conflict with each other, so that you do not do what you want. ~ Galatians 6:17

Even though I was saved and I was Spirit-filled, I was not "living by the Spirit" or I would not have danced with Julius the way I did that night. I would not have let my heart dictate my actions in that friendship. I would have resisted the temptation in both of those scenarios and steered clear of the trouble it caused. You see in both situations – along with many others – I had let what I *thought* and *felt* dictate how I *acted*. I was living according to my sin nature.

"Living by the Spirit" is *choosing* to live, having your soul - or sin nature - completely submitted to the Spirit of God. The Spirit is controlling your thoughts, actions, and emotions.   Remember the scripture in Romans by the Apostle Paul...

> *I know that nothing good lives in me, that is, in my sinful nature. For I have the desire to do what is good, but I cannot carry it out. For what I do is not the good I want to do; no, the evil I do not want to do - this I keep on doing.*
> ~ Romans 7:18-19

When we are saved and invite Christ into our hearts, we receive His Spirit. We *can then choose* to live according to the Spirit rather than our sinful nature, but it requires self-discipline.

> *Those who live according to the sinful nature have their minds set on what that nature desires; but those who live in accordance with the Spirit have their minds set on what the Spirit desires. The mind of the sinful man is death, but the mind controlled by the Spirit is life and peace...*
> ~ Romans 8:5-8

Even Paul struggled with this. We all do. I still do. The sinful nature is all about instant gratification. It bows easily to temptation.

> The sinful nature is all about instant gratification... It has an appetite for the things in life that will hurt us the most.

It has an appetite for the things in life that will hurt us the most. Sin is fun ...for a few minutes.

Unfortunately, we will wrestle until we cross over into eternity and give up our mortal bodies. At that time we will also joyfully resign our sin nature.

However, when we nurture our spirit and spend time with the Lord, as I stated in the first section, our spirit grows in strength.   It becomes easier and easier to live by the Spirit and resist sin.

As our human spirits get stronger, the Spirit of God takes precedence over the desires of our souls. We are able to walk according to the Spirit rather than the sinful nature.

There are two primary benefits of walking according to the Spirit: you can hear the voice of God clearly, and you are able to protect yourself from the enemy.

Let's trace back to the first section of the book. In *Renewing the Spirit*, the scriptures there show us that God is a Spirit and when we are born again He communicates to us through our spirit. When we make a conscious effort, on a daily basis, to choose to walk in the Spirit, we have a constant and clear stream of communication with the Father. That communication is enhanced with supernatural power when we are baptized in the Holy Spirit.

> If we cannot hear God clearly, we become open to deception by the enemy.

However, when we are walking according to the sin nature, our soul dictates. What God is saying to us must first filter through our thoughts, imaginations, and confusion of our mind. Then through the pain, brokenness, anger, and resentments in our emotions. Then through the consequences of the choices we have made. And finally, through any other stress we may be experiencing. The clarity of His voice gets lost in all these elements of our soul and God's direction for our lives is weakened or lost. If we cannot hear God clearly, we become open to deception by the enemy.

I need you to remember that the stories I told you in the first section about how the Lord graciously used me to minister to Darla and Connie were years *after* my personal story you just read. The chronology is backwards. I just wanted to remind you. The rest of the book is set in flashback - in years previous to now. I am walking in freedom and abundance today and have been for years. But you and I still have a bit of a journey, in order to finish our spiritual handbook.

So again, hearing God's voice is essential for spiritual growth. However, there is another reason that Christians must walk in the Spirit. This is just as crucial. We must be able to protect our soul from the attack of the enemy.

Remember how I fought the voices in my head? The nightmares?
Thoughts of suicide? Even a physical manifestation that night in my
car with the steering wheel, and outside my car with the goat? All of
those are examples of what the Bible calls *"flaming arrows of the evil
one."* In some translations they are called *"fiery darts of hell."*

They are real. And they are evil. We see people succumb to them all
the time. The evening news is full of stories where someone actually
acted on the voices in their head. We see people take their own lives
in order to make the voices stop. Sometimes they commit a heinous
crime - such as murder - and can't even remember it. These people
are suffering from the flaming arrows. They suffer and, just like me,
they have no idea they can actually *do* something about it.

People are locked in cycles of sin, guilt, and shame. Even worse, they
are harassed and helpless against the devil's schemes...

> *Put on the full armor of God so that you can take your stand
> against the devil's schemes. For our struggle is not against
> flesh and blood, but against the rulers, against the
> authorities, against the powers of this dark world and
> against the spiritual forces of evil in the heavenly realms.*
> *Therefore put on the full
> armor of God, so that
> when the day of evil
> comes, you may be
> able to stand your
> ground, and after you
> have done everything,*

For our struggle is not against flesh and blood, but against the rulers, against the authorities, against the powers of this dark world...

> *to stand. Stand firm then, with the belt of truth buckled
> around your waist, with the breastplate of righteousness in
> place, and with your feet fitted with the readiness that comes
> from the gospel of peace. In addition to all this, take
> up the shield of faith, with which you can extinguish all the
> flaming arrows of the evil one. Take the helmet of salvation
> and the sword of the Spirit, which is the word of God.*
> ~ Ephesians 6:11-17

When you and I are walking in the Spirit, not only can we hear the
voice of God, but we have access to all kinds of new weaponry. When

we choose to put on the full armor of God, we are protected by the shield of faith.

I want you to think of the shield of faith differently. Not as you would see it on a knight, but more like an invincible, impenetrable force field that covers you entirely. Think of it as having some kind of fluid that immediately quenches fire. Those flaming arrows thrown at your heart, at your mind, and at your body are immediately extinguished by the shield of faith. *The blood of Jesus is that fluid.* His royal blood *does indeed* cover you. It atones for every sin. Every crazy thought. Every wrong action. Every infirmity of your soul. And every sickness of your body.

Isn't that great news? Hallelujah!

Chapter 22
...The Prayer of Submission

Okay. So here is a quick summary of the last few chapters.

We need to learn to walk in the Spirit, not the sin nature. It is a daily choice. The word I like to use is to "submit." Our souls must *submit* to our spirits.

For some of us, the word "submit" brings up a negative connotation. We don't like that word. Especially when we filter it through some of our personal experiences with abusive parents or spouses. However, this was *The Key* to my freedom, and it is also the key to yours.

Here are some definitions of the word **submit:** [1]To come under the protection of. [2]To yield - accept somebody else's authority or will. [3]To defer to another's knowledge, judgment, authority, or experience. (Ref: Webster's Dictionary)

Now, let me ask you... in light of my story on the road that night, wouldn't it be a good idea to submit? To defer to the authority of the Spirit of Christ? To come under the protection of the Lord? Yes. It saved my life!

Here is a simple prayer that changed my life. I pray this daily. Sometimes when I am wrestling with temptation, I pray it several times. I actually speak out loud to myself. I choose to use my mind to force my body and soul into order and submit to (come under the protection of) my spirit.

Now, the last section of this book is all about the Body, so this prayer will make more sense later. Remember how I said I intentionally began to gain weight to protect myself? The flesh is a funny thing. Its appetites never cease. Whatever you feed, expands. Literally. Physically *and* spiritually. But I have control over my mind, will, emotions, and my body. This prayer works!

> "Father, thank you for saving me. Thank you that I am the temple of the Holy Spirit and that my spirit is controlled by the Spirit of God.

Soul - submit to my spirit right now. My mind, will, and emotions will *not* control me. I choose to come under the protection of the Spirit.

Body - line up under my soul. You will not control me either. I do not cater to the flesh. My spirit will control my soul *and* my body. I choose to walk in alignment. Spirit, Soul and Body, come under the covering and protection of the Spirit of God. Amen."

When we continually discipline the desires of our souls and the appetites of our body, our souls eventually get used to it and submit more easily. Our bodies will submit as well. We are then finally able to hear the voice of God. We are also protected by the Spirit from a very real enemy ...one that throws very real flaming arrows.

After a period of time without the onslaught of arrows, our souls begin to relax. We can actually lie down and rest without the continuous barrage of negativity in our heads. Sleep comes more easily. The loud accusing voices soften and then eventually cease. The sleepy fog of confusion dissipates. The heavy weight of depression begins to lift from our shoulders. Sick thoughts of worry, anxiety, and fear are no longer our constant companions. Guilt and shame bow to grace and mercy. Under the protection, guidance and authority of the Spirit, we are able to resist temptation and choose to walk in His ways.

In summary, I just wanted to clarify a couple of things. As I attended these ministry classes, nearly every week there was a new concept. And each concept challenged me. It challenged how I looked at the Word of God, and it certainly challenged how I looked at myself. As I walked through this new information, I fought through many things.

However, as I worked through and began to assimilate this new knowledge, I started to realize that there was a light beginning to appear at the end of the tunnel. Hope began to stir in my life. I had to fight to get to the classes each week, but in the end I gained invaluable spiritual tools.

I learned the foundational basics of spirit and soul, and I learned to walk in the Spirit and say "no" to my sin nature.

It was only then, after several weeks of practicing my new spiritual tools, that my soul finally began to rest from the onslaught of "flaming arrows" enough to handle the deeper teachings coming up in the next several chapters.

Read this scripture again, and look at the last half this time. After we resist the enemy, the God of all grace promises to restore us and make us strong, firm, and steadfast. What a great promise!

> *Be self-controlled and alert. Your enemy the devil prowls around like a roaring lion looking for someone to devour. Resist him, standing firm in the faith ...and the God of all grace, who called you to his eternal glory in Christ ...will* **Himself restore you** *and make you strong, firm, and steadfast.* ~ 1 Peter 5:8-10

If you just read this page and you don't feel strong, firm, and steadfast, then the next few chapters may be for you - because we have *much more* to cover.

When we begin walking in the Spirit, we are able to finally discipline ourselves against the desires and appetites of our sin nature. We are then able to open up the lines of communication with the Spirit of God, and He can begin to actually shore us up. Finally, the touch of the Father's hand can begin to restore our souls to their original beauty and splendor.

It can be a painful process, but so worth it! I said in my introduction that you might want to have someone praying for you as you read through the material here. If you haven't done that yet, now might be a good time. Because if you are like me, you may be about to encounter some information that could change your life and set you free.

However, I feel compelled to inform you that the path to freedom will require some work on your part. It could be emotionally painful. Thus your need for prayer cover...

I am also compelled to place a caveat here. Earlier I spoke of three categories with regard to your thoughts on the Holy Spirit. There are three categories of people at this point in the book as well.

The first category is that you are shocked at my story. You have never had anything traumatic happen to you. You have never done anything remotely like what I did that night in the Dominican Republic. Maybe you have never behaved in that manner or placed yourself in a situation similar to my massage clinic experience. There are some people out there that just have phenomenal lives. They have always just been ...good! No trauma or tragedy. No devastating personal sin. I greatly admire those people! If that is you, then perhaps this book is not for *you*. However, keep reading, and consider that it may be for someone you know, or maybe a family member. Remember that 7 out of 10 people around you... are silently hurting.

The next category is that you haven't ever been molested, contemplated suicide, or had sex with someone else outside of marriage, but you *have* done some things in your life that need healing. The Lord is working with you right now, and you know that you need to "press on."

The third category is that my story pales in comparison to yours. You view your sins as so much worse than mine. And you are hearing things like, *"Amy thinks she was bad? What if I told her MY story!? She would blush with shame and completely judge me! My story makes hers look like a freakin' fairy tale!"* ...

If *that's* what you are hearing in your head right now, *THOSE* are the voices I am speaking of! And they *DO NOT* belong to you. I know it sounds like your thoughts but believe me, they are *not your thoughts*. And they certainly aren't God's. They are the thoughts of the father of lies and they are *camouflaged as yours*. Trust me, I remember them well. I lived with them for years!

Chapter 23 ...*Jesus Came to*

134   Amy Sever

His approval is
money, not s
approval. ↑

Transr
to a'

Those voices! How I hated those vo
to my introduction when I talked ab
They are responsible for those voi
struggling with that statement. Ma
have demons, but I am here to dis
Christian. And I *definitely* had
taking up *real residence* in my body.

I have been laying that foundation for several chapters. I guess I've been easing into it. I don't know if that was for your sake or mine. Even still, I have just been sitting here staring at my computer screen for hours now. Praying. How do I get started with this part? You may think I'm crazy from here on out!

> How do I get started with this part? You may think I'm crazy from here on out!

This is again the precise reason why I have continued to put the book down and not pick it up for years at a time. But I know what this knowledge and the subsequent deliverance did for me. And what it has accomplished for those I've had the privilege of ministering to on an individual basis. So I pray that you or someone you love can absorb this and let the Father use it to heal and restore as well.

Even as I write this, I have been wrestling.

I have been running from this ministry for over a decade. My fear of judgment has been the catalyst. However, I've decided that I will no longer acquiesce to the fear of how this book will be received. You see - I see faces. Connie's face, Darla's face, and the faces of so many others who are dear to me – a few of which I'm about to introduce you to – who are free today, as a result of this information.

And I guess I have finally come to the conclusion that my job is not to care what people think of me. It's really none of my business, is it? My job is transparency and information. It's God's job to do the rest.

e only thing that matters to me anyway. Not
...ess in business, not the applause of men. God's
...t's it.

...ency is a curious thing. It is one of the most difficult things
...ow, and yet it *is* what set me free. It wasn't until I was
completely transparent, that
God restored my soul.

> ...my job is not to care what people think of me. It's really none of my business, is it? My job is transparency and information.

One of Satan's tactics is to keep things hidden. He hates the truth. And he hates truthful people. Even as I write this book, I have to actively force my soul submit to my spirit and take my thoughts captive. It is indeed *a fight* to expose the tactics the enemy used in my life and tell you the truth!

For the next several chapters I'm going to move toward the 5-hour experience that changed my life and set me free. That 5-hour experience could have made a great movie if someone had actually had a video camera! Even though it was years and years ago, I still remember it vividly.

But I am getting into future pages here, so let me back up. In the last several chapters you have become familiar with these scriptures:

> *Be self-controlled and alert. Your enemy the devil prowls around like a roaring lion looking for someone to devour.*
> ~ 1 Peter 5:8

> *For our struggle is not against flesh and blood, but against the rulers, against the authorities, against the powers of this dark world and against the spiritual forces of evil in the Heavenly realms.* ~ Ephesians 6:12

> *The thief comes to steal, kill, and destroy...* ~ John 10:10

Unfortunately, these scriptures concerning your enemy have been front and center for a while now. I just had to establish the fact that he is indeed real and he is relevant to your situation.

So let me balance things a bit. Let's talk about our Savior for a few minutes. Because He is *also real*, and He is *also relevant* to your situation! Praise God!

Seven hundred years before His birth, the prophet Isaiah looked down through the tunnel of time and wrote one of the most beautiful, promising, and accurate portraits of Jesus. This was a perfect description of the coming Messiah.

> *The Spirit of the Sovereign Lord is on me, because the Lord has anointed me to preach good news to the poor. He has sent me to bind up the brokenhearted, to proclaim freedom for the captives and release from darkness for the prisoners, to proclaim the year of the Lord's favor and the day of vengeance of our God, to comfort all who mourn, and provide for those who grieve in Zion - to bestow on them a crown of beauty instead of ashes, the oil of gladness instead of mourning, and a garment of praise instead of a spirit of despair... ~ Isaiah 61:1-3*

You may recognize that passage from my original prayer for you in my introduction. You see, Jesus called us to take up this same mantle and He gave us this same mandate.

Let's look at some other scriptures. Do you realize that one-third of Jesus' ministry was delivering people from demons? As you can see, people in His time were just as *"harassed and helpless"* (Matthew 9:36) as we are today. Demons don't die. They are still here. And they are still doing exactly what they did then. I can personally attest to this. Let's examine these passages. This first one is Jesus himself, actually quoting from the above passage in Isaiah.

> *The Spirit of the Lord is on me, because he has anointed me to preach good news to the poor. He has sent me to proclaim freedom for the prisoners and recovery of sight for the blind, to release the oppressed... ~ Luke 4:18-19*

> *News about him spread all over Syria, and people brought to Him all who were ill with various diseases, those suffering*

severe pain, the demon-possessed, those having seizures, and the paralyzed, and He healed them. ~ Matthew 4:24

While they were going out, a man who was demon-possessed and could not talk was brought to Jesus. And when the demon was driven out, the man who had been mute spoke... ~ Matthew 9:32-33

On a Sabbath Jesus was teaching in one of the synagogues, and a woman was there who had been crippled by a spirit for eighteen years. She was bent over and could not straighten up at all. When Jesus saw her, He called her forward and said to her, "Woman, you are set free from your infirmity." Then He put His hands on her, and immediately she straightened up and praised God. Indignant because Jesus had healed on the Sabbath, the synagogue ruler said to the people, "There are six days for work. So come and be healed on those days, not on the Sabbath." The Lord answered him, "You hypocrites! Doesn't each of you on the Sabbath untie his ox or donkey from the stall and lead it out to give it water? Then should not this woman, a daughter of Abraham who Satan has kept bound for eighteen long years, be set free on the Sabbath day from what bound her?" ~ Luke 13:10-16

Then they brought him a demon-possessed man who was blind and mute, and Jesus healed him so that he could both talk and see. ~ Matthew 12:22

*When evening came, many who were demon-possessed were brought to Him and He drove out the spirits with a word and healed all the sick. This was to fulfill what was spoken through the prophet Isaiah: "**He took up our infirmities and carried our diseases.**"* ~ Matthew 8:16-17

I put those words in bold, because I am going to come back to them in a few minutes.

Those are passages that show you Jesus constantly delivered people from demons - individually and corporately. Sometimes a demon was responsible for a particular physical malady. These are amazing scriptures!

How many of our loved ones are unnecessarily suffering from physical diseases? In many cases that person could be healed by being delivered from the demon that is tormenting them.

> ...doctors today would give it a name and prescribe drugs to mask the symptoms. But *The Healer* did not spend time naming it - He just cast it out.

I love the passage above about the lady in bondage for 18 years. It sounds a lot like osteoarthritis, doesn't it? You see, our doctors today would give it a name and prescribe drugs to mask the symptoms. But *The Healer* did not spend time naming it - He just cast it out.

I pray for an army of believers that will actually *do* what Jesus commanded us to do! What are we afraid of? There aren't nearly enough brave men and women of God who are actually walking in the power and authority of the Holy Spirit and doing the things Jesus did! He sent the disciples to continue in His ministry then, and He is *still* sending us today...

> *He said to them, 'Go into all the world and preach the good news to all creation... And these signs will accompany those who believe: In my name they will drive out demons; they will speak in new tongues... they will place their hands on sick people and they will get well. ~ Mark 16:15-18*

> *I have given you authority to trample on snakes and scorpions and to overcome all the power of the enemy; nothing will harm you. However, do not rejoice that the spirits submit to you, but rejoice that your names are written in Heaven. ~ Luke 10:19-20*

I tell you the truth, anyone who has faith in me will do what I have been doing. He will do even greater things than these, because I am going to the Father. And I will do whatever you ask in my name, so that the Son may bring glory to the Father. You may ask me for anything in my name, and I will do it. ~ John 14:12-14

My prayer is not that you take them out of the world but that you protect them from the evil one. They are not of the world, even as I am not of it. Sanctify them by the truth; your word is truth. As you sent me into the world, I have sent them into the world... My prayer is not for them alone. I pray also for those who will believe in me through their message, that all of them may be one, Father, just as you are in me and I am in you. May they also be in us so that the world may believe that you have sent me. ~ John 17:15-21

You see? We are to be doing even greater things than Jesus did. Even as I write these verses, I am currently challenged in my own walk. Everywhere I turn, people are hurting. Physically, mentally, emotionally and spiritually. I have the answer! I have watched this information work for myself and others. I must *always* be ready and willing to aid a brother or sister in need.

After my own personal experience many years ago, I actually got some training on the deliverance ministry. I studied all the stories in the gospels where Jesus set someone free. As I learned more and more, I began to write it down in my journal. I also prayed for opportunities to help others.

And God immediately started placing people in my life who were struggling. They were saved and loved the Lord but were walking the same path I had just traveled. They were trapped in bondage, just as I had been. These were people who loved the Lord, but were wrestling with demonic influences and didn't know where to turn or how to rid themselves of the oppression.

God allowed me to minister to people one-on-one. Daybreak Coffee House became my favorite hangout. I sat for hours at a time and poured through this information with each individual person.

This allowed my own healing to be completed, while I also learned to trust that the information that I had penned – was indeed accurate. It began to transform other lives as well.

I began to do small groups. And then larger ones. Then women's retreats.   I spoke at youth camps and business meetings.   The information had the same life-altering effect in every genre.   The more I encountered the freedom of deliverance, the more amazed I became. It was such a privilege for the Lord to use me in the healing process of others!

In the next section, you are going to meet several of those people. Their stories are unique. And yet, they paint a vivid portrait of not only how our enemy works, but the magnificent joy and freedom that we, as God's children, are entitled to receive.

Chapter 24 ...Elaine's Story:
Possession vs. Oppression

Elaine is the first person I want to introduce you to. I had led her to Christ and she had been a Christian for a while. She absolutely loved the Lord and there was no doubt that she had been saved. However, she was struggling with some common and familiar characteristics of someone wrestling with demonic bondage. Elaine wanted to walk in joy and freedom.

So, several intercessors got together one evening and she came prepared for her deliverance. As we began to work through some of her issues, I noticed that her eyes kept changing. They would sort of "glaze over." She would blink extremely slowly. And then not at all... for several minutes at a time.

> I couldn't get her to respond at all. I would call her name loudly just inches away from her face and she would just stare through me with no response.

One minute she was listening intently and "with me" as I spoke of scripture and told her my own story of deliverance. The next minute it looked as though she had gone into a trance. Like she was asleep, only with her eyes wide open. I couldn't get her to respond at all. I would call her name loudly just inches away from her face and she would just stare through me with no response.

Finally she would fight through it and "resurface." She desperately wanted to be rid of the entities that she was sure were plaguing her. When Elaine would blink again, she would ask me to repeat everything I had just said. She told me she couldn't hear anything because the voices were just too loud. They were telling her, "*we will handle this...*"

I will resume Elaine's story in a few minutes, but I need to explain several things.

First, Elaine was a Christian. So how could demons be controlling her? If I had become a Christian at age 10, then how did *I* have demons?

> Elaine was a Christian. So how could demons be controlling her? If I had become a Christian at age 10, then how did *I* have demons?

If you are reading this and are saved, then how could *you* possibly have demons?

For some, just the thought of demonic activity in our lives is hard to believe. However, there are many Biblical examples of, not only unbelievers harassed by demons, but *believers* as well. Remember our friend Simon the Sorcerer? He obviously had demons because he was using their power to perform magic.

> *Now for some time a man named Simon had practiced sorcery in the city and amazed all the people of Samaria ...all the people, both high and low, gave him their attention and exclaimed," This man is the divine power known as the Great Power," They followed him because he had amazed them for a long time with his magic. But when they believed Phillip as he preached the good news of the kingdom of God and the name of Jesus Christ, they were baptized, both men and women. Simon himself believed and was baptized.*
> ~ Acts 8:10-13

Even though Simon believed in Christ and was baptized, he still struggled with demonic influence. Peter rebuked him when he tried to buy the Holy Spirit, remember? Peter told him to repent of his wickedness. But, this is the scripture I want you to focus on...

> *For I see that you are full of bitterness and captive to sin.*
> ~ Acts 8:23

So let's go back to the question, how can a Christian have demons?

It is the difference between possession and oppression. Another word for oppression is bondage. This is a very important nuance.

These are two terms that are often confused concerning the influence of Satan and the workings of his demon forces in our lives. Some people think that possession and bondage are the same thing. They are not.

We must understand that these two words actually refer to and occur in two separate parts of our being, the spirit and the soul. Even though the manifestation is almost the same - demons living in, harassing, and manipulating someone.

We have covered the fact that when we ask Jesus Christ to come into our hearts and be our personal Savior and we repent of our sin, we are born again. When this miracle takes place, our spirit has been renewed. Jesus is now living inside the spirit (see the first few chapters of the book). You are possessed by the Spirit of God. Therefore once a person is born again, he/she can never be possessed by Satan. The human spirit can only be possessed by one Spirit. Praise God!

Oppression or bondage - in contrast to possession - is "whoever controls the soul." As we have already established, Satan *does* have access to that area of our being. He knows that he cannot possess a born-again Christian, so he seeks to manipulate us by gaining access into our soul. This is how he establishes a "foothold."

A "foothold" is simply an area of sin. It can be any area where you miss the mark. In this particular example, the sin of anger can give the devil a foothold.

> *In your anger do not sin. Do not let the sun go down while*
> *you are still angry and do not give the devil a foothold.*
> ~ Ephesians 4:26-27

These footholds are lodged in your soul – not your spirit. This becomes clear if we pause to consider how all sins involve the mind (how we think), the will (how we act), and the emotions (how we feel). These are areas of sin where we have allowed the devil a foothold, as in the above scripture.

A few other examples of demonic footholds are: fear, lust, depression, addiction, rejection, sexual perversion, lying, worry, and bitterness.

In my case it was self-hate and condemnation. Only these weren't just footholds; they were strongholds.

Let me explain "strongholds." A stronghold is just that.   It is something that has a "strong hold" on your life. This is a great way to describe an area where a demonic spirit has a legal right to oppress a person – even when that person is a Christian.

> If you are suffering from either devastating guilt or the repeating cycle of sin and forgiveness, chances are you are dealing with a stronghold.

Strongholds are areas of bondage that manifest two separate ways: falling to the same sin repeatedly, or being plagued with condemnation over something you did previously.

In my case, I was no longer committing the sin, but I was plagued with guilt and condemnation. Even though the sin was years earlier and I had been forgiven, I was not free from that sin at all. I was not living in joy or abundance. I was oppressed. Again, oppression, bondage, and strongholds are synonymous.

If you are suffering from either devastating guilt or the repeating cycle of sin and forgiveness, chances are you are dealing with a stronghold.

Strongholds usually start in one of several ways: word curses, sin, generational curses, soul ties, or unforgiveness.

The first is a word curse. The next several chapters address this.

The second is to give in to a temptation and sin. The devil will throw all kinds of temptation at us just to see if we will take the bait, so he can establish the hook. The bait he throws is usually according to your given sin nature (your astrological sign). It really doesn't matter. As I have stated, sin is sin. Satan's goal is to ensnare your soul. It doesn't matter what the bait looks like. As long as it sets the hook. If the devil can tempt you and get you to sin, he gains a foothold. These footholds can quickly become strongholds if you allow them.

The third way he establishes a stronghold is through generational curses. I will speak more of this later. For now, just log it away. It is certainly life-changing information.

The fourth is through soul ties. If you've been wondering when I would ever get back to my own story, then keep reading.

The fifth way the devil establishes a stronghold is through unforgiveness. The chapter titled "Forgiveness" will prove to be interesting as well. It is the culmination of my story and my freedom. It's the whole point of the book.

Obviously, we still have a bit more to cover when it comes to restoring the soul. Unfortunately, most of us never discover the true source of our problems ...and we stay "broken."

We've spent a lot of time together so far, so thank you. Here is what I ask. Please buckle in for the rest of the journey. Because to travel through the first half of the book and not through the second half still leaves so many unanswered questions. Besides, the stories make for interesting reading. You don't hear stories like these in Sunday School...

Notes and Reflections

Notes and Reflections

...Thoughts Turn Into Words

Remember my "voices"? The thoughts that constantly plagued my mind?

Let's talk about those thoughts for a minute. You may think that "your thoughts are your thoughts and no one else knows what is inside your head."

I know that in some cases my thoughts were in first person and sometimes they were in third person.

Sometimes they came in the form of *"I am an adulteress."* Sometimes they came in the form of *"You are an adulteress."* In both cases, it was the enemy of my soul. They were NOT my thoughts. But, because I *accepted them as my own*, they had creative power and they were absolutely leading to my spiritual imprisonment!

This is truth: if a thought (even if it comes in the form of a "voice") stays in your mind long enough, it begins to set things in motion within the universe. Especially if it has emotion attached. Science is finally advanced enough to prove this through quantum physics.

Thoughts have particular frequencies. And one frequency attracts another just like it. The creative power of the universe – which God fashioned for his children to utilize – is simply amazing. I could write another book on this subject.

But for now, let's explore what actually happens in the spiritual realm when the thoughts in our heads actually become words we speak out of our mouths...

Make no mistake; once a disempowering thought becomes a word and *is released, it has life*. Satan loves it when that happens! Especially when those words come from the thoughts *he* placed there! If he can get you to actually *speak* what the voices are saying, you become ensnared.

That is why the Bible gives us explicit instructions to take thoughts captive when they go against the knowledge of God.

> *We demolish arguments and every pretension that sets itself up against the knowledge of God, and we take captive every thought to make it obedient to Christ.* ~ 2 Corinthians 10:5

Why is this so important? Why is it so absolutely imperative that we take our thoughts captive? And what is the big deal when those thoughts turn to words that tumble carelessly from our lips? *Satan remembers the words you say,* and he uses your own words against you. The Bible says that Satan is:

> *...the accuser of our brothers, who accuses them before our God day and night...* ~ Revelation 12:10

The enemy of our soul stands before the Father like a prosecuting attorney. He accuses us day and night. When we speak words, Satan has all of the ammunition he needs to have a **legal right** to torment us. All he has to say to the Father is *"Amy actually said this. She said that she 'would rather be fat than beautiful,' so she 'wouldn't be molested again.' She also said she would 'never be free' from her guilt! So the spirit of condemnation has a legal right to torment her, as well as bind her with an inability to lose weight."* And **God must grant it**, because we are in sin. We are snared by our own words.

> *Set a guard over my mouth, O Lord; keep watch over the* **door of my lips**. ~ Psalm 141:3

> When I learned that my lips are actually *a door to what was taking place in my life,* it sobered me...

When I first heard that concept, and learned that those last four words are crucial, this scripture hit me hard. Again, I had never been taught any of this in church. When I learned that my lips are actually *a door to what was taking place in my life*, it sobered me, because all kinds of garbage had been coming out of my mouth. This was one of the first concepts that God used to actually initiate my healing and restore my soul. I learned to take my thoughts captive – and certainly keep them from carelessly coming out of my mouth! Here are a few more scriptures that might startle you...

*A fool's lips bring him strife, and his mouth invites a beating. A fool's mouth is his undoing, and **his lips are a snare to his soul**. ~ Proverbs 18:6-7*

*From the fruit of his mouth a man's stomach is filled; with the harvest from his lips he is satisfied. The **tongue has the power of life and death**, and those who love it will eat its fruit. ~ Proverbs 18:20-21*

*You have been trapped by what you said, **ensnared by the words of your mouth.** ~ Proverbs 6:2*

He who guards his lips guards his life, but he who speaks rashly will come to ruin. ~ Proverbs 13:3

The tongue is a fire, a world of evil among the parts of the body. It corrupts the whole person, sets the whole course of his life on fire, and is itself set on fire by hell. ~ James 3:6

The Bible says we can speak life or death, health or sickness, blessings or curses upon our lives through our words. Most people have no idea how powerful the spoken word really is. We don't realize that we actually have the creative power to loose the powers of hell upon our lives. *We are bound by the very words we speak.*

Often we don't see dramatic evidence that we have loosed hell in our lives by the power of our words. The tactics of Satan are very subtle. Knowing that he cannot touch our born-again spirit, the enemy will try to entrap and strangle our soul, bit by bit.

Although we can bring about immediate destruction to our lives by our words, most often the bondage occurs much more slowly over a period of time, or even years later. Many times we can't even remember the words we have spoken. Christians wonder why they cannot live victoriously. This is one key. They have spoken against themselves.

God has given us the authority to use the power of words. This is a gift! He intends for us to use that gift to unleash *His* abundant blessing on our lives. Health, freedom, fulfillment, joy, knowledge, wisdom, provision, and protection are all readily available to God's children *if* we properly use this powerful ability.

Again, the key is emotion. When I first learned the concept of the creative power of words, I was constantly worried that my casual words were creative.

However, every little word you speak doesn't set the universe in motion. They must have power backed by belief and emotion in order to "create". Words that are deeply rooted in emotion and fueled by belief have creative power. Both good and bad. Your lips can absolutely manifest good or evil in your life.

> *Jesus replied, "I tell you the truth, if you have faith and do not doubt, not only can you do what was done to the fig tree, but also you can say to this mountain, 'Go, throw yourself into the sea,' and it will be done. If you believe, you will receive whatever you ask for in prayer."*
> *~ Matthew 21:21-22*

... Created In His Image

> *God spoke and everything that ever was and is and is to come came into being.* ~ Hebrews 11:3

When He created us in His image, He gave us the same power to create with the spoken word. The universe was created by Jesus. And the universe is a creative substance. We can tap into that substance by our thoughts and words, and manifest the very image of the thoughts. We are constantly doing this.

> *By the **word of the Lord** the heavens were made, and all the host of them by the breath of His mouth. For He **spoke, and it was done**; He commanded, and it stood fast.* ~ Psalm 33:6, 9

> *When God sent His only son into the world, the Word became flesh and made it's dwelling among us. We have seen His glory, the glory of the one and only, who came from the Father, full of grace and truth.* ~ John 1:14

Jesus spent much time teaching his disciples how to use the power of the spoken word. They watched as He used the power of words to perform all kinds of miracles. Jesus told his disciples:

> *All authority in Heaven and on earth has been given to me.* ~ Matthew 28:18

It was because of that authority that Christ's words impacted every realm around Him, the physical elements of nature, the individual lives of people, and even the forces of the kingdom of darkness. They had to submit to Christ's words. Jesus has that authority and He gave it to us!

If you take the time to really meditate on these scriptures, it creates a fascinating picture of creation and also of the power of the spoken word. When God sent Jesus to earth, He brought glory with Him. That glory has creative power. He also came with the same authority He used to create the universe. Jesus used that authority to alter history. And then Jesus *intentionally gave it to us*. He gave it to us so that we could continue doing the things He had been doing...

> *I have given them the glory that you gave me.* ~ John 17:22

> *And I will give you the keys to the Kingdom of Heaven, and whatever you bind on earth will be bound in Heaven and whatever you loose on earth will be loosed in Heaven.* ~ Matthew 16:19

These words of Jesus have significant meaning for not only our lives, but also the lives of those around us. They say that we can literally bind (or hold back) the powers of hell and at the same time, we can loose the works of God to fulfill our lives.

On the other hand, this same power can have just the opposite effect.

We also have the ability to loose the works of hell and bind the works of God, preventing fulfillment of God's plans and purposes for our lives. Unfortunately, this is the principle that is at work in most of our lives *most of the time*. Because of ignorance, we constantly allow this wonderful authority to work against us.

> *My people perish for lack of knowledge.*   ~ Isaiah 4:6

> *A fool's lips bring him strife, and his mouth invites a beating.*
> *A fool's mouth is his undoing, and **his lips are a snare to his soul**.* ~ Proverbs 18:6-7

We're going to talk about word curses. *"We have the authority to bind on earth as it is bound in Heaven"* with the power of the spoken word. However, instead of advancing the Kingdom of God, we are constantly advancing the kingdom of darkness by speaking word curses over our lives. Let me introduce you to Jade.

Jade is a beautiful girl that I met several years ago.

The first time I saw Jade was at the gym. I had come full circle physically. I had already lost all my weight and was competing in fitness competitions. I think I had already won the North American Nova Fitness Championship by then. That was such an amazing season. I was able to minister to so many women in that arena.

Women who would never set foot in a church, but needed the Lord's love and acceptance desperately.

In Jade's case, as you will read, she was indeed a Christian. She loved the Lord with all her heart. Yet she was in that sin, guilt, shame cycle that I had once been locked in, only it was with bulimia. As you read her story, think back on some of the information you have previously read and see if you can't pinpoint the devil's plan for her. Remember that I said your sin doesn't have to be sexual? That you could be prone to something else? This is a prime example. It doesn't matter the hook that Satan uses. As long as he can get you to take the bait, he can ensnare your soul. He does it through your mind first. If he can get you to use your will to sin, he then has legal access to wreak havoc in your emotions. Jade's situation is textbook!

> ...she was a perfect example of how so many people wrestle quietly. They are Christians but are privately locked in all kinds of unseen prisons.

I had her get up and share her testimony at one of my seminars. She is precious. I didn't edit her comments at all. I had her introduce the section on Words and Strongholds because she was a perfect example of how so many people wrestle quietly. They are Christians but are privately locked in all kinds of unseen prisons. However, there is FREEDOM!

This next chapter is an exact transcript of Jade's heartfelt testimony that day. She stood in front of the room and nervously addressed the audience, with her journal in her hand and a smile on her face...

 **Chapter 27** *...Jade's Story*

Jade began: "I'm just going to start with reading a few journal entries from last semester.

'Not only do I let myself down, I feel like I let everyone else down as well. I feel like I don't live up to this expectation that everyone has for me and they will be disappointed in me. It's like there's more to it that I'm just not getting. There's more to this disease than I'm seeing. Something is not letting me go. I'm still holding on to it for some reason. It also makes me wonder why is it that I have this eating disorder, this disease, when there are so many people in my life who love me for who I am and think I'm special and wonderful.

'Why do I think that the only thing people see is the outside? Why do I think that for some reason if I were to lose a few pounds they would love me just a little bit more, or think I'm a better person? Maybe that's it; maybe I just think that they will be so proud of me and look at me as though I'm a better person, which I know is such a lie. I know it is and I continue to believe it. Why do I allow my mind to deceive me so much?

'Why can't I just know the truth and believe it, believe that I am a wonderful person? The Lord made me who I am for a reason and He is proud of what He created in me. I know He is. He looks down on me and He smiles because He knows He made something great. Isn't it funny how you can hear people say things about you your whole life, really good things, but choose only to believe what Satan has told you? That you are fat, worthless, and people will only like you if you look a certain way? Why is it so much easier to believe the bad stuff ...even and especially when believing the good stuff feels so much better?'

"That was written probably at the beginning of last semester. And I struggled with bulimia for about 4 years. It was one of those things where, and this may not relate to any of y'all – struggling with something every day – but it's one of those situations where you don't understand.

"You know that you don't want to do it, but yet you continue to do it every single day. Every time I would do it, every time I would eat so much food and then throw it back up, it was one of those things where I would get on my knees and ask for forgiveness and say I would never do it again, God, I promise. And then the very next day I would do the same exact thing.

> I would get on my knees and ask for forgiveness and say I would never do it again, God, I promise. And then the very next day I would do the same exact thing.

"I couldn't understand, I couldn't comprehend why, if I kept asking for forgiveness, why I was still dealing with it. Until I was just praying all the time, I was just like, 'God, I don't know why I'm doing this and I don't know what's going to happen.' But throughout that whole time people would say eating disorders are something you're always going to struggle with. You are just always going to just repress it and make it to where it's not such a big deal.

"And I didn't believe that in my heart because I believed that my God was so much bigger than that and that He could completely set me free from it. That's what I believed. I remember my dad telling me, because he had done some research about it, and he said, *I read somewhere, if you have an eating disorder, you're going to have it your whole life.*' And that just made me want to scream because I was like, *I'm not going to have this my whole life. It's not going to be like that.* But at the same time, the whole time, nobody could understand.

"The worst part about it, it was like an addiction, and I hated to use that word because it sounded so... much like control. *Food cannot control me; it can't be that big of a deal.* And yet it was. It was all I ever thought about. When I was with my boyfriend and my family, all I thought about was the next time I could eat and it was just awful. It was horrible.

"And then I remember praying one time, I think I wrote it in here... it said, *I pray that the Lord would put someone in my life that could hold me accountable. Someone who wants to eat healthy and workout. That would be so great because not only would I be doing it for myself, but also for this person because they are counting on me to do my best in the same way I would be counting on them. We could push each other and pray for each other.*'

"I remember the first time I saw Amy in the gym; I had never seen her before. She walked in, in a pair of jeans and a sports bra and I was like *'Holy Cow!'* Because I wanted to compete in fitness. And I was like *'Where did she come from? Who does she think she is? And she needs to put her shirt back on!'* You know, the typical thing that any woman would think. The first thought is jealousy.

"Not in a million years if someone had said, 'do you think she's a Christian?' I would've said, *'no way!'* Then she came to kick-boxing and I saw her there and we talked a couple of times and I looked at her website and it was really cool. And then we started meeting at Daybreak Coffee on Tuesdays and Thursdays for like 3 hours at a time.

> "As we began to work through the information in her book, I started counting the days that I didn't make myself sick."

"As we began to work through the information in her book, I started counting the days that I didn't make myself sick. I think since we first met, I was on day 30 or something; it was really incredible. And it was really amazing because the Lord gave me such a heart for everything that y'all are about to learn. I just ate it up and it was so incredible! The one thing that she taught me, which y'all are fixing to learn, was about word curses and strongholds. I knew that I had a stronghold and I knew that it was bulimia, an eating disorder, an addiction, debauchery, all these incredible things.

"But the one thing that I didn't know is that not only do you have to consciously turn from sin, not only do you have to ask for forgiveness, but you also have to take that next step and renounce that spirit and speak blessing into your life. And it's incredible, y'all.

Once I did it, I spent a whole night just praying over it and reading that prayer that y'all will see here in a bit. It was amazing!

"The thought will appear every now and again, but it's to the point that there's no way it will ever happen again and right now today is day 185 and I'm still counting the

> "...not only do you have to ask for forgiveness, but you also have to take that next step and renounce that spirit and speak blessing into your life."

days. It's been over 6 months and it's been amazing, and the Lord has continually shown me things about myself that I need to work on. The coolest part about that is how God works for the glory of all of us and in everything. Through the suffering and through everything, His glory has been revealed.

"My dad and I made a pact whenever I told him about all of this. My parents have been amazing, and he said that if I got rid of my stuff that he would quit smoking. So I called him whenever I hit the 6 month mark and I said, "All right, you got a promise to keep," and so I think he's on day 13 or 14 with no cigarettes.

"It's really been amazing. I don't know if eating disorders apply to any of y'all, but what I would really like for y'all to go away with, from everything that I've been saying, is that our God is so much bigger than anything you're struggling with right now and He's so willing to set you free from anything that you've been dealing with, no matter how long you've had it, no matter who did what, or who said what. He just wants to pour His love all over you and just completely set you free and it's amazing. A friend of mine wrote this letter to me: 2 Chronicles 20:15 says, *Thus says the Lord to you, do not be afraid nor dismayed because of this great multitude, for the battle is not yours, but God's.'*

"And she said, *'I was reading this today and thought it was awesome. We are always in a battle, whether it be mentally, physically, or spiritually. But realizing since we've been born again in Christ, which must mean that Christ is in it as well... Just knowing that there's no need to fear when you know that God is in the fight. No need to be afraid when you are on the side of the winner.   How different should I act knowing I'm winning, not losing?'*

"And that was just amazing to me because so many times we think, *'Oh, my gosh, I can't do this. I'm not going to get over this. I'm going to have this for the rest of my life. I'm going to struggle with this and deal with this and it's just something I'm going to have to accept.'*

"But it's not something you have to accept because you are on the side of the Lord and He is ready to fight for you and ready to win the battle for you. And all you have to do is get on your knees and say, *'Okay, God, I'm ready for you to win because I think I'm losing.'* And I promise you, no matter how hard you try, no matter how many times you say, *'Please, forgive me, Lord, I'll never do it again,'* you're going to do it again and again. It's a hard lesson to learn, but, gosh, freedom is the most amazing gift the Lord could ever give us!

"And so I guess just open your heart to what Amy's teaching you because it has completely changed my life. It has completely changed my relationship with my fiancé, with my parents, with myself. Just to be able to look in the mirror and say, *'You know what? God created something great in me.'* And it's the most amazing feeling in the world.

"And like Amy said yesterday, just ponder the thought of how much the Lord loves you. I think the best part about it is that through your suffering and through your trial, God will bring something great from it and He will use it for His glory.

"And I know now that I have such a passion for girls that struggle with eating disorders. I want to help them. I don't know how and I don't know where or when, but I know that I do. And I mean, 1 in 4 girls struggle with this. It's terrible! Satan knows that he can get girls there - and it's awful. So I know that through my suffering I've been able to talk with girls already and told them what I did and that I hope it helps them.

"Just be open to whatever the Lord is going to do in you today and keep looking through this information. I look back on it almost every week. Just believe in how big God is and how much He loves you."

Chapter 28 ...Breaking Word Curses

Jade's story gave me resolution to keep writing. Steve actually found the transcript of one of my seminars. He had recorded the whole thing. Turns out it's pretty priceless. I had actually forgotten some of the stories, but they are certainly encouraging!

Back to words...

Jade was just like me. She had grown up in church but was never told that her lips could be a snare to her soul, *and* they are potentially a door for spiritual torment. She was not taught that she had creative power in her tongue. And that her thoughts, as they became words, were unleashing an open-ended demonic invitation upon her life.

The most damaging thoughts are usually the "voices." Those are a little harder to take captive. Those tend to rattle around in your head all the time. We actually let them take up residence in our minds instead of just saying, *"I rebuke that thought in Jesus' name!"*

I believe a big key is when we speak with emotion behind the thought. *That* helps enforce the enemy's legal right to set a spirit in place and establish a curse. Here are some examples of words that can establish word curses: "No matter what diet or exercise I try, it *never* works! I'm *never* going to lose this weight!" or "I fail at everything I try! *Nothing works!*" or "I don't think my marriage is *ever* going to get any better!" or "No matter how I try to stay healthy, I *always* get sick! I will *never* get well!" Debt is another subject where we struggle. "We are *never* going to get out of this debt!" What you focus on, expands.

All of these are damaging, but one of the most common and devastating forms of word curses – responsible for breaking up so many marriages – is sexual fantasy.

This is a whole other chapter in the book. I will bring that back around in a few minutes.

It warrants its own chapter because it's so common and such a huge trap!

You see, God's people are in chains of bondage because of the power of the spoken word. But the Word of God is still alive and powerful and ready to set us free.

> *But the Word of God is not chained.* ~ 2 Timothy 2:9

> *And you shall know the truth and the truth shall set you free.* ~ John 8:32

> *For the Word of God is living and active, sharper than any double edged sword. It penetrates, even to dividing soul and spirit, joints and marrow; it judges the thoughts and attitudes of the heart.* ~ Hebrews 4:1

When the Word of God is spoken with the authority given to us by the Holy Spirit, demonic forces have *no choice but to flee.* However, we must *know* the Word before we can use it as the powerful, effective weapon that it is. And it is indeed a weapon! I believe this next scripture applies to us even though Jesus was speaking to the Sadducees...

> *You are in error because you do not know the scriptures or the power of God.* ~ Matthew 22:29

When we know God's Word, the Holy Spirit is empowered to bring back to our minds the right scripture during any given circumstance. We, as God's children and as His ambassadors, have the incredible responsibility to learn to speak the words that align with the Spirit rather than to speak the words that align with the sin nature.

Even though this is our intent, we are still human and make mistakes. We often fail. The Apostle James understood our dilemma when he wrote this scripture:

> *For we all stumble in many things. If anyone does not stumble in word, he is a perfect man able also to bridle the whole man.* ~ James 3:2

This is a huge battle ground for us. I still wrestle with thoughts and words all the time. It is a never-ending process. The devil continues to speak. Trust me! When I fail, I just recognize it quickly, repent, and use my knowledge of the truth to get back on track.

> *God will grant them repentance, leading them to a knowledge of the truth that they will come to their senses and escape from the trap of the Devil who has taken them captive to do his will.* ~ Timothy 2:25-26

The truth is that curses are real and we can unwittingly trap ourselves with our words. But Jesus came to bind up the broken hearted and set the captives free. He actually *became* a curse for us so that we could be redeemed.

> *Christ redeemed us from the curse of the law by becoming a curse for us.* ~ Galatians 3:13

So let's start figuring this out. Here is the first key to gaining victory over word curses...

> *We demolish arguments and every pretension that sets itself up against the knowledge of God and we take captive every thought to make it obedient to Christ.* ~ 2 Corinthians 10:4-5

> The Bible is clear. Just as the power of our spoken words can get us *into* bondage, the power of our spoken words can also get us *out of* bondage.

If a thought enters your mind and it appeals to a negative emotion, or if it appeals to your sin nature, then you need to *take it captive*. And certainly do *not* speak it out of your mouth and give it life!   Say something like this instead (out loud if you are alone): *"I rebuke that thought! It is not my own. I reject it in Jesus name!"*

The next thing is to know the Truth. The Bible is clear. Just as the power of our spoken words can get us *into* bondage, the power of our spoken words can also get us *out of* bondage.

Your own words are the most effective at destroying curses. As you speak, the power of the Holy Spirit within you is released upon the curse and destroys it. The key to deliverance from self-inflicted word curses is for you to break them by the power of your *own spoken words again.*

Let's say you're struggling with a particular issue: unforgiveness, anger, depression, anxiety, guilt, or bulimia, etc. They are all the same. You've had people pray for you but the prayers are ineffective. If this sounds like you, then chances are you're struggling with something *you spoke over your life* and it is something that *you need to break.*

Let's look at Jade's example.

In her case she was struggling from her own spoken words. According to God's ordained plan and the laws of His Kingdom, she had used the power she has to create - and had cursed herself. Jade struggled with bulimia. She had given it a name and had told people she struggled with it. *Those words* gave the spirit *legal right* to be there. On one hand Satan doesn't really fight fair. But he *does* however, fight by the rules. We just have to know the rules!

Because she had spoken those things on herself, only her own spoken words again could deliver her from the bondage they created.

She had to go back and break so many word curses. Not only that *she* had spoken, but also word curses from counselors and other people that had authority in her life. Even her father said *"This is something you will have to deal with the rest of your life."*

When someone in authority speaks over your life, and you receive it into your heart as truth, then it can easily become

> When someone in authority speaks over your life, and you receive it into your heart as truth, then it can easily become a word curse.

a word curse. You constantly see examples of children walking out the exact curses their parents spoke over them.

For example, if you have an area of unforgiveness in your life and you just can't seem to overcome and other people may say, *"You can forgive, but you're always going to have to live with that anger. It's just always going to be there."* – If you receive that statement as truth – then you have received a word curse.

After walking through all these scriptures and Jade gained knowledge of these truths, we asked the Holy Spirit to show Jade the curses of others that she had allowed into her life as truth. We then prayed and broke those as well.

Then we went back and addressed the words Jade had spoken over herself. As the Holy Spirit brought things to her mind, she was appalled at what all she had said. We took each "life sentence" and broke it.

We walked through the 5 steps in this chapter. They are simple and precise. They had set me free and, as you can see, they were effective on Jade as well!

I encourage you to pray right now and ask the Lord to reveal any word curses you have either received from someone in authority over you, or you have spoken yourself. Are there areas that you are struggling with? See if there are any sentences you have spoken that are "sentencing your life." If the Lord brings anything to mind, or you have a "favorite saying" that is not in alignment with what God says about you, then write it down. Take yourself through these 5 steps. They are effective at breaking word curses.

The first step is to **repent** to God for the words that you've spoken that have loosed hell upon your life.

The second step is to address the "voices" and **renounce the demon spirit** that was given the legal right to torment you because of the curses you spoke.

The third step is to use the name of Jesus. Invoke the power of the Spirit of Almighty God and **break the curse**. Break off the effect of the words. Close doors of darkness that the words have opened in your life.

The fourth step is to *speak the truth from God's Word* that counters the negative words and curses from your past.

The last step is to ***speak scriptural blessing*** into the area of your life that's been affected by the curses. Let that verse be one of your life verses. Anchor yourself to it. Speak it every day and never stop.

Jade went through the steps perfectly. Following her repentance, she renounced the demon spirit that had been assigned to exercise its right of control over the curse brought on by her own words. Then because of her repentance and the choice of her will to renounce both the curse and the spirit controlling the curse, she had the spiritual authority to break the curse and cancel its power over her life. She then spoke the spiritual truths of God's eternal Word concerning her particular situation.

Now, this is a key. Once you repent, renounce, and break the curse, you need to go to the Word of God and find a scripture that counteracts the word curse. − I can promise you there is scripture for everything that you need to break in your life − Find one that destroys the lie you've been buying, and speak *that* instead.

And I promise you, God is intimately close throughout this process. He will bring the right scriptures to anchor your soul. He longs to see you walking in freedom and in the full measure of the glory, blessing, and anointing that He has for each of his children. Breaking words off of your life is critical for those promises to manifest!

Breaking words curses will also prepare you to learn about the next way Satan has a legal right to torment you − through "giving in" to temptation and choosing to sin.

Notes and Reflections

Notes and Reflections

Chapter 29   ...Temptation to Sin

If we give in to temptation and choose to sin against God, we unleash the destructive forces of darkness and open our souls up to demonic torment. We become a slave to that sin. This is no small matter.

These are the words of Jesus:

> *I tell you the truth, everyone who sins is a slave to sin.*
> ~ John 8:34

> *For the wages of sin is death...* ~ Romans 6:23

> *...let us throw off the sin that so easily entangles...*
> ~ Hebrews 12:1

> *But each one is tempted when he is dragged away by his own desires and enticed. Then, when desire has conceived, it gives birth to sin; and sin, when it is full-grown, brings forth death.* ~ James 1:14-15

First, temptation does not come from God. It comes from Satan. And we have the Lord on our side helping us through our temptation.

> *When tempted, no one should say, "God is tempting me." For God cannot be tempted by evil, nor does He tempt anyone...*
> ~ James 1:13

Satan is the one behind the temptation of mankind. Scripture is full of examples of Satan tempting man: Eve in the Garden of Eden, Judas, the disciple who betrayed Jesus, and even Jesus in the wilderness.

However, God is merciful to His children. He knows how we are formed. He is true to His Word. God will not allow the enemy to tempt us beyond our threshold to resist that temptation. God will always provide a way of escape.

And God is faithful; He will not let you be tempted beyond what you can bear. But when you are tempted, He will also provide a way of escape so that you can stand up under it.
~ 1 Corinthians 10:13.

Jesus also helps us in our weakness.

Because He himself suffered when He was tempted, He is able to help those who are being tempted. ~ Hebrews 2:18

Obviously, by these two scriptures, we do not have to give in to temptation! We *can* be victorious over every temptation of the enemy. It is imperative that we understand that God has provided a way of escape through His Son, and we need to look for that escape.

Second, Satan is not omnipresent like God. He is a created being, a fallen angel. So since he cannot be everywhere at once, he must rely on the help of the rest of the fallen angels that also rebelled in Heaven and were thrown to the earth. Together, Satan and the rest of the fallen angels (demons) make up the kingdom of darkness. Their purpose on earth has never changed. It is to tempt man to sin so that they can unleash Satan's plans of destruction upon God's beloved creation. This is explained more in-depth with scripture references in The Premises (Premise 5) in the front of the book

Thus, whenever there is temptation to sin, we can conclude that there is a spirit of evil behind that temptation trying to get us to succumb to that sin. If they can get us to fall to the temptation, they have a *legal right* to gain a foothold in our soul.

Scripture has already proven that we can give the devil a foothold.

*In your anger do not sin. Do not let the sun go down while you are still angry and **do not give the devil a foothold**.*
~ Ephesians 4:26-27

That passage is referring to anger. I will speak more on anger in a few minutes. For now, just know that if we sin in our anger, we give the devil a foothold. This is just one example of how sin opens that door. There are many sinful doors that the enemy uses to gain footholds into our soul. Those footholds, if not confessed, repented of, and renounced, will eventually become strongholds. Those strongholds, if left alone, will completely bind us with unseen spiritual chains and ultimately bring destruction into our lives.

> *The evil deeds of a wicked man ensnare him; the cords of his sin hold him fast.* ~ Proverbs 5:22

> I have explained that the devil doesn't fight fair. In most of our lives, the devil tries to open doors and gain footholds through sexual sin.

I have explained that the devil doesn't fight fair. In most of our lives, the devil tries to open doors and gain footholds through sexual sin. Regretfully, one of the most cunning and yet overlooked ways he creates a door for sexual sin is through childhood friends and their parents. This tactic goes completely unnoticed. Often we struggle with these doors of sin when we are adults and can't even remember how they opened in our lives.

Dr. Kevin Lehman is a renowned child psychologist. He had a rule that goes against the grain of most parents in our society. He almost never allowed his children to do sleepovers. He gives this great advice:

> "Perhaps my experience as a counselor has made me unusually sensitive here. But the truth is, it's impossible to know what's going on at other people's houses. In my counseling office, I talk to some of the seemingly most respectable families in town, only to discover that crazy and even perverse things happen behind closed doors." (Ref: *Adolescence Isn't Terminal ...it just feels like it*)

The point that he does not make, is the spiritual fact that if your children are in a place where something of an immoral or perverse nature is going on – *spiritual doors are opening.*

If the spiritual head of that home is allowing something into that home – a spirit of pornography, lust, or any other perverse sexual spirit – it can gain access to your child. And your child can consequently live with and struggle against that spirit for years.

That is why this next bit of information is so crucial to the Body of Christ. We are crippled with sexual sin. We must gain the correct knowledge to finally become victorious in this most critical area.

Chapter 30 ...Leah's Story

Let me introduce you to Leah.

I met Leah in one of my weekly small groups. Leah was a beautiful woman and was married with a five year old son. Although she would politely interact at the beginning of class each week as the ladies made their coffee and casually chatted, Leah never contributed to the discussions about the previous week's homework. She listened intently to every word and took copious notes, but she never really opened up.

> I was thankful for the time alone with her, because I was aware of the pain behind her eyes. It looked excruciatingly familiar.

After the session on Strongholds, Leah stayed after class to help me pick up coffee cups and straighten the chairs. I was thankful for the time alone with her, because I was aware of the pain behind her eyes. It looked excruciatingly familiar. I had lived that pain myself. She was struggling with condemnation.

I knew not to "press." I figured she would talk when she was ready. Staying after class to help pick up was a step in the right direction. So as we washed empty coffee mugs and dirty plates, threw away plastic forks and crumpled napkins, I gently asked about her life. As she answered my non-threatening questions, she began to open up a bit. I thanked her for her help.

The next week was a carbon copy. We had finished the section on "Word Curses." As usual, Leah was painfully intent as we walked through the workbook. She didn't say a word during the discussion but stayed after to help me pick up.

This time she asked a few questions about my deliverance. Her eyes widened as I gave her explicit details. She was amazed at my transparency and she said so. *"You know, Leah,"* I said, *"If I can help someone else experience freedom by laying my life down and showing all the cards, then it is worth it. Otherwise, my journey has been in vain."* As we pushed in the final chairs, Leah hugged and thanked me, as tears welled up in her beautiful but sad green eyes.

"Leah, I'm here if you ever need to talk. There is joy and freedom at the end of this road you are traveling. I promise." She smiled a faint, half-hearted smile as she got in her car and drove off. I began to pray for her right then. I could tell she was struggling immensely. I could literally feel the spiritual warfare surrounding this young woman. I prayed for her safety.

> She smiled a faint, half-hearted smile as she got in her car and drove off. I began to pray for her right then.

Several times throughout the week, the Holy Spirit impressed me to pray for her. I always prayed in the spirit since I had no idea how to pray. I knew the Holy Spirit was lovingly guiding her toward freedom.

I was relieved when Leah walked in the next week. She was late. The first 30 minutes of coffee and dessert usually allowed everyone plenty of time to arrive and get settled. Leah had never been late. When she did show up, I knew she had been crying. She walked in and sat at the back of the room, just as we opened our workbooks and I began to teach.

As I covered the information you just read about children, open doors, and about how the devil can gain a foothold through those doors, Leah stiffened. When I covered Proverbs 5:22, Leah's head dropped. She hung her head so that her long black hair conveniently covered the sides of her face. Although she was on the back row, it was obvious she was going to great lengths to hide the constant stream of huge tears rolling down her cheeks. As I talked about how Satan can establish a stronghold through our sin, Leah struggled. She never made a sound, but I could tell that she was sobbing inside.

Her shoulders and chest silently heaved under the invisible load she carried.

I prayed that she would stay after class and talk to me. As soon as class ended though, she darted out of the room. I was disappointed and prayed that she would turn around. Often, if we miss the opportunity when it presents itself, it is hard to get it back. I knew that this room was a safe place. I had prayed over every chair and had been ready for this moment all morning. If she got out of this environment, I knew that the devil would continue to strike devastating blows to her battered soul and she may not ever come back.

As I washed the cups and plates, Leah walked back in. I silently thanked God.   She had been so heavy on my heart! I had been interceding for this woman all week long. I barely knew her, but she had been in the forefront of my mind for days. Leah's face was swollen from crying.

"Oh, Leah, I was praying you would come back! Please don't miss this opportunity to get healed! I have been there. I know how you feel. I may not have the exact same story, but I know guilt and condemnation when I see it. You are safe here. Please open up about what is going on. I promise there is no judgment! Nothing you say will surprise or shock me. I understand how the devil works. If he can keep you in fear about confessing what is really going on; he can keep you locked in this torment. The Bible says in James 5:16 'Confess your sins one to another, and pray for one another so that you may be healed.' Please tell me what is going on..."

Now, let me place a huge caveat here. You must use wisdom and discernment on James 5:16. Please. I am not advocating that you ever "filet yourself" to just anyone. I knew that Leah was imploding. And I knew that this was her moment to gain permanent freedom. There is a difference. When James 5:16 is handled correctly – with the Holy Spirit's guidance – it will be the catalyst to healing. When James 5:16 is handled incorrectly – with Satan's guidance – then it can have even more devastating effects.   Remember, he knows scripture too, and he will use it to create havoc when he can!

Leah sat down in the chair and just looked at me. *"I can't cry anymore. I have no more tears. My heart is broken. I guess I just need to tell you my story and hopefully you can help me."* *"Leah,"* I said, *"I can't help you, but the Lord can. He is right here with you, and this is your moment to gain freedom over this constant torment. You are safe here. I promise. Please just start at the beginning and don't stop. Get it all out. Don't be embarrassed. If God is for you, who can be against you? He loves you. You are forgiven."*

Leah took one huge breath, and then she began to speak.

Chapter 31 ...Leah's Childhood and Beyond

"I grew up with a single mom. My dad left before I was born. I never met him. And my mom was constantly dating new men. She worked at night and hated to leave me by myself. I was only 9 at the time ...but I liked being alone. I was pretty self-sufficient.

"Mom had a fun personality, and when she wasn't working, there were always people at my house partying. Our apartment was a constant stream of unfamiliar faces. There was always loud music and people laughing. Every week-end, the smell of alcohol and marijuana permeated my home.

> *"Sometimes at the end of those nights, several people would end up in Mom's room with the door locked. I hated those nights."*

"Sometimes at the end of those nights, several people would end up in Mom's room with the door locked. I hated those nights. I sensed what was happening in there. At the time, I thought it was painful to her. I was always glad to see her fine the next day. She was hung over, but she seemed okay.

"Mom changed jobs a lot, and sometimes she worked all night. I hated those nights. She would leave me with Susan, a new friend she had met in our apartment complex. Susan was a lot like my mother ...single and fun-loving. I liked her. She was sweet to me and I remember she laughed a lot. She liked my hair and called me "black beauty." She kept me when Mom was working. Susan had three kids. John was about 15 at the time, I think. Drew was a little younger, and Kayla was about my age.

"But, Susan was also gone a lot at night. And she would put John in charge...

Leah's eyes had begun to focus on the past. The next part came slowly. *"As soon as his mom would leave, John got out his dirty magazine. "*

Leah looked at me and breathed deeply. She had been staring out the window and talking non-stop without a breath. Her eyes searched mine, I think to see if I was in shock yet. *"Leah, I told you, nothing you tell me will surprise me. You are safe. Go ahead."*

A fresh tear rolled down Leah's cheek. *"John kept telling us how great it was. He said, 'It's called having sex. It's normal.'*

"I'll never forget the first time I saw that magazine. I could barely read, but I stared at the pictures. John showed it to us and said we were all going to get to pretend we were adults.   It was pornography, but how could I know that then?"

A fresh tear rolled down Leah's cheek. *"John kept telling us how great it was. He said, 'It's called having sex. It's normal. It's what adults do.'*

I was uncomfortable, but I didn't know what to do.

"He always wanted us to pretend we were the people in the magazine. And he was the photographer... Her voice trailed off again. I waited.

"The three of us would pose just like the pictures. And then we would switch around. John would be a model and Drew would take pictures. They always posed Kayla and me just like the girls in the magazine.

"I didn't want to play. But anytime I said that, the boys made me feel like I was wrong ...not to. To this day, I don't know what ever became of Kayla. The boys convinced us to do the things they saw in the pictures ...and they convinced us we could never tell anyone, because we would all get in trouble.

"Anyway ...John made me and Kayla get on the bed. And Drew would get behind us and... and ...he always wanted Kayla and me to kiss...

As she wiped the single tear on her cheek, she glanced at me. *"Well, you get the point. We always played the same game. And it happened almost every time I spent the night, and their mom was gone. The first few times we played, I felt guilty ...but, the more we did it ...it didn't bother me as much. I even developed a crush on Drew. ...Is there something wrong with me?!"*

"No, Leah," I quickly responded. *"Oh, if only you knew how common this is. It's not you. And it wasn't anything you did."*

"I know that now ...but there's more," she said. *"It went on for several months."* Leah paused for a long time. *"...John started making us have oral sex. He made us do it with him and Drew ...and with each other. Eventually, John said it was time for the sex scene. By now, I was so much more reluctant. I know Kayla was too. But John kept pushing us. Amy, I was trapped. What could I do?"*

I encouraged my struggling friend. *"We're working toward your freedom right now, Leah."* She hesitated for a moment more. *"Drew got on top of me that night. John was with Kayla..."*

> This beautiful woman was a million miles away. She was no longer a wife and mother... She was a 9 year old little girl, in that apartment, reliving her trauma all over again.

Leah looked up at me. Her eyes seemed blank. *"Susan made fish sticks and macaroni and cheese for us that night... I liked fish sticks. Especially with ketchup..."* Leah trailed off again. This beautiful woman was a million miles away. She was no longer a wife and mother. She was no longer sitting at the table with me and the rest of the dessert plates and coffee mugs. She was a 9 year old little girl, in that apartment, reliving her trauma all over again.

Her voice thinned and grew faint. *"Kayla and I were on our backs side by side; John made us hold hands and start kissing. ...And then we both screamed in pain at the same time..."*

Leah burst into tears. I grabbed her and hugged her while she cried for several minutes. *"Don't say anymore. I understand. That's enough."*

"But that's not the end," she cried. *"There's more I need to tell you   ...from college."*

Leah wiped her tears. I got her some water. She sipped, took another deep breath, and continued.

> Leah burst into tears...
> *"But that's not the end,"*
> she cried. *"There's more
> I need to tell you"*

"Mom and I finally moved away. I don't know whatever became of Susan or her kids. I never saw them again. Kayla crosses my mind a lot. But, to this day, I never told my mom about any of it.

"Besides, Mom seemed much better after we moved. The parties stopped and we started going to a small church, which I really loved. The people were so nice. She met a guy there and they got married. Eventually, I just let all the pain fade away... At least I thought I had.

"I went on to high school and college. I was in a sorority." Leah paused again. *"Then one night at a mixer, several of the girls had been drinking a lot. We were all playing drinking games. Anyway, I got dared to kiss the girl sitting next to me. We'd had a lot to drink... So, I did. And Amy, I just kept thinking about Kayla. I know it was wrong, but ...it was too easy for me. At the time, I felt like I actually enjoyed it... Do you know what I mean?"*

I nodded. Leah had strengthened slightly. I know she was beginning to feel the love of the Holy Spirit surrounding her. As I just continued to listen quietly with no interruption and no condemnation, she fast-forwarded one more time.

"Nothing ever came of that. I soon met my husband, and we were married two years later. After three years we had our son, Josh. And after all the baby weight, it took a while for me to start feeling attractive again. Then Josh started preschool, and I wasn't as tired, so... Anyway, one night, John told me he had been buying magazines. He had been looking at the pictures, and reading the stories. I know I should have been bothered by it, but I wasn't. I felt

bad that I hadn't been there sexually for him like the first couple years of our marriage.

"Then he started talking about how he liked seeing women together. I was not surprised. I told him about that one night at the college mixer. I never even got her name.

"And that's when we started bringing fantasy into our sex life. When we would make love, he would make up these stories that almost always involved me with someone else.   ...It was usually a woman."

I could see where this was going. *"You're forgiven, Leah. The Lord knows your heart,"* I encouraged.

"Well ...three months ago my husband and I went on a cruise. It was our first one. It was really great ...at first. There was a lady at our dinner table. She was with a group from her work. The last four nights she sat next to me. She was really pretty ...red hair. I could tell John thought she was attractive.

"The last night of our cruise, we all drank more than usual at

"We all ended up together in our stateroom that night. We were all pretty drunk, and ...well ...it just kind of happened."

dinner. After we ate, a whole group of us went to one of the lounge bars on the ship. At one point, my husband ordered a round of tequila shots. There was a great band and the mood was festive. We all sat around and laughed. And we danced some. As the night unfolded, I began to realize that this woman was attracted to me. It was weird. ... John picked up on it too ...and we had more tequila shots..."

Leah had been very detailed in her story, until now. She simply said, *"Anyway, I'm sure you can guess the rest. We all ended up together in our stateroom that night. We were all pretty drunk, and ...well ...it just kind of happened. We had gotten back to the room sometime after 2:00 am, and I got up to take a shower at 5:00, so she wasn't there very long. She was gone when I got out of the shower, and I never saw her again.*

Amy, I felt so disgusted. I turned the shower as hot as I could stand it, and cried the whole time. I begged God for forgiveness.

"When I came out of the bathroom, my husband grabbed my hands, looked me in the eyes, and apologized. He knew he had made it happen. He felt as terrible as I did. His apology was so sincere. We got on our knees and repented, and renewed our vows to each other, and to God.

"You see, we had found a church a couple of years before and we were both saved. We were baptized together. I didn't understand how something like this still could have happened, until I listened to you today. I'm so disgusted with myself!

"And since that night, I've had three women come on to me! I'm sure of it. That's never happened before! I'm so embarrassed and ashamed! I am just sick with guilt. I'm happily married! I know we messed up that one night. But now you have me thinking that everything I've done ...is somehow related."

Chapter
32   ...My Response

I got up and got us each another cup of coffee. *"Leah, thank you for trusting me. Let me explain a few things. First, you are completely forgiven. The Bible is full of scripture that assures you of that fact. Psalm 103 says:*

> *'The Lord is compassionate and gracious, slow to anger, abounding in love... He does not treat us as our sins deserve or repay us according to our iniquities. For as high as the heavens are above the earth, so great is His love for those who fear Him ...as far as the east is from the west, so far has He removed our transgressions from us.'*

"I know you don't feel forgiven, but you will in a few minutes. This guilt is not coming from God. It is coming from demonic influence. There is Godly sorrow, and then there is worldly sorrow.

> *Godly sorrow brings repentance that leads to salvation and leaves no regret, but worldly sorrow brings death.*
> *~ 2 Corinthians 7:10.*

"The condemnation you are feeling is another word for "worldly sorrow." There is a difference between conviction and condemnation. The first brings about repentance and renews your relationship with the Lord. The second heaps guilt and shame on your life. And it devastates your relationship with Him because it drives you out of His presence rather than into His loving embrace."

Leah nodded. She had certainly been feeling the latter. I was glad that she was tracking so closely with what I was explaining.

*"The second thing you have to understand, is what Jesus actually did for you on the cross. He took our sins upon Himself. He didn't just **die** for our sin; He **became** sin. And when He died, the price for all our sin was paid **in full**. Because of His death, God looks at you and He doesn't see your sin. He sees the righteousness of Christ.*

You are covered. Jesus also disarmed every demon harassing you right now. You just have to know how to get rid of them.

"Jesus came to earth to do so much more than save you and make sure you go to Heaven. He died for the emotional pain, and the fear you felt in your childhood as you watched your mom abuse drugs. He died for the physical and psychological pain you felt while acting out the magazine photographs. He died for the kiss at the sorority mixer that night. He also died for the sexual fantasy you guys allowed into your marriage, and for that last night on your cruise.

"Jesus came to set you free from not only the sin, but the shame. From the cross He saw it all; He was there. Right there with you through every bit of it. Leah, these are the 'iniquities' the Bible talks about in Isaiah. Listen to these scriptures, and take heart!"

> *Surely He took up our infirmities and carried our sorrows, yet we considered Him stricken by God, smitten by Him, and afflicted. But He was pierced for our transgressions, He was crushed for our iniquities; the punishment that brought us peace was upon Him, and by His wounds we are healed.*
> ~ Isaiah 53:4-5

> *...He forgave us all our sins, having canceled the written code, with its regulations, that was against us and that stood opposed to us; He took it away, nailing it to the cross. And having disarmed the powers and authorities, He made a public spectacle of them, triumphing over them by the cross.*
> ~ Colossians 2:13-15

> *He himself bore our sins in His body on the tree, so that we might die to sin and live for righteousness; by His wounds you have been healed.*   ~ 1 Peter 2:2

"Leah, the punishment that brought you peace was upon Him. You WILL feel peace. Trust me!"

Leah's deep breath was different this time. It was one of hope-filled relief rather than crushing condemnation. She was beginning to absorb the scriptures. This woman was a new Christian. She had not been saved that long and wasn't really even familiar with the Bible.

She was hearing these scriptures for the first time. There were so many more that I wanted to give her, but I didn't want to overwhelm her.

I continued, *"The third thing you need to understand, is that you are wrestling with what the Bible calls a 'perverse spirit.' You asked why you have been 'propositioned' by other women in the last couple of months, since the night on the cruise. There is a very definite reason. You are caught in what the Word calls 'a snare.'*

"You see, people don't realize that when they sin, it literally opens a spiritual door to the demonic realm. That's why there is so much scripture warning us away from sin. Especially sexual sin. Satan always tries to open doors in this area early in a child's life, so he can set the hook later.

> *"...a whole generation of people are suffering from the implementation of a Satanic agenda... to break up marriages, and destroy the next generation all in one strategic blow."*

"Let me explain what happened with you, Leah, because it's textbook. And a whole generation of people are suffering from the implementation of a Satanic agenda – to attack the home and family, to break up marriages, and destroy the next generation – all in one strategic blow.

"I have no idea what kind of childhood your mother had. But it obviously created pain that she didn't understand, or know how to navigate. To fill the void in her heart, she eventually turned to sex, alcohol, and drugs. Your mother was probably hurting deeply in order to intentionally abuse her body like that – especially with a young daughter nearby. Unfortunately, those activities just exacerbated her emotional trauma.

"The challenge with sin is that it opens doors to your children. When the adults in a home are participating in stuff like that, it has the potential to rain down onto the children. This is what happened to you as a 9-year old. I'm not sure about Kayla's mom, but chances are she was also participating in sexual sin. John, Drew, and Kayla obviously felt the effects.

"So, let me explain your situation. When you participated with Kayla, it opened a small door.   When you grew up, that door opened just a bit wider and created space for you to kiss the girl at your sorority mixer – and enjoy it. That sin became a 'foothold.' It was the bait the devil used to set the hook on the cruise with your husband.

*"It's not a matter of being attracted to women instead of, or in addition to men. In our world today, this is one of the greatest areas of confusion and debate. This matter is not genetic... It's spiritual. There was a spirit that **did** attach itself to you that night. When you and your husband opened that door completely, that spirit had a legal right to step right into your soul and establish a stronghold. The reason women are coming on to you right now is because they also are carrying the same spirit... And those spirits recognize each other. Most of the time, those carrying the spirit aren't even aware of it. That's why there are so many people in the world today claiming it's genetic. It's not. It's demonic."*

> *"That's why there are so many people in the world today claiming it's genetic. It's not. It's demonic."*

Leah sat back in her chair and gasped. She had been listening intently. When I said that, she looked at me incredulously, *"Are you serious!? What do I do?"*

I took a sip of my coffee and continued.

"People don't realize that there is the 'seen realm' and the 'unseen realm.' Humans are in the 'seen realm.' Angels and demons are in the 'unseen realm' (2 Corinthians 4:18). I call it the natural and the spiritual realm.

"Angels are created beings, and are just as real as you and me. Some are fallen angels – 'spirits of wickedness' is another term the Bible uses. Because of the sin, one of those spirits did indeed attach itself to you. Let me ask you a question. When you walk into a room full of people, do you recognize the people you know?"

Leah nodded.

"Okay, well, it is the same in the spiritual realm. 'Like' spirits recognize each other. A spirit recognizes a similar spirit. Once the foothold is there, it can quickly become a stronghold.

> "Angels are created beings, and are just as real as you and me. Some are fallen angels..."

"If you weren't in this class, and if you hadn't recently been saved, and if you hadn't experienced the love of Jesus in your life... chances are, you and your husband might be tempted to sin in that same area again. It gets easier and easier once the door is opened. Just like when you eventually began to get comfortable with those nights at Susan's house, before it turned worse.

"You were innately aware that it was wrong, but after a while it just became normal. Even enjoyable. That's how all sin is. It's a trap. And it eventually ensnares people so completely that they almost never discover the truth and escape. Marriages have certainly been known to break up when one spouse 'discovers' what they've mistaken for the truth about their sexuality, and leaves their spouse for someone else.

"Leah, what you are dealing with is so common. And it can be un-done. So take heart, and don't feel disgusted. Sin is sin. And Jesus paid the price for it all. No sin is worse than another. It is all forgiven!

"However, we **do** need to break some things off your life and close some doors. There are some simple steps you need to take, and you will be fine. I promise!"

I will come back to Leah's story again, but I want to say a couple of things here. I know this information will set some people free. It is the very knowledge they have been praying for.

I also understand that it will infuriate some. I'm okay with that. Especially since I know I'm not actually infuriating *that person*. I'm infuriating the spirits which have attached themselves to that person... And that person is angry, under those spirits' influence.

I know it's Truth. I have watched the Lord set many people free from this type of bondage. I have cast this same spirit and many others out of people, and those people are walking in complete freedom today. *And* thankful for it.

Leah is living proof. I have her permission to tell her story. And I use it often when explaining how these spirits work.

It isn't just a perverse spirit... although that sexual-based spirit is extremely common. There are many spirits, by many names. I teach in-depth on these, in my seminars.

We need to think of spirits as "parasites which have attached themselves" to us through open doors of sin. And those parasites can see other parasites...

There are many kinds of spirits which attach themselves in clusters. For example, a seducing spirit will attract another seducing spirit – like a magnet. Some spirits are also repelled by each other. For example, the spirit of jealousy *hates* a seducing spirit. Keep reading, because there are several more pieces of this puzzle coming in the next few chapters.

*"You can't tell anyone what happened, because those things just **don't happen** if you're Christian!"*

When those pieces all come together, hopefully they will assist in healing many in the Body of Christ. I see people all around me who love the Lord, but are locked in silent prisons and bound by unseen chains. Those prisons become more impenetrable because of shame. *"You can't tell anyone what happened, because those things just **don't happen** if you're Christian!"* ...Those are the demonic whispers that keep families in quiet torment.

I believe this is an edgy, but relevant and necessary message to the Body of Christ today.   We need to walk in personal freedom and power, so that we can then turn around and help others. We live in a depraved generation. As we "do church" as normal, our kids are being consumed by pornography streaming live through their cell phones ...and right into their souls.

I pray for the day when we as Christians lay down our religious tendency to judge those struggling brothers and sisters around us, and instead, *help them out of sin.*

> I pray for the day when we as Christians lay down our religious tendency to judge those struggling brothers and sisters around us...

Brothers, if someone is caught in a sin, you who are spiritual should restore him gently. But watch yourself, or you also may be tempted. Carry each other's burdens, and in this way you will fulfill the law of Christ. ~ Galatians 6:1-2

Sexual sin might be appalling to you. But I promise, if your family has not been "touched by it" in some form or another, then you are a rare minority! This next story is about a couple I met from a very large church in the States, several years ago. I was speaking at a Three R's Seminar for their city. Again, it is textbook, and it validates Leah's story...

There are couples like this all around you. This may in fact be your story as well. Or the story of someone you love. Believe me, it is more common than we'd like to think.

Notes and Reflections

Notes and Reflections

Chapter 33
...Deborah and Braden's Story

The Three Rs Seminar affects people profoundly. Going in, they don't really know want to expect. However, as the information unfolds, the Holy Spirit begins to gently reveal things to individuals. He is the Comforter and the Counselor. And that environment is conducive to both of those things. The section on Strongholds is particularly moving.

Coupled with examples from movie clips, as well as my own story, "Strongholds" is usually a point of breakthrough for many attendees.

On this particular day, when I spoke of how sin opens a door to demonic influence, and the very real fact that sexual fantasy can destroy marriages – a young woman on the front row began to cry softly.

She came up to me at the next break and asked if I would meet with her and her husband. After my seminar ended, the Pastor of the church, his wife, and I met with the young couple.

Deborah and her husband Braden were both nervous. From the moment we walked in, the tension was thick. When the five of us sat down, she apologized to their pastor. You see, this couple was actually on his staff – at this very large church. The pastor had hired them to oversee and lead the children's ministry. Remember the words of Dr. Kevin Lehman in Chapter 29? You never know who is hurting, or what their story is.

Deborah grew up in a "Christian home." Her dad was a deacon in their little church. Yet when she was 10 years old, her dad divorced her mother and married a girl who was 18.

Deborah's new step-mother was only 10 years older than she was. This devastated Deborah, and she didn't like her ...at first. Sonja was her name. Deborah grew up with her dad and his very young wife having crazy sex right next door to her bedroom... Eventually, Deborah's dad lured her to become part of the sexual games they played. Deborah had been introduced to sex in a twisted fashion. Incest was normal for her. As expected, her Dad's marriage eventually disintegrated and Sonja moved away.

Unlike Leah, who was very detailed about her life, Deborah was very succinct. She skipped over all of the details. I wondered what became of her relationship with her father after Sonja left.

> Eventually, Deborah's dad lured her to become part of the sexual games they played. Deborah had been introduced to sex in a twisted fashion.

Deborah grew up and married Braden. One night, Braden confessed the fact that he had been molested when he was 15. He described the time when he spent the night with his friend, and the friend's dad molested him. When Braden got to college, he began drinking heavily. He told Deborah there were a couple of instances when he experimented with homosexuality. He had assured her that he was *not* gay, but he had experimented with it a few times with some guys on campus.

So many times, when children are abused early, those demonic doors are open and normal sex with a spouse is almost boring. These spirits drive people to ever increasing levels of perversion. That's one reason why people turn to fantasy. So many couples get sucked into this!

This was the exact case with Deborah and Braden. When he discovered that speaking of other sexual partners turned Deborah on, this became regular in their marriage. When they made love, he talked and she listened. At one point in fantasy, they talked about having a threesome with someone.

Deborah said, *"You know who comes to mind?"* She mentioned her stepmother that she hadn't seen in years. Deborah explained to Braden what Sonja had been like; she had seduced her father and was "into kinky stuff."

Less than a week later, Deborah answered the doorbell, and guess who was standing there? Sonja. She had just ended another marriage and had nowhere else to turn. She asked if she could stay with Deborah and Braden for just a few days... until she could get on her feet.

Tell me, how coincidental do you think that was?

And so they invited her in – and you guessed it - within two days the three of them were in bed together.

Now, let me stop here for a second.   Because there are several key points I want to make. The first is that I am not just relating "steamy" stories to intrigue the reader, but to reiterate how the enemy works. He is cunning, and he is ruthless. These are real stories of real people. And the devil hardly ever gets exposed, because people walk in shame.

> These are real stories of real people. And the devil hardly ever gets exposed, because people walk in shame.

The second is that being a Christian, or even in leadership in the church, does *not* make you immune to sin. Even what some might call extreme sin. Although according to Jesus, *all sin is equal.* Being Christian, or in leadership, can actually make you *more of a target.*

The devil loves to quietly work behind the scenes when we are young. He then opens the doors when we are older.   He eventually sets the hook – when the absolute *most damage* can be done. In the *most public fashion.* This tactic has worked time and time again.   Just look how the mighty have fallen...

As we have already discussed, sexual sin which is perpetrated on children and young teens almost always opens doors for that same sin to take effect, and wreak havoc later in their adult years.

Remember when we were discussing "Words" and I talked about how powerful the spoken word is? When a thought – even if it is a temptation from the enemy – is spoken out of your mouth, it has life...

*A fool's lips bring him strife and his mouth invites a beating.
A fool's mouth is his undoing and his lips are a snare to his
soul.* ~ Proverbs 18:6-7

*You have been trapped by what you said, ensnared by the
words of your mouth.*   ~ Proverbs 6:2

The enemy of your soul is going to make certain that if you speak
something out of your mouth, at some point, that temptation will be
right in front of you. It's amazing. The very person you speak of will
show up. And if the devil can get you to actually *sin*, then he has a
legal right to set the hook.

*The evil deeds of a wicked man ensnare him. The cords of his
sin hold him fast.* ~ Proverbs 5:22

I tell you the truth, everyone who sins is a slave to sin.
~ John 8:34

*...but each one is tempted when, by his own evil desire, he is
dragged away and enticed. Then, after desire has conceived,
it gives birth to sin; and sin, when it is full- grown, gives
birth to death.* ~ James 1:14-15

This may not mean physical death. At least not immediately. Death
happens in many forms. In this case it meant the death of Deborah
and Braden's marriage. Remember, the devil comes to steal, kill, and
destroy.

Deborah and Braden and
Sonja had their threesome.
Instantly, all hell broke loose
in their marriage. Literally.

Let's get back to the story.
Deborah and Braden and Sonja
had their threesome. Instantly,
all hell broke loose in their
marriage. Literally. Deborah and
Braden had immediately kicked
Sonja out, but the damage had already been done. And it was
massive. It seemed to have disintegrated their marriage overnight.

Since that night 9 months earlier, they had not even been able to have
a full conversation without a huge fight. They had rarely been in the
same room together during the day (unless they were leading the

children at church). And at night, Braden was on the sofa, while Deborah slept in the bedroom.

If the enemy can cause you to tumble into sin like that, the very next reality is a huge flood of anger, guilt, and shame. They had been through counseling, but she was so riddled with guilt and with anger toward Braden for opening the door to fantasy, she was completely closed to reconciliation. Although he had taken the lead role in trying to reconcile, he was also angry at her for suggesting Sonja in the first place. They had been isolated and stuck in that same place for months on end.

This situation *seems* like it happened over the course of a couple of months. But hopefully, you are beginning to see that the enemy of your soul is patient. This set-up was *years* in the making. It had woven its way into the fabric of both of their lives, and waited for the right moment to set the hook and destroy each of them at once... Not to mention what it was doing to their ministry.

It's stories like these that caused me to finish writing this book and get back into my seminars. I know I will "feel the heat" for this type of raw, authentic information. I'm sorry if it makes you blush, makes you uncomfortable, or even makes you mad. I don't want to offend. That's not my purpose at all. This book is not about shock and awe. I fully understand there are millions of people immersed in these types of lifestyles and *do not* want to be delivered from them. *Wanting* your freedom is a critical prerequisite.

This book is about real lives. It is for people who are hurting deeply and don't understand the cause.

> In the meantime, Satan continues to decimate homes and families – while the Church sleeps.

Those who feel hopelessly confined to silence, and completely bound by choking guilt. But they can't figure out *why*, much less *what* to do about it.

I was one of those people. And now I have keys. I will be accountable to the Father for those keys. And as I watch the signs of the times... I am convinced that the Great Deception is near... So I need to get on with my life message, and be obedient to the call.

I've watched and waited. And I've noticed that very few people in Christian circles are willing to walk in submitted obedience – using wisdom, transparency, and authority. We all have sinned, but if the devil can make us think *our* sin is somehow "worse" than everyone else's... he can keep us locked in shame.

Or worse yet, if he can keep the church itself locked in self-righteousness, then the spirit of religion keeps us from talking about the real issues people are facing. In the meantime, Satan continues to decimate homes and families – while the Church sleeps.

When I told Leah's story, it gave Deborah enough courage to talk to me. She realized I had helped someone else fight through this particular kind of marital trauma. I'm so glad she did! I will share more of their story in a moment.

> The truth is... what happens behind closed doors, *does not* stay behind closed doors. It *does not, cannot*, and *will not*.

Right now though, I want to tie both of these stories to an unfortunate truth. In each case, the sexual sin of the parents was the common denominator. The truth is... what happens behind closed doors, *does not* stay behind closed doors. It *does not, cannot*, and *will not*. Remember the unseen realm? *Everything* is exposed in the unseen realm. And the unseen realm *trumps* the seen realm.

For example, someone sitting in their bedroom with the door closed, watching porn on their computer, *with* headphones on... *is indeed* affecting the spiritual atmosphere in that home! As I said earlier, the spirits that are allowed into a home based on the sins of the parents *do not* play fair, and they *do not* play nice. They seek out your children. And they attach themselves like parasites, looking for the first chance to walk through any open door. Even to the third and fourth generation... which brings me to the next chapter.

Chapter
34   ...Generational Curses

Hopefully, by now you have a working knowledge of the fact that when we are born again, we become a new creation. God renews our spirit.

> *Therefore, if anyone is in Christ, he is a new creation; the old has gone and the new has come.* ~ 2 Corinthians 5:17

However, that does not mean established strongholds of the soul are not *still there*. This is a common area of deception for many Christians. They think that just because they've asked Christ into their lives everything should be fine. But when you read each of the examples I have given you in the last several chapters, things were *not fine*. They weren't fine in my life, or Jade's, or Elaine's, or Leah's, or Deborah and Braden's. Why?

Because the spirit may be renewed, but what about the soul? Again, the soul needs to be *restored*. We can love God with all our hearts, and still be completely enslaved in the private recesses of our souls.

Just because we now love the Lord, does not mean that the habits and patterns we wrestled with before Christ, are not *still there*.

A renewed spirit doesn't mean that we no longer have a sin nature. And most of the time,

> A renewed spirit doesn't mean that we no longer have a sin nature. And most of the time... we still have strongholds...

especially if we are saved later in life, we still have strongholds – patterns of iniquity, along with the spirits that accompany those particular sins. These spirits had established a *"strong hold"* in our soul *before we accepted Christ*.

Unfortunately, some of those habits and patterns of iniquity were established in our family's bloodline – to the third and fourth generation before us. If our forefathers have sinned and opened doors of bondage, *those same doors could be opened to our lives. Even at conception.*

> *Surely I was sinful at birth, sinful from the time my mother conceived me.* ~ Psalm 51:5

King David wrote that verse. Remember him? Remember his sexual sin with Bathsheba? His son was King Solomon. Solomon's propensity to sin sexually with foreign women eventually became his downfall. This is one example of generational sin.

Let's look at this next scripture, and then we will examine it for a moment.

> *For I, the Lord your God, am a jealous God, visiting the iniquity of the fathers upon the children to the third and fourth generations of those who hate me.* ~ Exodus 20:5, Deuteronomy 5:9

This is a tough scripture. A lot of people would like to dismiss it, because it is part of the Law of the Old Covenant. We simply cannot do that. Jesus' life, death, and resurrection did not abolish the Law. It fulfilled it.

> *Do not think that I have come to abolish the Law or the Prophets; I have not come to abolish them but to fulfill them. I tell you the truth, until Heaven and earth disappear, not the smallest letter, not the least stroke of a pen, will by any means disappear from the Law until everything is accomplished.* ~ Matthew 5:17

The bad news is that sin cannot go unpunished. God is Holy. He is just. And He cannot look upon sin.

The Old Covenant required a yearly blood sacrifice for the atonement of sin. The good news is that we are under the New Covenant. Jesus became that blood sacrifice for sin - once and for all! As I stated to Leah, Jesus' death was sufficient.

> *For the wages of sin is death, but the gift of God is eternal life in Christ Jesus our Lord.* ~ Romans 6:23

But He was pierced for our transgressions, He was crushed for our iniquities; the punishment that brought us peace was upon Him, and by His wounds we are healed.
~ Isaiah 53:5-6

So, even though the iniquities of the father are visited upon the son, they are covered and atoned for by Jesus Christ Himself. He paid the penalty of death, for not only our sin, but the sin of every generation before us and after us.   Unfortunately, that marvelous truth is lost on most, and families continue to suffer from generation to generation... Because of their lack of knowledge on how to abolish those generational iniquities.

Now, why the sins of the fathers? What about the mothers?   Even though Eve bit into the apple first, it was still classified as *"Adam's sin."* The sin nature was passed through the blood line of Adam, not Eve.

Therefore, when a husband stands by – even if his wife is the one who opens the door to sin – the Bible makes it clear that the husband will be held accountable. Remember what my husband has always said? Any time there is a physical situation between a man and woman, and that situation goes wrong, it is always the fault of the man.

> The fathers are the spiritual leaders of the home. Whatever spirit – good or evil... As the man goes, so goes his family.

The fathers are the spiritual leaders of the home. Whatever spirit – good or evil – they either bring themselves, or allow into the family, *is* the direction the family will lean.

As the man goes, so goes his family. Even if that man is no longer around, either through death or abandonment. The only exception would be if another man steps in to be the spiritual leader of that home, and he knows how to close the open doors.

In a single-mother household, this still holds true. Even though a marriage may have broken up and the father is no longer in the physical picture, his spiritual leadership - or lack of it - still affects his wife and children. *But,* a single mother can also come under the headship of the Lord. You also have the same ability to control the spiritual atmosphere in your home.

> *For your Maker is your husband, The Lord of hosts is His name... ~* Isaiah 54:5

In addition, the fathers of previous generations also account for the "spiritual leanings" of a family. Those bloodlines are still an open invitation for spirits to flow down to the new generations of children bearing the same name.

Now follow me here. Have you ever seen five generations of family living at the same time? I haven't. It's very rare. Occasionally there are four generations. So what happens when the fifth generation has passed away?

Here is how generational sin works. Demonic forces will work to establish a sinful pattern in a family. Think about alcoholism for a moment. It starts as a sin committed by one man. That sin can open the door to his wife. And then it becomes a spiritual, generational trait that is passed down. That "trait" eventually establishes a demonic pathway that weaves its way through a family line... for generations at a time. Again, it's something we try to pass off as "genetic." It is not. It is spiritual.

Rage is another huge spiritual stronghold that is often disguised, and therefore overlooked. I see it all the time; parents (or step-parents) who flare in anger and scream at their children. Often, the child is misbehaving to some small degree, but the parent completely over-reacts. That parent loses control. They throw a "temper-tantrum" themselves. In doing so, they have *no clue* what kind of damage they are causing that young soul. I'm not talking about normal discipline. I'm talking about rage. When people "just snap" and cannot control what comes out of their mouths. The kind of anger that makes people slam doors, throw things and say emotionally damaging words to the people they love. The kind of anger that makes one want to hit. That is not normal. It is a *spirit of rage.*

Now, we all get angry sometimes. But there is a difference between getting angry, or having a heated debate with a spouse, or disciplining your children.... and rage.   In all of the previous examples, the person is still in control.   Rage takes over at that moment, and causes damage.   And once a spirit of rage gains a foothold, then a stronghold, if often attracts a spirit of abuse.

> *In your anger do not sin. Do not let the sun go down while you are still angry and* **do not give the devil a foothold**.
> ~ Ephesians 4:26-27

Have you ever wondered why children who have been abused often become "abusers" themselves?   How could someone who has experienced the devastating emotional, psychological, and in extreme cases, the physical trauma of child abuse – actually turn around and abuse their own children?   When interviewed, these people usually communicate a common response: *"I don't know why. I hate doing it. It's as if something is controlling me."*

Why does depression, poverty, addiction, or rape run through a family line? These are just a few examples of generational sins. And when you study a family's history, this phenomenon often becomes painfully, yet fascinatingly apparent.

Demons have the ability to *possess* us if we *are not* saved, or to *oppress* us if we *are* saved... the manifestation is basically the same.

Let me explain why it happens. Demons have the ability to *possess* us if we *are not* saved, or to *oppress* us if we *are* saved. We've established the fact that the manifestation is basically the same. It is really a matter of what area of the body they occupy - the spirit or the soul.

We also know that demons are fallen angels. They don't die. When you think of a demon as a parasite, and a parasite's "host" dies, what happens to the parasite? It will look for a new host.

Therefore, if a demonic spirit has a legal right to oppress your great-great grandfather in an area, and then your great-great grandfather dies, where does the spirit go? Every demonic spirit's main agenda is to destroy families. So it doesn't look for another family. It packs its little snake-skin suitcase and goes down *that same family line* – looking for the next person with the same open doors, the same tendencies, the same personality type, and the same weaknesses – as the host it just departed.

Demons know what weaknesses to look for, and people are usually easily inhabited. And demons know exactly *how to tempt us*, because our weaknesses are encapsulated in our individual sin nature.

They tempt each person in the area of their individual weakness. And if that person chooses to fall to the temptation and sin, then that spirit has a *legal right* to gain access to its new host. They've been doing it for thousands of years.

Now, let me ask you, how well do you *really* know your parents? Do you know all of the hidden things that took place in the privacy of their bedroom?   Do you know what sinful doors they may have quietly, accidently opened throughout their lives? Most of us have no idea. Well, that's your first generation.

How well did you know those things about your grandparents? That's your second generation. How about your great-grandparents? Most of us don't even know our great-grandparents' names, much less what kind of sinful doors they may have opened, or what kind of strongholds they may have established. And that's only your third generation.

Your great-great-grandparents are your fourth generation. You see, you could be silently struggling with something that comes from your great-great-grandparents and there's no way you could know it.

So follow me now. That's two parents, plus four grandparents, plus eight great-grandparents, plus sixteen great-great-grandparents. Altogether, that's thirty people. If you're married, it becomes sixty people... because the two become one flesh. More on that in the next section.

After reading this last part, you may be overwhelmed. Don't be. This is easily fixed. I'm about to give you a simple, yet effective way to break generational sin off yourself, and off your children and grandchildren, etc. God is good!

Let's jump back in here though, because this is real, and it has been wreaking havoc on our families since the beginning of time. As I said earlier, demons don't play nice. They look for any open door. And if they find one, our children could suffer the consequences. Our children can inherit those demons looking for a new host. There are lots of Biblical passages that speak of demons in children, but I chose this one because I want to honor a young mother that I will introduce to you in a moment. Her story breaks my heart. We have much to learn from this particular passage. I am challenged by it even as I write. I pray for the self-discipline, wisdom, and authority of Jesus!

> *A man in the crowd answered, 'Teacher, I brought you my son, who is possessed by a spirit that has robbed him of speech. Whenever it seizes him, it throws him to the ground. He foams at the mouth, gnashes his teeth and becomes rigid. I asked your disciples to drive out the spirit, by they could not.'*
>
> *'Oh unbelieving generation,' Jesus replied, 'how long shall I stay with you? How long shall I put up with you? Bring the boy to me.' So they brought him.*
>
> *When the spirit saw Jesus, it immediately threw the boy into a convulsion. He fell to the ground and rolled around, foaming at the mouth. Jesus asked the boy's father, 'How long has he been like this?'*
>
> *'From childhood,' he answered. 'It has often thrown him into the fire or water to kill him. But if you can do anything, take pity on us and help us.'*
>
> *'If you can'? said Jesus. 'Everything is possible for him who believes.'*
>
> *Immediately the boy's father exclaimed, 'I do believe; help me overcome my unbelief!'*
>
> *When Jesus saw that a crowd was running to the scene, He rebuked the evil spirit. 'You deaf and mute spirit,' He said, 'I command you, come out of him and never enter him again.' The spirit shrieked, convulsed him violently and came out.*

The boy looked so much like a corpse that many said, 'He's dead.' But Jesus took him by the hand and lifted him to his feet, and he stood up.

After Jesus had gone indoors, His disciples asked Him privately, 'Why couldn't we drive it out?' He replied, 'This kind can come out only by prayer.' ~ Mark 9:17-29

Chapter 35 ...A Young Mother's Story

I will never forget the day I heard an eerie, unfamiliar sound at the front of my church. A young mother and her son caught my attention. It was after the service was over. Steve and I were visiting with family and friends before heading to lunch. It was a beautiful Sunday afternoon in March.

There was quite a commotion near the altar, so we came closer to observe. Our pastor, along with several prayer workers, were already standing there with her. The boy must have been about 3 years old. She was still holding him, so he couldn't have been much older than that.

The first thing I noticed was this little boy's hair. He was almost bald. My first thought was that maybe it was because he had been through chemotherapy. But it wasn't. It was because he was grabbing handfuls of it himself, and ripping it out. And he was growling.

Steve and I both watched in sad disbelief. Not only was he growling, he was completely rigid. I had never witnessed anything like this. The second thing I noticed was that this little boy's eyes were sunken into his head ...and they were pitch black.

To my knowledge, this woman was not a member of our church. I had never seen her before.   She had just braved the whole scene in order to bring her son to someone who could pray for him. She seemed to be at a complete and total loss, and could not handle him.

> No one commanded the spirit to *"Come out of him and never return."* They just prayed a nice prayer. And absolutely *nothing* happened.

The whole scene definitely drew a crowd. It was almost a carbon copy of the passage you just read. Only it didn't end the same way. Steve and I stood there and watched our pastor quietly talk with her, while the boy was in a complete melt down. The altar workers gathered around her and prayed while tears slid down her face. The boy continued to writhe, growl, hiss, pull his hair out, and gnash his teeth at anyone that even came close to try to touch him. Not one person addressed the demon controlling that little boy. No one did what Jesus did. No one commanded the spirit to *"Come out of him and never return."* They just prayed a nice prayer.

And absolutely *nothing* happened.

They felt badly for her and gave her some ideas to get some counseling. Then, they all quietly, sheepishly walked away. It was apparent that they had no idea what to do. Or if they did have the knowledge, they certainly didn't possess the confidence. I don't fault them. Because I just stood by and watched. I did nothing either.

As she struggled to carry her son back toward the door, the hope she had mustered to come to our church that day vanished with every step. Her young arms were trembling as she continued to hold her son, who constantly switched from rigid to limp. Her embarrassment almost rivaled the obvious ache in her biceps. As people pointed and whispered while she trekked to the doors, she gritted her teeth. She couldn't get him out of my church fast enough. Her face still haunts me to this day. It was after that sad incident that I decided to get training in the deliverance ministry.

You see, that 3 year old little boy did nothing to deserve the spirit that was tormenting him. Somewhere in the bloodline above him someone opened an unseen, yet deadly door. The generations above him were not protecting their children. Somewhere, someone's sin had invited a demon spirit to have legal access to that family. Demons don't have the right to do that to just anyone. They have to have a *reason* to be there. Unfortunately, we - or someone above us - all too often give them that reason.

I'm not sure we realize how deadly sin can be. And when we are in the middle of temptation, it is increasingly difficult to count the cost. The longer we look at the bait, the less resolve we maintain.

And it only takes a second of lost resolve for the enemy of your soul to set the hook. After writing these last few paragraphs, I had to stop and pray for a fresh understanding that my actions - both good and bad - have lasting consequences.

So! Let's take a breath and start figuring out how to break this stuff off, and learn to walk in freedom and abundance!

...Onward!

...*Breaking Generational Curses
and Demolishing Strongholds*

In order to free ourselves from any kind of demonic stronghold, whether they come from any of the three subjects we've already covered: Words, Sin, and Generational Curses - or the next two we've yet to cover – Soul Ties and Unforgiveness, we need to recognize that we *do* have authority over them! And when we exercise that authority *they must depart.* They have no choice. However, they *will remain* unless we demand that they leave!

The steps are simple. Just like the steps for word curses: **Repent**, **Renounce**, use scripture to **Break the Stronghold**, and then **Speak Blessing** into that area.

Let's get back to Sin for a moment. Our second area of demonic entrance.

We've established that sin opens the door, and if that sin continues repeatedly, it begins to turn the foothold into a stronghold. We've also established that any sin, no matter what kind, can create the same demonic strongholds. Although sexual sin is a huge tactic from the enemy, it is certainly not the only one.

For example, it can be lashing out in anger. If that behavior continues, eventually it could open the door for a spirit of rage and abuse. It can be abuse of drugs – either street or prescription - that eventually opens the door to the spirit of addiction. It can be over eating that eventually opens the door to a spirit of gluttony. It can be playing with a Ouija board as a kid at a slumber party that opens the door to a spirit of witchcraft.

You get the point. One sin, if repented of quickly, doesn't necessarily set up a demonic stronghold. However, when that sin is recurring, it gives a spirit the legal right to establish an outpost in your mind, will, or emotions, and torment you in the area of your sin.   That stronghold will either cause you to fall into that sin again and again, or plague your soul with so much guilt and condemnation that it renders you ineffective.

And, as we have just established, habitual sin left to its own devices, will absolutely open the door for those spirits that have been tormenting us – or the generations above us – to attach themselves to our children.

That's why it is so important to turn away from sin. When we get alone and command our souls to line up under our spirits, the Lord can then communicate with us. He will

> When we get alone and command our souls to line up under our spirits, the Lord can then communicate with us.

speak to our spirits and show us the hooks. He wants us to be free to live in the joy and abundance that His Son's death purchased for us.

The instructions to us are exactly the same as the Apostle Paul's instructions to Timothy. Paul encouraged Timothy to teach the people how to escape the snare of the devil. Truth never changes.

> *They are to come to their senses and escape the snare of the devil, who has taken them captive to do his will.*
> ~ 2 Timothy 2:26

Remember, demons don't die. Their methods are the same today as they were 2000 years ago. In fact, they are literally the *same* demons today...as back then!

I encourage you to take a systematic approach. Write down everything you currently struggle with. If you have a propensity toward something you know is harmful to you or someone else, or you have areas of known sin, or a family trait that seems to run through generations, write them down. And pray through these steps...

Repent

When we recognize the truth of God's Word that opposes the bondage in our soul, there must be a deep, heartfelt repentance and turning away from the sin that placed our souls in bondage. That is what the word repent means; it means to *turn around*. To turn away from the sin. Without this crucial step, we can never break the power of that sin and the foothold it creates. We do not have the choice as to whether or not we will be tempted. We *do* have the choice to give in to that temptation.

> *...let us throw off everything that hinders and the sin that so easily entangles, and let us run with perseverance the race marked out for us.* ~ Hebrews 12:1

> *...I will judge you, each one according to his ways, declares the Sovereign Lord. Repent! Turn away from all your offenses; then sin will not be your downfall. Rid yourselves of all the offenses you have committed, and get a new heart and a new spirit. Why will you die? For I take no pleasure in the death of anyone, declares the Sovereign Lord. Repent and live!* ~ Ezekiel 18:30-32

Renounce

After we repent or turn away from the sin, our relationship with God has been renewed. This second step is that we must renounce the demonic spirit that has gained a foothold in our soul as a result of that sin. When we repent, we are looking up at our Father. When we renounce, we are looking down at the enemy, as we speak directly to the wicked spirit. This is one of the most overlooked, yet most powerful scriptures in the entire Word of God.

> *But we have **renounced** the hidden things of shame...*
> ~ 2 Corinthians 4:2

This step is the most important step in gaining freedom, from not only falling to sin again and again, but also in abolishing the condemnation that plagues our souls. The enemy doesn't mind us repenting, as long as we don't follow through with *this step*. If he can keep us from *renouncing the spirit* that has a legal right to be there, then he can keep us locked into that vicious cycle of sin and guilt.

Use Scripture to Break Strongholds and Speak Blessing

Once we identify an area of bondage in our soul, we can go back to the Word and find scripture that opposes that lie. When we learn to use the weapon of the Word, we are well on our way to spiritual freedom!

Take the helmet of salvation and the sword of the Spirit, which is the word of God. ~ Ephesians 6:17

For the Word of God is living and active. Sharper than any double-edged sword, it penetrates even to dividing soul and spirit, joints and marrow; it judges the thoughts and attitudes of the heart.   ~ Hebrews 5:12

All scripture is God-breathed and is useful for teaching, rebuking, correcting and training in righteousness, so that the man of God may be thoroughly equipped for every good work. ~ 2 Timothy 3:16

If the stronghold has been there a long time, the spirit may resist leaving, as in the example of the little boy and Jesus. There are times when we may need to seek the help of strong brothers and sisters in the Lord – with knowledge of the deliverance ministry – and pray and fast before addressing a deep stronghold. This is the type thing we address and deal with in my seminars. But make no mistake, demons must leave! Satan is a defeated foe, and we have authority over the works of darkness in our lives. Jesus came to set the captive free, and no spirit of darkness can resist the power of His name!

> But make no mistake, demons must leave! Satan is a defeated foe, and we have authority over the works of darkness in our lives.

The seventy-two returned with joy and said, 'Lord, even the demons submit to us in your name.' He replied, 'I saw Satan fall like lightning from Heaven. I have given you authority to trample on snakes and scorpions and to overcome all the power of the enemy; nothing will harm you. However, do not rejoice that the spirits submit to you, but rejoice that your names are written in Heaven.' ~ Luke 10:17-20

Chapter 37

...The Rest of the Story

Let me get back to the stories I've left open-ended for the last several chapters. I've introduced you to a few of the people I've had the privilege of ministering to through the years. The first was Elaine. She had demons that were blanking out her mind causing her to fall into a trance, and she was fighting to stay alert. Her voices were telling her *"We will handle this..."* Remember?

You see, Elaine had opened the door to witchcraft. Her demons had a legal right to be there because she had actually invited "spirit-guides" into her life when she was younger. She had

> ...she had tried all kinds of experimental psychedelic drugs like LSD and cocaine, and dabbled in a smorgasbord of new age religions.

gone through a period in college when she was on a "spiritual quest" and she had tried all kinds of experimental psychedelic drugs like LSD and cocaine, and dabbled in a smorgasbord of new age religions. Several of the drugs she had taken had sent her on a spiritual trip into unseen realms complete with all kinds of cool "entities" that had stepped up to "guide her."

Elaine had grown up, married, had a daughter, and had become a normal adult. But when she found Christ and got saved, her old "spirit guides" were not the least bit happy about it. They had begun to torment her dreams. Things in her house began to change as well. Lights were flickering on and off. The television came on and off. Objects were moving. She saw shadows. She told me her house was haunted.

The night of her deliverance, I grew tired of the spirits harassing my friend. *"I command the spirit that 'blinds the minds of those who don't believe' to let me speak to Elaine!"* Her eyes blinked slowly and Elaine resurfaced and looked at me. *"What is going on? Why can't I stay awake?"* she asked.

"Remember when we talked about your personal history? You told me that you thought you had opened some doors through the drugs you've experimented with in college, and some of the mind trips you took..."
"That's right," she said.
"Well, I need you to pray a prayer and walk through some steps to get rid of these spirits that are plaguing you. Because right now, they have a legal right to be there."

Elaine agreed wholeheartedly. She desperately wanted to be free from her nightly torment.

This is the prayer I gave Elaine. I walked her through it and she prayed after me. We prayed it several times with a different spirit as the focus each time. The Holy Spirit guided her as He systematically brought particular sins to mind and she obediently repented, renounced, and used the Word to break the stronghold and speak blessing.

> *"Father, thank you for sending your Son Jesus to die for my sins. I repent for taking drugs that have altered my spiritual state and have opened the door to witchcraft. I repent of giving place to the enemy by abusing drugs. Lord, I turn from that sin now, and I receive your forgiveness. From now on, I choose to be a person who only looks to the Holy Spirit for guidance. In Jesus Name, Amen.*

> *"And, now, Satan I renounce you! I renounce every spirit of drug abuse and witchcraft in my life. I want nothing more to do with you, or with your works. You are the enemy of God and according to Psalm 139:21-22, I hate you with a perfect hatred. I count you my enemy. I also hate how you have manipulated my life through nightmares, trances, and haunting my home. I renounce you and I command you out of my life! In the name of Jesus, leave me now! I cancel every agreement I have made with you. I reclaim every part of my life I have given you. I break every hold you have had over me, every vow and covenant, every hex and curse, and every unholy soul-tie. I command you to remove your hook from my life. Leave me now in the name of Jesus and by His*

blood, shed on the Cross! I claim 2 Corinthians 3:17 that says 'where the Spirit of the Lord is, there is freedom...' In Jesus' name, I cast out drug abuse and witchcraft, and I ask the Spirit of the Lord to replace that void. I speak blessing over my life in the specific areas that have been affected by these spirits of darkness."

As Elaine continued to pray and cast them out, the spirits shook her, made her cough violently, and even made her throw up as they exited. She left that night exhausted, but a completely different person. Her nightmares stopped. Peace returned to her home, and she is still walking in freedom and joy today.

Let's talk about Leah.

She had several things we had to deal with separately. She was dealing with emotional trauma in her childhood, so we started with breaking off the perverse spirit. She prayed this prayer.

"Father, I repent of every sin that I have committed that has opened the door to a perverse spirit. I repent of opening the door to a perverse spirit during my childhood with Kayla. I repent of the night at the sorority mixer, and the kiss that opened the door. I repent of sexual fantasy. I turn from that sin. I repent of the night on the cruise, and every action that led to this stronghold in my life. I receive your forgiveness. Jesus, thank you for shedding your blood to die for my sins! I turn from them now, in Jesus' name.

"And, now, Satan I renounce you! I renounce every perverse spirit in my life! I want nothing more to do with you or with your works. You, spirit of darkness, are the enemy of God, and according to Psalm 139:21-22, I hate you with a perfect hatred. I count you my enemy! I also hate how you have manipulated my life through sexual sin. I renounce you, and I command you out of my life. In the name of Jesus, leave me now! I cancel every agreement I have made with you, and I reclaim every part of my life I have given you. I break every hold you have had over me – every vow and covenant, every hex and curse, and every unholy soul-tie. I command

you to remove your hook from my life and to leave me now, in the name of Jesus and by the Blood of His Cross! I claim 2 Corinthians 3:17 that says 'where the Spirit of the Lord is, there is freedom...' In Jesus' name, I cast out this perverse spirit! I ask the Spirit of the Lord to replace that void. I speak blessing over my life in the specific areas that have been affected by these spirits of darkness."

As soon as Leah prayed that prayer, she began coughing violently and choking. I commanded, *"You perverse spirit of sexual sin, in the name of Jesus stop choking Leah and come out of her, never to return!"*

> **Hope flooded her lovely green eyes, where despair had been moments earlier.**

Her whole body stiffened, and then immediately softened. She looked at me in surprise. *"It's gone. I feel different. I KNOW it's gone! Praise the Lord!"* She smiled. This was the first real smile I had ever seen on her beautiful face. Hope flooded her lovely green eyes, where despair had been moments earlier.

Leah and I talked about the other things she needed to break off. We prayed and asked the Lord for His guidance on the next steps of her deliverance. He walked us through several things that had established strongholds in her life. We broke off Depression, Anxiety, Insomnia, Soul ties, Unforgiveness, and Fear.

Because of her childhood, fear had established a hook, and she was overprotective of her son Josh. She constantly dreamed that Josh was being attacked by wild animals. As we prayed and broke off each stronghold and the spirits left her, Leah's countenance continually lightened. She was becoming more beautiful by the minute. As the spiritual heaviness departed, it was like she had received a supernatural facelift. It was hard to believe this was the same woman sitting at our little table just a couple of hours before. She and I are still friends today, and she is just as free now, as she was that day.

Now, let's talk about Deborah and Braden.

Because they were there together, and the relationship was still very tenuous, we started there. I asked Braden if he was willing to learn the things Deborah had learned in the seminar that day. When he agreed, I briefly explained how strongholds are established and went through the difference between possession and oppression. He was a quick study. Braden was precious. When I asked them if they were willing to ask each other's forgiveness and reconcile their marriage, he was so choked up he couldn't say yes. He just gently nodded. It was obvious that this was the first time Deborah had truly made an effort in 7 months, and Braden was overwhelmed.

> When I asked them if they were willing to ask each other's forgiveness and reconcile their marriage, he was so choked up he couldn't say yes.

He began to cry as I asked them to clasp hands and agree together to *"...take a stand against the devil's schemes. For [their] struggle was not against flesh and blood but against the rulers, against the authorities, against the powers of this dark world and against the spiritual forces of evil in the heavenly realms"* (Ephesians 6:11-17). They agreed. Then I asked their pastor to pray for us as we allowed the Holy Spirit to guide the reconciliation of their marriage.

The first thing I addressed was the perverse spirit that was implanted in Braden when he was molested at 15. So many men fight the same tendencies... for the same reason. They may not be walking it out, but they quietly battle in private. Why? Because this spirit is *implanted* ...and it is ravaging our generation.

You only need open eyes to notice the dramatic increase in the various perverse lifestyles in recent years. It isn't because people are just now coming out of the closet. It is because when people are abused in that area, as in Braden's case, that spirit steps up and settles in. The door can also open through childhood play, as in Leah's case. "The sins of the father (or mother) are visited upon the son (or daughter...)"

That spirit may lie dormant, but it will continue to tempt... And if that person finally gives in to the temptation (or tendencies), and chooses to sin in that area, the cycle repeats itself. If the spirit can cause a person to give in to the tendencies just once – then it initiates the process all over again. People think it's genetic. That is what the enemy of your soul *wants* you to think. It is not. Again, it is a spirit.

Knowing what you now know about how generational sin works, and how the devil will always use some form of sexual activity to set the trap, it is easy to see his evil, yet very effective agenda. The perverse spirit is one of the largest and most aggressive strongholds I've ever seen. But it *has to bow* to the mighty name of Jesus. I have also seen that. Many times.

Braden repented of the sin, renounced the spirit, and broke it off of his life in a matter of minutes. He prayed a version of the prayer you read with Leah. And when you pray that prayer and *mean it*, the spirit has no choice but to leave. This gave Braden and Deborah hope as they broke incest, and more, off her life. They held hands and repented of sexual perversion and sexual fantasy. They renounced all spirits that had attached themselves, both individually, and as a couple. They specifically addressed the night with Sonja and the sin they committed.

It was beautiful to watch the Holy Spirit work with them... and their willingness to walk through it.

Systematically, one after the other, they addressed their demons. They repented, renounced, broke the strongholds, and spoke blessing. In two hours, I watched God *completely reconcile* a marriage that had been completely irreconcilable for 7 months!

People spend thousands of dollars on marriage counseling. But Deborah and Braden went to THE Counselor, THE Comforter, THE Holy Spirit, and were completely healed. It was amazing. At the end of the night they were exhausted, but ecstatic. They were both free of spirits that had been plaguing them since childhood. And they had their precious marriage back. I got an e-mail from them recently, and they're still doing great. When the Holy Spirit does the work, it is complete and it is permanent!

Now, there is one more story that we need to revisit. The story of Amy Sever. And I take a deep breath, as I digress several years. Back before I was able to help Jade or Elaine,   Leah, or

Now, there is one more story that we need to revisit. The story of Amy Sever. And I take a deep breath, as I digress several years.

Deborah and Braden, and so many others. Before I was free of the demons that plagued *my* soul. Back when I was miserable. Back when I was still hearing voices.

I want you to flashback with me now...

Notes and Reflections

Chapter
38

...Flashback to Soul Ties Night;
My Story

Those voices were screaming at me loudly the night Steve and I headed to our weekly class and Bible study. *"You don't want to go tonight. This whole thing is ridiculous. Who believes this stuff anyway? I mean really - body, soul, spirit? Come on! People are going to think you have become a religious fanatic. And the leaders of this class know your family. If they find out about all the shit you have done, they will tell others, and it would get back to Steve. It's all too personal. This is going to end badly for you, Amy. You know this!"*

On and on and on. The voices never stopped. I was so sick of them! However, I had been learning through that class, about how to speak to myself. To command with my mouth. To use the *"sword of the Spirit which is the Word of God"* (Ephesians 6). I realized that my soul *had to submit* to my spirit when I prayed that prayer. And for the first time in years, for small windows at a time, I was able to make the voices stop. I was learning to use scriptures I had memorized to fight them off.

On this night though, they were particularly annoying. So even though I felt really stupid, when we arrived at the church that night, I went straight to the restroom. I looked at myself in the mirror and with full intensity said, *"Soul! You WILL line up under my spirit! And my spirit WILL line up under the Spirit of God who lives in me. I command my thoughts to line up with the Word of God that says 'I can do all things through Christ who strengthens me.' I claim the scripture that says 'No temptation has seized me except which is common to man. And God is faithful; He will not let me be tempted beyond what I can bear. But when I am tempted, He always provides a way out so I can stand up under it.' Whatever is tempting me to not come to this class tonight, I speak to you now and command you to STOP!!"* (Philippians 4:13; 1 Corinthians 10:13).

The voices instantly stopped. Peace immediately flooded my mind and emotions. The anxiety left. I could hear the worship music and it no longer sounded like fingernails on a chalkboard. It was actually beautiful and comforting. I walked out of the restroom. I was beginning to believe in the new spiritual tools I was acquiring.

After we sang and worshiped for a few minutes, we began to get into the teaching. It was then when I discovered why the devil had tried so hard to keep me from going that night. We learned about soul ties.

> As I began to absorb the scriptures from my workbook, I was absolutely sick to my stomach.

That specific term isn't in the Bible. I had never heard of soul ties. But they are very real. And I found out I was certainly suffering from them. As I began to absorb the scriptures from my workbook, I was absolutely sick to my stomach. The familiar emotions of guilt and shame came rushing back. I felt dirty. Even though I had been a Christian all my life, it felt like I was seeing these passages for the first time.

As I read, my soul came roaring back to the forefront and the voices started again. *"Do you see what a wretch you are? You are a whore! You are an adulteress! If Steve found out he would divorce you! You have to keep those damn tears from rolling down your pathetic face! No one must know what these scriptures are doing to you right now! Go to the restroom! Stop reading this shit! Put it down and walk out of here! This is ridiculous! No one can know what you've done! If you tell anyone, life as you know it will end!"* I blinked back my tears and forced myself to focus on the words in front of me.

> *Do you not know that your bodies are members of Christ himself? Shall I then take the members of Christ and unite them with a prostitute? Never! Do you not know that he who unites himself with a prostitute is one with her in body? For it is said 'The two will become one flesh.' But he who unites himself with the Lord is one with Him in spirit. Flee from sexual immorality. All other sins a man commits are*

outside his body, but he who sins sexually sins against his own body. Do you not know that your body is a temple of the Holy Spirit who is in you, whom you have received from God? You are not your own, you were bought at a price. Therefore honor God with your body. ~ 1 Corinthians 6:15-20

But among you there must not be even a hint of sexual immorality... ~ Ephesians 5:3

It is God's will that you be sanctified: that you should avoid sexual immorality; that each of you should learn to control his own body in a way that is holy and honorable, not in passionate lust like the heathen who do not know God; and that in this matter no one should wrong his brother or take advantage of him. ~ 1 Thessalonians 4:3-6

My son, pay attention to my wisdom, listen well to my words of insight, that you may maintain discretion and your lips may preserve knowledge. For the lips of an adulteress drip honey, and her speech is smoother than oil; but in the end she is bitter as gall, sharp as a double-edged sword. Her feet go down to death; her steps lead to the grave. She gives no thought to the way of life; her paths are crooked, but she knows it not. ~ Proverbs 5:1-6

Why be captivated, my son, by an adulteress? Why embrace the bosom of another man's wife? For a man's ways are in full view of the Lord and He examines all his paths. The evil deeds of a wicked man ensnare him; the cords of his sin hold him fast. He will die for lack of discipline, led astray by his own great folly. ~ Proverbs 5:20-23

With persuasive words she led him astray; she seduced him with her smooth talk. All at once he followed her like an ox going to the slaughter, like a deer stepping into a noose till an arrow pierces his liver, like a bird darting into a snare, little knowing it will cost him his life. ~ Proverbs 7:21-23

Through clenched teeth I whispered to myself, *"Soul! I command you to line up under my spirit. My spirit is under the protection and authority of the Spirit of God who lives in me! I will NOT listen to these thoughts. 'I take them captive and make them obedient to the knowledge of Christ!' (2 Corinthians 10:5) I know that I am forgiven! I am covered by the blood of Christ who died for my sins! Leave me alone right now!"*

This particular night I was wrestling my soul like I wrestled the steering wheel that night in the rain. It was constant. The voices were loud, accusing, and persistent. But, I continued to fight them off, using the Word of God. Each time I did, they would retreat for a short time.

Although the scriptures seemed extremely accusatory, I let them absorb into my spirit. I realized they are there as a warning to protect us from ourselves. Especially as the class continued, and I learned about Dinah...

> *And Dinah the daughter of Leah, which she bare unto Jacob, went out to see the daughters of the land. And when Shechem the son of Hamor the Hivite, prince of the country, saw her, he took her, and lay with her, and defiled her. **And his soul clave unto Dinah** the daughter of Jacob...* ~ Genesis 34:1-3 KJV

Wait a minute! What? She sounded just like me! That sounded like she was raped. And when I continued reading the rest of the story, it turned out that the guy actually had fallen in love with her. But he *had defiled* her. "And his soul clave unto Dinah" ...hmm. I was seeing this for the first time that night.

According to the Webster's Dictionary, the definition of "cleave" means *"to adhere to firmly, to lock together."*

Again, the word "soul tie" is not a term used in the Bible. It is the name for the spiritual tie that occurs when two people *"become one flesh."* **Thus, a soul tie is "the binding together of two souls."** In other words, a soul tie occurs during intercourse between two people. The Word states:

*...a man shall leave his father and mother and shall **cleave**
to his wife: and **they shall be one flesh.**   ~ Genesis 2:24*

The instructor was saying that God intended for a man to be joined to
his wife and a wife to her husband, body, soul, and spirit. This is an
incredibly powerful experience! When a husband and wife love each
other and they come together physically, the tie that occurs is
supposed to be binding. You not only exchange bodies, but your
souls become intertwined as well. In a loving relationship, this is a
beautiful phenomenon.   It is meant to give wholeness to both
husband and wife. We are to gain strength from our partner. And we
are to give strength as well.

However, this beautiful
experience has been
perverted through the
ages.   Satan has taken
this precious gift and
used it to wreak havoc on

> Because sexual intercourse is meant
> to have a "binding" effect, the enemy
> has been using it to entangle us, and
> keep us locked in unseen prisons.

the lives of humans for thousands of years.   Because sexual
intercourse is meant to have a "binding" effect, the enemy has been
using it to entangle us, and keep us locked in unseen prisons. That's
why Satan uses sexual trauma so often.   It not only has a binding
effect, but a lasting one as well.

 I stared at my workbook and tried to make sense of it all. *So... When
you have sex with someone, you actually become one flesh. Yeah, I
get that.   Okay, that's pretty obvious.   But... the **souls cleave
together as well?** The souls of two people actually lock together?
Surely not!*

As the knowledge of that sank in, my mind went rushing back to the
night in the Dominican Republic. The night on the moonlit path. A
night that changed my life...

As Julius ripped at my dress, I knew I was about to be raped. All I
could think was "Please, no.   Please, no!   I don't want to lose my
virginity this way! God, no! Please don't let me get AIDS!"

He threatened my life if I ever told anyone. And he walked away casually, leaving me in a crumpled, bleeding heap. The next day, as Julius' threats still rung in my ears, I vowed to never tell a soul. My virginity had been taken from me in the most terrifying way, and my body still ached. I could still feel his cold hard eyes staring into mine as he mercilessly ripped through me. At breakfast with my family on that last morning, I did my best to be delightfully cheerful and thankful for my dream vacation. On the flight back to Texas, the physical pain was a constant reminder that I would never be pure again. My fear that I had gotten pregnant – or worse – was overwhelming. I was dying inside, and I couldn't even tell my mother... who was sitting in the seat next to me. I was trapped...

Just then, still sitting in class, a sudden sharp pain hit my right side and brought me back to the present. I flinched as the pain began to intensify. Steve looked at me with concern. *"Honey, are you okay? You have been acting so strange tonight. Are you hurting?"*

It was either my ovary or my appendix. I couldn't tell. But it was hurting terribly. Steve was staring at me with concern on his face. *"I'm fine."* He had become very familiar with the lack of truth in those words.

> When two people have sex, they exchange more than just bodily fluid. Their *souls* blend together as well.

He didn't believe me, but I shrugged him off. He looked back down at his own workbook. I could tell that he was also trying to absorb the words and scriptures on the pages in front of him. So I forced the pain away and concentrated on this new knowledge I was trying to absorb.

My thoughts went back to what the instructor was explaining. *"Oh, no! Oh, no! Does this mean I have a soul tie with ...Julius?! But I'm married to Steve. I have a soul tie with him! What? Could this be true? If that's the case, what am I going to do?!"*

When two people have sex, they exchange more than just bodily fluid. Their *souls* blend together as well. So if your sexual partner has any demonic strongholds, sex with them creates an *open door for their demons to flow right into your soul* ...and begin to wreak havoc. Whatever spirits they have opened themselves to... now have a *legal right* to you.

Suddenly, the bloody nightmares I had been experiencing for years came to mind. There was no telling what Julius had opened himself up to... and now his demons were affecting me! Following the rape in the Dominican Republic, those nightmares started immediately... and had never ceased.

> *...For it is said* **'The two will become one flesh.'** *But he who unites himself with the Lord is one with Him in spirit. Flee from sexual immorality. All other sins a man commits are outside his body, but he who sins sexually sins against his own body.* ~ 1 Corinthians 6:16-18

As that knowledge sank in, I realized it wasn't just the nightmares that started that night. There were other things that had begun too. I had recently learned that depression, anxiety, insomnia, and fear were all demonic strongholds. All of those had begun with Julius, as well.

The pain continued to intensify in my right side. On a scale of 1 to 10, it had reached a 7. I was shifting uncomfortably back and forth as the next piece of new knowledge hit me like a ton of bricks...

When we have sex with someone, it isn't just *their* demons that we are exposed to. It is also the demons of *anyone they have slept with as well.* Sexual sin is literally a demonic highway, a spiritual web linking people together for generations.

I immediately flashed back to the teaching we got in high school about sexually-transmitted diseases (STDs). One afternoon, the bell rang and all of the kids in my high school were herded into the auditorium for a school assembly on sex. We were all snickering in feigned embarrassment when they told us they were going to talk about sexually-transmitted diseases.

When the teacher explained that when you have sex with one person you can still catch a disease from *someone else that person has been with*, I sat up and began to pay close attention. I didn't know that. I remember shuddering at the graph they showed us that day. It was like a huge spider web, and showed how multiple sexual partners filter down through bodily fluids.

So, you may have slept with someone and that was your only encounter. But, what if that one person was extremely promiscuous? You also have a chance to catch disease from *all of their partners as well as those people's partners, and so on.* That huge webbing of potential danger freaked me out. I felt like my sexually active friends were playing Russian roulette with sexually- transmitted diseases.

On this night though, we weren't talking about sexually transmitted diseases. We were talking about *sexually transmitted demons*. This new meaning for "STDs" sent a fresh wave of fear and dread through my whole body. I immediately became nauseated.

After the rape with Julius, I was scared to death that he had gotten me pregnant. Or worse, given me AIDS. The Dominican Republic is next to Haiti, one of the largest areas in the world for HIV. Waiting for my period that next month was excruciating. I cried with relief the day I started. One bullet dodged.

But the thought of possibly having a life-threatening disease plagued me for months. One day my family switched insurance companies. I still remember sitting at my family's dining room table giving blood. Fear gripped me almost uncontrollably as I laid out my arm for the lady to prick me. I watched my hand tremble in fear. The nurse noticed and asked me if I was afraid of needles. *"Yes,"* I lied. But as the thick red fluid flowed into the glass tube, all I could think was *"What if my blood test comes back HIV positive!? How in the world am I going to explain that to mom and dad!? They think I'm a virgin!"*

The pain on the right side of my abdomen had reached an 8 out of 10. Steve noticed. *"What's wrong, honey? You're in pain, aren't you? What's going on?"* he whispered. *"Do we need to leave? What can I do?"*

"I don't know what's wrong," I said through gritted teeth. *"I don't want to leave. Maybe it will subside in a minute."* I was sweating. A hot tear rolled down my cheek.

The instructor gave one more point; you create a soul tie with *every person* you have ever been with. Part of your soul cleaves to them and part of their soul cleaves to you. You don't get to pick and choose whose soul is cleaving to yours. If you have had sex, there indeed is a soul tie. People wonder why they have so many psychological problems. This is one of the main reasons. Their personalities are split among all those people. Soul ties are real.

Thoughts of my life flashed before me. After the rape with Julius, I just "quit caring" for a while. One of the strongholds from the rape was a passive-submissive spirit. The voices would say, *"What's the use trying to fight this? You're not a virgin anymore anyway. Just get it over with so he will leave you alone."* If I ever got in a situation that I was uncomfortable with, I just let it happen anyway. I married at age 21 in order to get away from it all.

> The instructor described how so many are suffering from splintered personalities because of multiple soul ties.

I felt nauseated as my mind flashed to that day at the clinic and yet another soul tie. The pain in my right side had hit a 9. Tears rolled down my cheeks.

The instructor described how so many are suffering from splintered personalities because of multiple soul ties. As he talked about extreme cases of abuse – even if it is generational – diseases like Multiple Personality Disorder, Schizophrenia, and Bipolar came to my mind.

Though I wasn't suffering to this degree, I thought the voices in my head were going to drive me crazy. The nightmares, the depression and anxiety, fear, insomnia, and suicidal thoughts were enough!

No wonder there was so much scripture, both from the Old and New Testaments, warning me to flee sexual sin! If I could have only realized how devastating it actually is!

> *Flee the evil desires of youth, and pursue righteousness, faith, love and peace, along with those who call on the Lord out of a pure heart.* ~ 2 Timothy 2:22

I had not followed this scripture. Righteousness, faith, love, peace, and a pure heart, were nowhere around.

It had started with the way I was seductively flirting with Julius. I was not *"fleeing the evil desires of youth."* I was enjoying them. And now I was spiritually tied to every person I had ever been intimate with. Parts of my soul were cleaving to others, and parts of other souls were cleaving to me...

Chapter
39   ...At the Emergency Room

I couldn't stand the pain any longer. I staggered to the restroom and threw up. I thought I was going to pass out. I was sweating profusely and white as a sheet. Steve found me crumpled on the floor in the restroom and immediately picked me up and carried me out to the car.

The ride to the emergency room was excruciating. Every bump in the road sent new shock waves of pain through my entire abdominal cavity.

When we arrived, they wheeled me back to the room and took all of my vitals. Then I went in for a CAT scan. By the time the results came back, several people had come to the hospital to check on me. I was embarrassed. With the scan results and some other tests, they had decided I had a large ovarian cyst rupture and fill my abdominal cavity with toxic fluid. I was thankful it had not been my appendix.

The physical pain that had been my constant companion for the last several hours had started to subside, which allowed me to finally focus on the information I had received earlier that evening. And my emotional and spiritual

> I asked Joe Hamilton how I could break them off. What he shared with me was the beginning of my freedom.

pain came back with a jolt. As we were rushing out of class that night, they were beginning to explain to the group that soul ties were just like strongholds. We **could** *break soul ties* and be restored.

Once I could concentrate, I asked Joe Hamilton, who had come from our class to check on me, how I could break them off. What he shared with me was the beginning of my freedom. He told me that if I prayed and **Repented**, **Renounced the spirits** that had attached themselves to me through an unholy soul tie, then **Broke the soul tie** in Jesus' name, and **Spoke Blessing** into my life and the life of the other person, my soul would be free. He told me to make a list of every person I had ever been with, and pray that prayer for each one.

Steve suddenly interjected, *"What if you can't remember them all?"* For some reason I thought that was so funny, and I glanced up from my hospital bed and laughed. The immediate pain that it brought made me regret it. It hurt to laugh. But, the way he said it... it was just funny. Everyone standing around laughed. He was serious though, and even though he had a sheepish grin, he wanted to know the answer to his question.

Joe returned his own cute, crooked grin as he said, *"The Lord knows the names of every person you have been with, Steve. Just do your best. Write down everyone that you can think of. It is amazing how the Holy Spirit will bring people that you have forgotten back to your mind. Even if you don't know their names, an instance will flash in your mind and you need to write the instance down. The Lord knows that person's name, so it still works. You both will be amazed at how freeing this is. It will do you so much good to take the time and do this right. Don't do this together. Get alone with God and let Him minister healing to you in a very private manner."*

Chapter 40

...Breaking Soul Ties

Late that night after I finally got home from the hospital and settled, I reflected on my evening. The voices had been nonstop as we were heading to our class. When I commanded the voices to stop, the physical pain started. It had certainly been a night that I had to fight through my body and soul in order to hear what the Lord what trying to say to my spirit.

The Lord wanted me to be free, whole, and abundant. Joyful. And I was none of those. I had let myself digress to the point that I hardly recognized Amy Sever. When I looked in the mirror, I saw a depressed, overweight woman with absolutely no joy. I had intentionally tried to cover my God-given beauty. And I wanted to change that. As hard as the night had been, hope had begun to stir at the hospital when Joe told me I could be free.

Thankfully *my* "list" was not that long. But I knew I needed to start immediately, and I needed to start with Julius. Steve left me alone in our living room, so I could have some privacy. I got out a piece of paper and pen as fresh tears streamed down my face. As I listed names, I couldn't help but be amazed at what Jesus did for me on the cross. A deep, heartfelt repentance flooded my soul. I could feel the loving presence of the Holy Spirit as I took a deep breath and softly prayed.

> *"Dear Heavenly Father, thank you for allowing me to come before you and repent of my sin. Thank you for sending your Son. Jesus, I love you. Thank you for dying for my sin with Julius. I repent. I turn from that now and I receive your forgiveness.*
>
> *And, now, Satan, I renounce you and every demonic spirit that has had a legal right to torment me as a result of my sin with Julius! You have been defeated by the blood of Jesus Christ, my Savior and Lord. You no longer have the right to torment my dreams or manipulate my emotions. I rebuke*

every spirit that is attached to me right now and cast you out of my life. Leave me now!

I now break the soul tie with Julius. I break any and all ties to Julius and anyone he has ever been with. In Jesus' name, I release all parts of his soul that are clinging to mine. And I ask you Holy Spirit, to retrieve my soul from Julius. Please cleanse it and return it to me pure and whole. Thank you for your power to restore my soul! I love you, Lord!

And, finally, I speak blessing into my life and in the life of Julius. I ask that you forgive him, and bless him. Please bless me, Lord. It is in the mighty name of Jesus I pray. Amen."

> By faith, I pictured the Holy Spirit going to those people and supernaturally retrieving parts of my soul...

I prayed that exact prayer for every person on my list. And with every finished "Amen," my soul became lighter. More whole. It was truly an amazing experience. By faith, I pictured the Holy Spirit going to those people and supernaturally retrieving parts of my soul, and returning theirs.

It was such a sweet time with the Lord. The Holy Spirit was so near to me that night!

I knew that I still had work to do as far as total freedom was concerned, but just this one step was life changing. When I coupled it with what I had learned about breaking the strongholds of generational curses, sin, and word curses, I knew it was a huge step toward my ultimate freedom. I felt as though heavy chains had been lifted from my shoulders. I could not believe the difference in how I felt, compared to 7 hours earlier! On my way to class that night, I was at one of the lowest points in my life. Now I was feeling freedom for the first time in years!

As I fell into bed that night Steve softly kissed my forehead. I was exhausted. Emotionally and physically. But I felt better. And when I woke up the next morning, I realized that it had been the first full night's sleep I'd had in years. No bloody nightmares. No insomnia filled with anxiety. I had slept soundly all night. Relief washed over me as I realized I had gained a huge spiritual key. I knew that someday I would be able to help others with this same information.

So, I encourage you to make your own list. Do exactly what I did. Walk through that prayer, and *mean it*. With every person you have ever been with. Then crumple that piece of paper and picture placing it at the foot of the cross. Picture the blood of Christ flowing down and covering that piece of paper. And then burn the list. Seriously. Get a match out and burn it. You will be amazed at the freedom it will bring you. And it will prepare you, as it did me, for the next chapter of the book. The fifth way the devil has a legal right to torment you... Unforgiveness.

Notes and Reflections

Notes and Reflections

Chapter 41   ...Forgiveness

It had been a week since I had a nightmare. I still had some voices but not like before I broke soul ties. It had been one of the better weeks I had experienced in years. I was beginning to actually look forward to going to sleep at night. I was more rested. So, when Steve and I headed to our last weekly class, I was feeling relaxed and hopeful. I was actually looking forward to it ...until I got there and started listening to the instructor talk about forgiveness.

He was saying that in order to understand what forgiveness is, we must first understand what forgiveness is not. Forgiveness is not liking the person or approving of their actions. Forgiveness is not allowing that person continued access to your life.

Forgiveness is not just tolerating the wrong in your life. Forgiveness is not pushing the hurt so far down inside your soul that you think it is no longer there. Forgiveness is not just trying to forget that someone has hurt you.

> **Forgiveness is not an option. It is not a choice. It is a commandment. God is serious about this issue.**

Forgiveness is not an option. It is not a choice. It is a commandment. God is serious about this issue. It is absolutely crucial to forgive. Not only for others, but also for our own *spiritual and physical* health.

I began to feel an uncomfortable knot in the pit of my stomach. *"This is going to be harder than I thought. But, why is that knot there? I've forgiven everyone in my life already."*

I grew up in church. I had heard sermons my whole life on forgiveness. I thought I had forgiven everyone in my life who had hurt me. When I broke soul ties the week before, I had said the words *"I forgive Julius. Please bless him."* I had also prayed that sentence for the guy at the clinic. Even though that incident had quietly happened several years earlier, I had pushed it under the rug and had never told anyone. I had forgiven him. He was at the top of my list. His name had been next to Julius. So, I thought things were good. But, as I learned what forgiveness really is and all the reasons I needed to forgive, several things began to bubble under the surface of my soul. A *deep* anger began to stir. I was extremely agitated, as I looked at my workbook that night and followed the instructor.

Forgiveness is allowing yourself to go back to the incident that hurt you. You need to come to a place where you can look that person in the face, if not in person, at least through your mind's eye, and give them a full pardon. It is a deep work of God. And the cost is tremendous. Forgiveness is not cheap and it does not come easy. It is a selfless act of love. It is allowing the person that hurt you to go without punishment or vengeance. So many times, it is absolutely impossible for us to forgive. You need to picture that person standing in front of Jesus. And Christ *through* you forgiving that person.

> *I can do **all** things through Christ, who strengthens me.*
> ~ Philippians 4:13

Forgiveness is the key to your own freedom.

My agitation grew worse. It wasn't like the week before, during soul ties. I wasn't hurting physically. I was just... angry. Really, really angry. I couldn't put my finger on it. I was angry at the instructor. At myself. At my life. And I was angry at God. *"This sucks!"* I thought bitterly. *"Who needs this? I've forgiven everybody I need to forgive!"*

> Forgiveness is the *anvil of Christianity*. Without forgiveness, there would not be eternal life with the Father.

Forgiveness is the *anvil of Christianity*. Without forgiveness, there would not be eternal life with the Father. Christ's death on the cross is the ultimate act of forgiveness, and without that selfless act, we are without hope. Christians have accepted that pardon for their sins. We cannot receive that pardon ourselves and refuse to pardon others.

Therefore, as God's chosen people, holy and dearly loved, clothe yourselves with compassion, kindness, humility, gentleness and patience. Bear with each other and forgive whatever grievances you may have against one another. Forgive as the Lord forgave you. ~ Colossians 3:13

Unforgiveness is a sin. You can't allow it to continue in your life. It will eventually destroy you.

"But, I have forgiven!" I thought again. "Where was this anger coming from? I had been completely numb in the area of forgiveness my whole life. It had started with Jeff's death. I "forgave" the people that left the door unlocked and the ladder open for my brother to have free access to a 48 foot fall. I forgave those people. And I "forgave" the girl who said, 'Jeff deserved to die because he has a bitch for a sister.' I had forgiven her. I "forgave" Jeff for dying and leaving me all alone without my twin. I HAD forgiven him! Where in the world is this anger coming from? Why was I thinking about Jeff on "forgiveness night?"

> *Where in the world is this anger coming from? Why was I thinking about Jeff on "forgiveness night?"*

You have heard that it was said to the people long ago, 'Do not murder, and anyone who murders will be subject to judgment.' But I tell you that anyone who is angry with his brother will be subject to judgment. Again, anyone who says to his brother, 'Raca' is answerable to the Sanhedrin. But anyone who says, 'You fool!' will be in danger of the fire of hell. Therefore, if you are offering your gift at the altar and there remember that your brother has something against you, leave your gift there in front of the altar. First go and be reconciled to your brother; then come and offer your gift. ~ Matthew 5:21-24

"Well, I can't very easily go and be reconciled to my brother, now can I, God?! Because he is dead! I know it isn't your fault. I get that. But YOU ALLOWED THIS TO HAPPEN. Now Jeff is in Heaven and I HATE MY LIFE!!!" ...Wow! Where in the world was this *anger* coming from? It was beginning to churn inside my gut. I wanted to hit someone!

> *In your anger do not sin. Do not let the sun go down while you are still angry, and do not give the devil a foothold.*
> ~ Ephesians 4:26-27

"Whatever, God. WHATEVER! I guess I've given the devil a f....... foothold then!   Because I'm ANGRY!!! Do you hear me, God?! Because this shit sucks! I hate my f.......life!!!   Do you hear me?!! F.... this!!!"

> *Do not let any unwholesome talk come out of your mouths, but only what is helpful for building others up according to their needs, that it may benefit those who listen. And do not grieve the Holy Spirit of God, with whom you were sealed for the day of redemption. Get rid of all bitterness, rage and anger, brawling and slander, along with every form of malice.   Be kind and compassionate to one another, forgiving each other, just as in Christ God forgave you.*
> ~ Ephesians 5:29-32

"FINE, God!! Very funny! I finally say the 'f' word to you, and the very next scripture is 'Don't let any unwholesome talk come out of your mouth?!' Really God?! F....ing REALLY?!!"

"Daughter ...be still ...shhh," the Holy Spirit whispered. "Shhh ....I am interceding for you right now. I love you. ...shhh." Instantly, I heard my prayer language in my spirit. I heard the Holy Spirit praying for me. It had been ages since I had "dialed in." My heartbeat slowed. I took a deep breath.

This anger that had suddenly risen to the surface of my consciousness was so foreign to me. *What in the world?* Where was this coming from? This internal battle. I had dealt with a lot of things, but never *anger*. Not anger like this. Wow. Especially at Jeff. I had never been angry at Jeff *in my life*!   I took another deep breath and looked back at my workbook. It felt like a serpent was coiling in my stomach as I tried to focus on what the instructor was saying.

One of the reasons that God commands us to forgive is because when we harbor unforgiveness, it opens the door to demonic influence. The enemy has a legal right to torment us and keep us in bondage. Nothing will wrap chains of iron around our souls and hold us captive like harboring anger and unforgiveness! Jesus knew how dangerous this particular sin is. It affects every area of our lives. That's why it was one of His main priorities as He taught His disciples how to pray. Jesus said,

> Nothing will wrap chains of iron around our souls and hold us captive like harboring anger and unforgiveness!

*Forgive us our debts, as we also have forgiven our debtors. And lead us not into temptation, **but deliver us from the evil one.** For if you forgive men when they sin against you, your Heavenly Father will also forgive you. **But if you do not forgive men their sins, your Father will not forgive your sins**.* ~ Matthew 6:12-14

This is another scripture that speaks of the devil, right after a sentence about forgiveness. You can give the devil a foothold through anger. "The evil one" can also have access to your life if you don't forgive your debtors. Satan knows this. Therefore, if he can cause things to happen in your life to make you harbor unforgiveness, he has a legal right to torment you. So many people are dealing with demonic interference because they haven't *truly* forgiven those that have hurt them. And they don't even realize it. They may have said the words, but the deep cleansing work of the Holy Spirit has not completely sealed that person from the hurt and pain. And Unforgiveness *will* eventually affect your health!

The "coiling" in my stomach grew worse. The anger stirred again. My breathing grew ragged once more as the instructor was wrapping up. Sin absolutely *does* affect your physical body.

O Lord, do not rebuke me in your anger or discipline me in your wrath. For your arrows have pierced me, and your hand has come down upon me. Because of your wrath there is no health in my body; my bones have no soundness because of my sin. My wounds fester and are loathsome because of my sinful folly. I am bowed down and brought very low; all day long I go about mourning. My back is filled with searing pain; there is no health in my body. I am feeble and utterly crushed; I groan in anguish of heart. All my longings lie open before you, O Lord; my sighing is not hidden from you. My heart pounds, my strength fails me; even the light has gone from my eyes. ~ Psalm 38:1-10

And the sin of unforgiveness is one of the toughest, because it is indeed *the acid that destroys its own container...*

> And the sin of unforgiveness is one of the toughest, because it is indeed *the acid that destroys its own container...*

What did he say about acid destroying its container? Because that's how my stomach felt ...like acid. I had a terrible taste in my mouth as I picked up my workbook and Bible. I didn't speak to anyone after class. I couldn't wait to get out of there. Steve could hardly keep up with me on the way to the car. When we got in the car, Steve said, *"Okay, Amy, what's wrong now? You never jet out of there like that. That was rude. What is going on with you?"*

"I don't know!" I snapped. *"I'm just sick of this damn class. It messes with me every week. I feel like I'm going to throw up. My stomach hurts. And I'm just mad. I don't know why!"*

But I did know why. Just when I thought the knot in my stomach couldn't get any worse and just as I was trying to wrestle down the anger over Jeff, that last scripture about sin had brought the incident at the clinic rushing back. I knew I had participated by allowing that friendship to get too emotionally involved. I had sinned. And even though I had broken the soul tie the week before, I still had not told Steve. It was still my sick secret. Every time the thought of telling Steve had quietly surfaced in my spirit, I had immediately dismissed it. But after tonight, I knew that I had to tell Steve about the clinic. I knew that in order for me to be truly free and for me to *truly forgive*, he had to know. Wait a minute! What was I thinking? *No!* Steve must *never* know!

The voices had started again at the end of class.

"You know that you are about to lose your marriage, right? Because if you tell him he will leave you. Savannah's first daddy is dead, and if you tell Steve, then she will be without the only Daddy that she knows and loves. You better not tell him! This is all so much better left unsaid! Don't you see how f....ing ridiculous this whole process has been? All of this 'cleansing' that you have supposedly been going through ...and for what? If you finish it, you will lose everything. You will be an embarrassment and a disgrace to your entire family!

"No one knows right now that you have committed adultery. Just leave it that way! Why would you break Steve's heart like that? What about your family? What about your parents? They think you are the perfect little Christian daughter. But you are a whore! You are an adulterous bitch! You know that! There is no changing that fact. So just accept it, move on, and quit thinking about telling Steve. That happened a long time ago. It was the last class tonight. You don't have to go anymore. Just let it die down. This 'need to confess' will go away. And if you let it, you will be fine. If you spill your pathetic guts, then all hell will break loose!"

Chapter 42 ...*Later That Week*

Our class had been on Monday night. By Wednesday, I was a completely different person. I could not get a grasp on the roiling in my stomach that had started two days earlier. The anger that had flared for the first time in my life on Monday was getting out of hand. It was a serpent, ready to strike at any moment. I had lashed out at both Steve and Savannah several times. Bless her heart, Savannah had no idea why. She just knew her mommy was mad. Steve was gracious, but my anger was wearing on him. Steve has such wisdom. He knew I was hurting deeply.

The voices in my head were nonstop. One week of peaceful sleep had been such a nice respite. But because I hadn't slept at all since the class, Wednesday afternoon I snapped. I had just yelled at Steve again, and he finally responded. *"What in the world is going on with you, Amy? For two days, you haven't even been remotely close to the person I married. I don't even know who you are! Where is this anger coming from? You've never lashed out like that. Especially at Savannah! I'm worried about you!"*

I screamed, *"I hate my life!! I hate myself! I hate my f....ing beauty!!"* I grabbed a pair of scissors and tried to cut my hair at my scalp. Steve and I fought over them as he wrestled the blades out of my hand. I had just come within an inch of whacking my hair completely off!

After the fight with the scissors, Steve got scared. He grabbed me, squared my shoulders, looked me right in the eyes and pleaded, *"I want my wife back!"* My body went limp and I fell to my knees. *"No, you don't. You don't want me. I don't deserve you..."*

Steve got scared. He grabbed me, squared my shoulders, looked me right in the eyes and pleaded, *"I want my wife back!"*

"Amy, tell me what's going on. I promise that whatever it is, I will always love you. No matter what! It will be okay. We will get

through it together. I promise you I will never leave you. Whatever you tell me right now will never change that. Please. Tell me ...I love you."

I began to cry. I was so scared. But I knew that for better or worse, I was about to tell my husband. *"I'm so sorry Steve. Please forgive me! I have to tell you what happened a long time ago."* ...and I told him.

We were supposed to serve at church that night. We drove in silence. Steve was still wrestling with the information he was processing. I was wrestling with shame and self-hate. Savannah, my beautiful little girl, was oblivious. She was sitting in her car seat looking out the window as we drove. Her pony tails bounced as she tilted her head from side to side. Her little legs were swinging back and forth, and she was singing "Amazing Grace" at the top of her lungs.

> I began to cry. I was so scared. But I knew that for better or worse, I was about to tell my husband.

Savannah is my song bird. She was born with perfect pitch. And she has been singing since before she could talk. When she was two years old we taught her "Amazing Grace" and she sang it all the time. All four verses came barreling out in her tiny voice as we drove. I glanced at Steve. He was staring straight ahead, his jaw set. I had no idea what he was thinking. Tears slid silently down my face. I was thankful for my dark sunglasses.

We walked into the sanctuary and the very first note of the very first praise song sent me over the edge. Because there was so much demonic interference, I couldn't even hear the praise music. I couldn't sit through one verse. Demons can't stand the presence of praise. And I had been in full manifestation for two days. I bolted up and ran out of the sanctuary. For some reason I ran up the stairs and ended up in the baptismal area behind the choir loft.

I got in the little closet where people change to get baptized and curled up in the fetal position. I began to sob. As the people worshiped in the sanctuary, the words *His grace is sufficient for me* floated up to where I was cowering in the baptismal. *"His grace wasn't sufficient for me. It may be sufficient for somebody else, but not for me."* I continued to cry. I cried the whole hour and a half. I had been crying all day.

I never even went into the service. I stayed curled up in that closet. After church was over, I was already at the car as Steve came out of church carrying Savannah. He didn't even recognize me when I took my sunglasses off. My eyes were swollen completely shut. It looked as though I had been in a fist fight. Indeed, I felt like I had been. I felt like an invisible presence was continually punching me in my stomach and in my face.

We drove home in silence. As soon as we got home, Steve put Savannah to bed. He came in, locked our bedroom door, and took me by the hand. He gently sat me down on the bed and got down on his knees in front of me. I looked at him with dread. I had no idea what he was about to say. He looked me deeply in the eyes and he said, *"I have to ask your forgiveness, Amy. I have not led you properly. You said that you didn't deserve me. Baby, that is not true. I take full responsibility for the state you are in at this moment. You are my wife and I love you. I forgive you. I need you to forgive me as well for things that I have opened us to as a result of the sin in my life. I have been dealing with my own set of soul ties previous to our marriage. I understand that as your husband, it is my responsibility to make sure all the "doors" are closed. God has been dealing with me as well. It is me who doesn't deserve you."* I stared at him in disbelief. I thought he was about to ask for a divorce. I just knew he was done with our marriage. *"Please forgive me, Amy"* he said gently.
"...I forgive you..." I stammered.

Steve took a deep breath. And he asked me to breathe deeply as well. I thought he was about to get up. But he didn't. He shifted, and took another deep breath. *"Now, ...there is something else that we need to do."* Steve paused for what seemed too long, never looking away. Then he said, *"I am Julius. And I have to ask your forgiveness for raping you. For taking your virginity from you in such a horrific way. Please forgive me, Amy."*

I stared at him. *"What are you doing? Why are you doing this?"* But he persisted.

Suddenly we were no longer in our bedroom. I was an 18 year old in the Dominican Republic. I saw the full moon. The rocks were there. I could smell the sweet scent of the hibiscus that lined the path. The trees softly swayed in the ocean breeze. I saw Julius' face. And a dark rage came out of me. I couldn't believe it. I wanted to scratch his eyes out. *Rage.* I had never experienced it. It was scary. The deep guttural moan of rage. ... I had no idea that kind of sound could come from me. *"Amy, PLEASE forgive me. What I did was wrong. I need to have your forgiveness. Please..."* he said softly, his eyes held my gaze.

I tried to get up. But Steve gently put his hands on my knees. *"Please forgive me, Amy."*

Somehow I knew that this was my moment. As difficult as it was, I could still hear my prayer language. I knew the Holy Spirit was involved. He had inspired Steve to stand "proxy" and initiate forgiveness. I could tell that I needed to be obedient to the Lord at this very moment. I literally felt the presence of Jesus with me on the moonlit path. He was there. So I looked Julius in the face and I forced the words *"I forgive you, Julius"* out of my mouth through gritted teeth. And although it was excruciating, I meant it. I had to picture Jesus standing in front of me as my shield and Jesus saying those words of forgiveness. I focused on the Truth. *"I can do all things through Christ who strengthens me."* (Philippians 4:13)

Steve knew every name on my "list." He said, *"I am _____, and I need you to forgive me."* And the rage manifested again. I worked through that rage, and eventually forgave.

Every time he said somebody else's name I *saw* that person ...and the rage resurfaced. I grabbed my head because it felt like my temples were about to explode. The muscles in my head, face, jaw, and neck rolled and contracted. I curled my hands into fists. It was everything

I could do not to hit him in the face.   My palms began to bleed from squeezing my fingernails deeply into my hands to restrain from hitting him.

Steve kept calm and continued with his God-given mandate to stand proxy and ask forgiveness for everyone the Holy Spirit brought to his mind. He witnessed rage, bitterness, and unforgiveness in a way he will never forget.   He went through every person on my "list." And then he began to speak names of other people who had hurt me deeply.   The Holy Spirit was giving him names he had never heard. Names he didn't know. These were not soul ties.

> He witnessed rage, bitterness, and unforgiveness in a way he will never forget.

Steve did not know those stories or the names. He was strictly going on the gift of prophesy from the Holy Spirit. And sure enough, he was dead on. The Holy Spirit knew *exactly* who had hurt me to the point that I harbored unforgiveness. He is the Great Counselor. Each time Steve got another name, he told me who he was and ask my forgiveness. That name would force me to go through it all over again. Each time he patiently waited for me to work through it. I had to force myself into the very heart of each situation, look the person in the eye, and *truly forgive.*

When he finally said *"I am Jeff ...and I need to ask your forgiveness for leaving you,"* the anger was different. It surfaced as rage, but then quickly morphed into a deep, despairing grief that rocked my entire body. I never realized how angry I was at Jeff for climbing up that ladder that day. For stepping off the catwalk, through the ceiling tiles and accidentally falling to his death. For leaving me and the rest of my family to pick up the pieces of our shattered lives in shock and sorrow. The heartache was overwhelming. I staggered under the weight of it. Steve patiently waited while I wrestled. *"I forgive you, Jeff. I miss you and I love you. I forgive you..."*

As I said the words, my body literally crumpled. I thought I was done. I took a huge breath and started to shift. But Steve pressed in yet again.

"Now, Amy, you need to forgive yourself. You are the last person. You need to look into the mirror and tell yourself that you forgive you..." He handed me a mirror. I knew he was right. I had just been through one of the most difficult experiences of my life. The whole day had just been brutal. But I knew I had one more person to forgive. The most difficult one of all.

Chapter 43 ...Forgiving Amy Sever

As I stared at her in the mirror, I allowed the hatred and rage to manifest one last time. A deep feeling of self-loathing surfaced. I allowed the Holy Spirit to supernaturally transport me from one situation to another. Places where I had sinned against myself. I stared at the swollen face in the mirror. No light, no laughter, no joy anywhere in sight. For the first time in my life I actually let the Holy Spirit take me to that barren place inside the soul of Amy Sever. I looked at the young seductive teenager who had placed herself in harm's way. I looked at the girl who had stopped caring and had created a "list."

I looked at the deep disappointment of my first failed marriage. I looked at how Gary's death might not have happened if I had just "tried a little harder." The car wreck that had taken Savannah's father's life took place just six months later, the day before Savannah's second birthday. Gary was driving to the lake with one of his many girlfriends. I looked at the woman in the mirror. The one who apparently wasn't good enough for him.

I looked at the woman that had allowed an emotional affair. I looked at the pain on Steve's face as I had explained the incident at the clinic. I looked at it all. And instead of suppressing the self-hate that came back I let myself *feel* it.

Then I looked for my Lord. And I found Him. In every circumstance. In every situation of sin, Jesus was right there.

Then I looked for my Lord. And I found Him. In every circumstance. In every situation of sin, Jesus was right there. Through the trauma and tragedy, Jesus was there. I could literally *feel* His constant presence and His steady stream of love and acceptance..

I ripped off the mask I had been wearing for years and I took a hard look at the exposed, battle-weary woman underneath. *"Jesus, I know you died for my sins. Thank you for your sacrifice on the cross for my freedom. You not only died for my salvation, you died for my iniquities. You died for my infirmities. Thank you! I know you have forgiven me. So now please help me to forgive myself."* I paused. Then I took a long shuddering breath and deliberately said *"I forgive myself. I forgive Amy Sever,"* as a new set of tears rolled down my cheeks.

I made sure I meant it. I had learned that the devil doesn't mind you repenting as long as you don't take the next steps and address the spirits that have a legal right to be there as a result of the sin. I wasn't about to let that happen again this time. This whole process had been much too painful and I had come this far... So I gathered myself and mustered the last bit of strength I had, to finish it. I called on the Holy Spirit to help me. I quoted the Word of God out loud. And then addressed the enemy of my soul.

> *...God will grant [me] repentance leading [me] to a knowledge of the truth, and [I have] come to my senses and escaped the trap of the devil, who has taken [me] captive to do his will.* ~ 2 Timothy 2:25-26

> *...And what I have forgiven – if there was anything to forgive – I have forgiven in the site of Christ ...in order that Satan might not outwit [me]. For [I am] not unaware of his schemes.* ~ 2 Corinthians 2:10-11

"Satan, I renounce you and every spirit that has been given legal right to torment me as a result of my unforgiveness. I renounce self-hate, rage, and bitterness. I renounce depression. I renounce insomnia. I renounce every voice of accusation from the enemy. I break every unholy spirit off of my life. I renounce a spirit of rape and abuse. I renounce grief and despair, suicide, and death by accident. I renounce a spirit of heaviness. Leave me now! By the blood of Christ, I am forgiven! And I have now forgiven myself. I speak blessing into the lives of every person I have forgiven here tonight. And I speak blessing into my life."

As soon as those words left my lips, I began to cough. I coughed and gagged. I ran to the restroom and threw up. I coughed and gagged again. And I threw up again. I couldn't breathe. I grabbed my throat

as I choked. Steve rebuked the spirit and commanded it to let me go.
As I wrestled, I could faintly hear Steve quoting scriptures, praying in
the spirit and commanding the demons to leave me.

Suddenly, it was over. The spirits left. A supernatural peace filled
the room. I was free! The tormenting spirits were gone. I knew it
instantly. And I was suddenly so exhausted...

Steve helped me get under the covers. He got a cool wash cloth,
placed it on my swollen face and sat next to me just softly praying for
the Lord to minister to me. After he was sure I was comfortable and
safe, he quietly left the room.

I was so fatigued. But the deep coiling serpent of rage was gone. And the spirit of self-hate that been my constant companion and had tortured me for years had left me. I could tell the voices were gone. I knew that a deep work of the Lord had taken place. It was as if I had undergone spiritual surgery. I was at complete peace – for the first time in years.

> It was as if I had undergone spiritual surgery. I was at complete peace – for the first time in years.

I prayed and thanked God for the deep work He had done in my life.
I thanked Him for Steve and his wisdom to listen to the Holy Spirit
and initiate my freedom. I thanked God for my beautiful little girl
who sang "Amazing Grace" to me on a day *I desperately needed those
words.* I thanked the Holy Spirit for interceding for me with *"groans
that words can't express"* and for supernaturally giving Steve the
names of people I needed to forgive. I thanked Jesus for dying for
me. And for resurrecting so that I could spend eternity in Heaven.
And for sitting at the right hand of the Father interceding for me. I
thanked God that I would get to see Jeff again. I thanked Him for the
journey. And for all of the trials I had experienced in my young life.

I thanked Him for my parents and my brother Jason and his family.
I thanked God that I was free from the tormenting spirits, and asked
that someday He would be able to use me to help someone else walk
through these same steps into freedom. I asked Him to show me how

to help others through the process of restoring their souls ...and I fell into a deep sleep.

Chapter
44   ...*The Next Day*

When I woke the next morning I was surprised to find that I had started my period. I wasn't anywhere near that part of my cycle. But I soon discovered that this was not menstruation at all. It was something else altogether. It was a jet black, thick, tar-like substance that flowed from my system.

My body cleansed for three days. Whatever it was, I knew it was a *direct result* of the deliverance that I had just experienced the night before. After that physical cleansing, I felt completely different. The depression, anxiety, and insomnia were gone. The self-hate and rage, the constant, loud and accusing voices in my head were all gone. My soul was at complete peace for the first time since I could remember. Hallelujah!!

After that experience I can't help but look at disease differently. I wonder how many cases are misdiagnosed. I wonder how many people are suffering from disease, and yet, it is actually a direct physical manifestation of demonic influence caused by sin? Especially the sin of unforgiveness.

I wonder how sick *I would be* today if I had not experienced true forgiveness and cast self-hate and rage out of my life? What would that black tar have turned into? I don't

> I wonder how sick *I would be* today if I had not experienced true forgiveness and cast self-hate and rage out of my life?

know. But I do know that whatever left my body those three days most certainly would have turned into something *bad,* if given enough time. And I am certainly glad I don't have to find out what that would have been. I also know beyond the shadow of a doubt that unforgiveness *will eventually affect you physically! It is indeed the acid that destroys its own container.*

In summary, there are a couple of key things I want to reiterate.

One of the major lessons I learned through that whole process is that true forgiveness does not happen overnight. And it is proportional to the size of the offense. The bigger the offense, the deeper the forgiveness. The ability to forgive is not a one size fits all simple equation. I wish it was. You can't just say *"I forgive you"* ...and everything be okay. In some cases, it takes a deep work of God.

Here is how gracious God is... He knew what I could and could not handle. The Holy Spirit is the Comforter and the Counselor. Right? And He has promised us that He will never give us anything more than we can bear. So He did not allow me to experience the *need to forgive* until my   soul *could truly handle it.*

> When I did my "mental checklist" on forgiveness, it was clear, remember? I honestly thought I *had* forgiven.

When I did my "mental checklist" on forgiveness, it was clear, remember? I honestly thought I *had* forgiven. It wasn't until the layers of words, sin, generational curses, and soul ties were broken that I was even *able* to understand that I needed to forgive. It wasn't until my soul had come under the protection of my spirit that it was able to pause, rest, and prepare for the deeper work of God that was about to occur in my life. There are a couple of scriptures that speak to this process...

> *Now the Lord is the Spirit, and where the Spirit of the Lord is, there is freedom. And we, who with unveiled faces all reflect the Lord's glory, and are being transformed into His image with ever-increasing glory, which comes from the Lord, who is the Spirit.* ~ 2 Corinthians 3:17-18

There are several phrases in this verse that I love. *"Where the Spirit of the Lord is, there is freedom."* Take that phrase and memorize it. Believe it! *"Unveiled faces."* You see, I had to take the mask off. The mask I had been hiding behind my whole life. God can work with unveiled faces. He can transform them into His image. *"Ever-increasing glory."* That's a beautiful promise. True freedom is a process. And the Holy Spirit is gentle. He will take you through freedom at your own pace. He will not put anything on you that you cannot handle. So it may have to take place in layers. That's okay. I encourage you to commit to the journey. It is so worth it!

> *In a large house there are articles not only of gold and silver, but also of wood and clay; some are for noble purposes and some for ignoble. If a man cleanses himself from the latter, he will be an instrument for noble purposes, made holy, useful to the Master and prepared to do any good work.*
> ~ 2 Timothy 2:20-21

This scripture sums up my journey perfectly. I was a wood-and- clay Christian. I loved the Lord. I was on my way to Heaven. But I was not useful to the Master or prepared to do any good work. I was battered and bruised. I was "ignoble". However, I cleansed myself from those *ignoble things* – the things that were causing my soul harm. Now I am on a constant, ever-increasing journey toward a *gold and silver* life. I am living this next scripture...

> *Dear friends, now we are children of God, and what we will be has not yet been made known. But we know that when He appears, we shall be like Him, for we shall see Him as He is. Everyone who has this hope in Him purifies himself, just as He is pure.* ~ 1 John 3:2-3

I am a child of God. I have no idea what I will be in the coming months and years. But I do know that I have a beautiful hope. And I am preparing. I *am* purifying. I want to be used for noble purposes.

So now you know the rest of my story. This last section has taken days to write. Again, it was very difficult. I almost quit again a couple of days ago. The temptation to do so was overwhelming. I was hearing this:

"Amy, you don't want to expose yourself like this. Why would you do this? You are going to be an embarrassment to your family! You are also going to stir things up in people they aren't prepared to walk through. You could damage more people than you help. You know that people are going to ridicule you and judge you now, right? You know that some of the stuff you wrote will stir up all kinds of controversy. Are you prepared to pick a fight with me?"

Was that another voice of oppression? Was I in bondage all over again? No. The enemy of your soul will always be an accuser. The difference is that today I have the keys to take those thoughts captive and immediately get rid of the voices. They are coming from *without... NOT within.*

> *For though we live in the world, we do not wage war as the world does. The weapons we fight with are not the weapons of the world. On the contrary, they have divine power to demolish strongholds. We demolish arguments and every pretension that sets itself up against the knowledge of God, and we take captive every thought to make it obedient to Christ.* ~ 2 Corinthians 10:3-5

"Well, Satan, I guess I am. Because I have to be obedient and finish the work the Lord has called me to. I am useful for any good work. I am purifying myself just as He is pure. I can do all things through Christ who gives me strength."

Besides that, I have one more section to finish. Reconstructing the Body.

Notes and Reflections

Notes and Reflections

Part Three
Reconstructing the Body

Chapter 45

...Victim vs. Responsibility

I realize that after the last section on Restoring the Soul, this next section might feel a little anticlimactic. Consider this last section the "cool down" after an intense spiritual workout. You know how you are supposed to spend some time stretching and cooling down after exercise? Well, since this last section covers the body, consider this the final stretch.

I still have more to say regarding the spirit and the soul. So again, please read all the way to the end of the book. As I was praying this morning, I realized that I do need to finish some thoughts and tie it all back together. So hang in there with me through the epilogue. Take hold of the knowledge you have and keep it until the end of the book. Don't get too caught up in the baby carrots and sugar snap peas of the following pages. I am going to ask you to do some things for me at the end of our journey together. The message of the spirit and the soul come back around.

> I know so many people that have an amazing walk with the Lord and are spiritual giants, yet they don't have their health.

However, this section on Reconstructing the Body is *just as important*. Because I know so many people that have an amazing walk with the Lord and are spiritual giants, yet they don't have their health. Diseases are ravaging our society. One in two people is affected by cancer. Auto-immune diseases, as well as heart disease, diabetes and Alzheimer's – along with so many others – are on the rise. We are an unhealthy society! So, work through the next couple of chapters with me. You might learn a few things that could make the difference for, not only your health, but also the health of those you love.

Interestingly enough, this is the section that people ask me about most. Especially when I was competing in fitness and my before-and-after pictures were floating around the internet. I appeared in

Oxygen Magazine a couple of times, and became a fitness model. Back then, people associated me with my fitness career, and they wanted to know how I lost my weight.

Now that it has been a decade, most people who know me don't even realize that fitness was part of my past. They associate me with business. But, when they find out that I used to weigh 170 pounds, they want to know how I have kept the weight off all these years. They ask what my diet and exercise regimen is like now. For most people, the focus is on the struggle with their body.

> For most people, the focus is on the struggle with their body. But, I know for a fact that most of the time the real issues are in the soul.

But, I know for a fact that most of the time the real issues are in the soul. I struggled with my body because of shame, self-hate, and unforgiveness. When someone hurt me, I didn't truly forgive that person. I turned that deep anger *in* and pointed it at myself. Doing that created all kinds of physical ramifications.

Once I was set free from self-hate, along with all of the other spirits that were tormenting my soul, I could finally see clearly enough to look at my body correctly. And I actually *wanted* to lose weight. I realized the weight had been a false sense of security I had created. It was a security blanket to keep sexual sin from happening. I also realized I had used the rapes as an excuse for my lack of self-discipline and weight gain.

I came to a point that I took *full responsibility for everything that had ever happened in my life*. Situations I had created, and also situations others had created. And it wasn't until I took *100% ownership* of my spiritual and emotional state that I was able to do anything about my physical state. I blamed my weight on circumstances that were out of my control. So, subconsciously I had taken the reigns out of my hands and placed them elsewhere.

Here is an important truth: As long as I blamed Julius, or anyone else in my life, I had no ability to change my current circumstances. The same goes for you. Take 100% responsibility for *everything* in your life. Even if it happened in childhood. It is the most powerful thing you can do, because it rips your circumstances *out of the devil's hands*. He can no longer hold your life hostage – based on what happened in your past.

And if you refuse to hold them, but actually take the broken pieces of your life and turn them over to the Lord instead, then the Master's hand can touch you. When you allow that, He will restore the beauty and innocence of your soul.

> One of Satan's main tactics is to keep people in "victim mode." ...then we are powerless to change our circumstances.

One of Satan's main tactics is to keep people in "victim mode." If he can keep us in "victim" instead of "responsibility", then we are powerless to change our circumstances. If we take *full ownership*, then our circumstances are completely under *our* control and, together with the Lord's guidance, we can absolutely change them.

This was a big realization for me. I was blaming so many habits and patterns on the fact that I had been raped. But when I took responsibility and decided I wasn't a victim anymore, things began to change. I now had the desire and the self-discipline to do something about my body.

First of all, I want to state that I am a registered massage therapist and a certified fitness trainer. I am not a doctor or a nutritionist. All of the knowledge that I have is strictly based on my own research. I do not pretend to be an expert on these matters. As a matter of fact, compared to all of the data that is available, I know very little. That said, I have learned a few things over the last several years that have changed my life. I actually lost my weight many years ago. And I have maintained health. I no longer compete in fitness, but I am still very active and very healthy.

Chapter 46   ...*Making Changes*

So how did I do it? Well, I took a good hard look at myself and decided I needed to set a goal. A date. Something to inspire and motivate me into an exercise routine. I found a picture of someone that was a realistic goal and said "I want to look like her," and I set the date. I flooded my mind with all kinds of before and after pictures of women who had made the trip. I constantly looked at pictures. I cut my head out of photos and pasted it on the bodies of women I wanted to look like. I visualized myself thin. And I talked about it all the time.

I began to push through my daily headache and *exercise anyway.* I just pushed through it. I started doing 10 minutes of some kind of cardio. That is all I could handle. I added one minute each day. I eventually worked up to 30 minutes of intense cardio. I was thrilled that my perseverance had paid off! Much to my surprise, my headaches, not to mention my sluggishness, were vanishing. I realized that my body actually began to *crave* exercise. I noticed that when I felt lethargic and lifeless, if I would exercise for 30 minutes instead of nap I felt so much better!

I also experimented with water. I knew that lemon was alkalizing, so I squeezed a fresh lemon into a huge glass of water with a spoon of xylitol, and make lemonade. (Xylitol is a natural sugar.) I discovered after I began to *force myself to drink water,* I eventually began to crave it! I slowly began to wean myself off of soft drinks. I went from a soda junkie to only water with lemon, and eventually no xylitol, throughout each day.

> I learned that the body has the same mechanism for thirst as for hunger... a growling stomach! So, I ignored the hunger pangs and drank water instead.

I discovered that many times when I felt hungry, if I gulped about 20 ounces of water, the hunger pangs vanished. I had been chronically dehydrated. I learned that the body has the same mechanism for thirst as for hunger... a growling stomach! So, I ignored the hunger pangs and drank water instead. It worked.

As I started seeing results, I was encouraged to continually challenge myself each day for a few more minutes. I began to train with weights. Then I *really* began to see my body change! I was not just getting smaller. I was actually *reshaping* my body. It was so neat to realize that I had a strong, healthy body underneath all that fat! You must realize that same thing. No matter what your body looks like at the moment, remember that underneath it all, is a solid set of bones and a solid set of muscles. They are still there. I promise you. So don't get in a hurry. Just start making small choices on a daily basis.

> Then I *really* began to see my body change! I was not just getting smaller. I was actually *reshaping* my body.

My choices began to cluster and compound. I got a journal. I recorded *everything* I put in my mouth. One piece of candy went into my journal. I recorded how I felt spiritually and emotionally. I talked to God. I asked the Holy Spirit to help me exercise. (He is the best physical trainer on the planet.) I kept that journal with me at all times. If it went in my mouth, it went in that book. It was a huge part of my process. I also kept the pictures of how I wanted to look in that journal. I looked at it constantly. I created affirmations about my "strong healthy body." And I used my soul to call my healthy body into manifestation.

It took me a year to lose my weight and get in great shape. Then I set a goal to compete in the fitness arena. And just like anything worth doing, it took a while to accomplish my goal. When I entered the North American Nova Championship, the first year I placed 37th. I had worked so hard. I was bitterly disappointed, but my body looked as good as the girl who won. I was just nervous on stage, and not fast enough on the military obstacle course. So, I worked another year. And then I placed 4th. I was still a bit nervous and not quite as fast as I needed to be. So I worked another year. The third year, I placed 1st in the North American Nova Championship. I placed 1st on the Military Obstacle Course and 1st in Swimwear. It was a triumphant moment! Not just because I had won, but because *I* knew where I had come from. I knew the *whole journey*. I knew what my victory represented. It made it so much more meaningful!

You can accomplish anything you set your mind to. It may take three years, but you can do it! The key is to *set your mind*. Learn to *use* the power of the soul. When it is submitted properly under your spirit, then you can tap the power of your mind, will, and emotions the way God *intended*.

We can use the power of the universe that God created and manifest *great things* in our lives! We have the authority to use faith – the thinking substance of the universe – to manifest health. What we *believe*, we can *achieve*. And believe me what you focus on (good or bad) – expands. So get some great pictures and start *focusing, believing and speaking words of life* to your body!

> *Now faith is the substance of things hoped for, the evidence of things not seen.* ~ Hebrews 11:1

> *...All things are possible to those that believe.* ~ Mark 9:23

I'm not going to lie to you. I worked hard at it. Regaining my health became my key focus for a couple of years. But it was so worth it! I still have that health today. And when I look around, great health is becoming less and less prevalent. It is a rare trait indeed. Neither Steve nor I have been to the doctor in years and years. Unless it's for an insurance checkup, we just don't go. We don't take anything except supplements. We enjoy good health. But it is an ongoing process. Especially in today's environment. That said, the next three chapters are dedicated to several key factors that have led to my success physically. These are certainly not all inclusive, but it will definitely get you started on the path to great health.

I am a huge fan of using the internet. I read and study all the time. The information available to us now leaves no room for error in judgment, due to lack of knowledge. So I've spent time pouring through hundreds of articles and websites over the years and have asked the Lord for guidance with regard to my health. I credit the internet for all of the knowledge I have, and continue to learn. The statistics and facts in the following chapters are not my own. They are pulled from all kinds of articles and posts.

I am certainly no expert. But I can point you in some of the directions the Lord has taken me.

The next three chapters are practical advice, tips, and ideas. They are not intended to treat or cure any health issues. If you have serious health challenges, please check with your doctor before incorporating anything in these chapters.

That said, these are things that I believe wholeheartedly. They are keys not only for weight loss, but great health in general. I also have several websites linked to www.AmySever.com that list the products and supplements I use and refer. My website will constantly be changing to include new information from my continuous study. So visit often!

Notes and Reflections

Notes and Reflections

Chapter 47 ... *Personalized Nutrition and Water*

1) PERSONALIZED NUTRITION

As soon as I started my health journey, I began to research nutrition. I quickly discovered that nutrition is the only thing that feeds the body. Not food. Nutrients. I also discovered that perfect nutrition was extremely hard to find. So I began to supplement. It made a huge difference in how I felt. But, I always knew the method needed improvement. Because my body is different from yours. Everyone has a unique system with different kinds of nutritional needs.

That's why I am so excited about this incredible technology in health and wellness supplementation. I didn't have this when I lost my weight. With all my years of exhaustive research on nutrition, I had never been able to find *exactly* what my body needs. All nutritional supplements on the market have been "one size fits all."

The latest in nutrition technology is software that creates your *personal nutritional data* from an in-depth assessment, based on your answers to specific questions regarding your personal health history. This includes your activities, your habits, and your diet. It also takes into account your health issues and if you have any type of diagnosis. It asks what medicines you're taking. It even asks allergies and what kind of physical environment you live in. All of these have nutritional implications. The personal assessment creates the *perfect nutritional regimen* for your individual needs!

In addition, the human body has a circadian rhythm that causes different organs to need nutrients at different times. This technology tells you not only what to take, based on your individual assessment, but *when to take it*. Personalized nutrition gives your body *exactly what it needs, exactly when you need it the most*. I'm a huge fan of this concept. It is a complete game-changer for the health and wellness industry! Check out my site for the link. You can take the free assessment there.

2) WATER

I used to despise water. I hated it. I had to force down just one glass. My staples were coffee in the morning and about noon I switched to soft drinks. I drank a lot of milk at night. I look back now and shudder! My body was dangerously dehydrated... just as most people are right now. Let me give you some information.

Water makes up nearly 85 percent of our brain, about 80 percent of our blood, and about 70 percent of lean muscle. Our bodies are one-half to four-fifths water. Studies show that 75% of Americans are chronically dehydrated.

Dehydration causes people to be less able to perform at their peak and sets us up for weight gain, joint and muscle pain, fuzzy thinking, disease, and fatigue. Dehydration can cause irritability, anxiety, depression, food cravings, and allergies. Emergency thirst signals include feeling sick upon rising in the morning, heartburn, migraines, angina, joint pain, back pain, colitis pain, fibromyalgia pain, constipation, late-onset diabetes, and hypertension. And *ALL* you needed was water!

Among people over 65, dehydration is one of the most frequent causes of hospitalization. Thirst isn't always a reliable gauge of the body's need for water, especially in children and older adults. Even slight dehydration can deplete your energy and make you feel lethargic. A mere 2% drop in body water can trigger fuzzy short-term memory, trouble with basic math, and difficulty focusing on the computer screen or on a printed page! Even mild dehydration will slow down one's metabolism as much as 3%. Athletic performance can drop by as much as 20 to 30% if you lose as little as four percent of your body's water during exercise. Lack of water triggers daytime fatigue in many people.

> A mere 2% drop in body water can trigger fuzzy short-term memory, trouble with basic math, and difficulty focusing...

Some studies show that 70% of pre-school children drink no water at all during the day. Some have a diminished thirst mechanism and mistake it for hunger. And just like I did, they feed their thirst with food. In a university experiment, one glass of water shut down midnight hunger pangs for almost 100% of the dieters.

Dehydration is prevalent among people who drink caffeinated coffee, tea, and sodas. Americans consume about 21% of their calories from beverages. That statistic alone is staggering. Think about how much weight we could lose if we drop sweet tea, soda, and coffee dessert drinks, and pick up water with lemon instead.

Preliminary research indicates that 8-10 glasses of water a day could significantly ease back and joint pain for up to 80% of sufferers. Additionally, drinking five glasses of water daily is said to decrease the risk of colon cancer, breast cancer, and bladder cancer. Currently the recommendation for water consumption per day is eight 8-ounce glasses per day, but to me that isn't enough. I do better with more than that.

...drinking five glasses of water daily is said to decrease the risk of colon cancer, breast cancer, and bladder cancer.

You will find yourself taking a trip to the restroom more often as you dramatically increase your water. But those visits subside once your body adjusts. And it's worth it! Your bathroom visits should happen about every hour and your urine should be mostly clear and odorless. If not, then you are dehydrated!

Dehydrated cells shrivel. Imagine a prune instead of a plum. Most people don't think of dehydration as a cause of pain, but this shriveled state of our cells can cause headaches and muscle and joint pain. This is one of the ways my body tells me I'm thirsty. I get a headache and my neck starts hurting. Every time.

First thing in the morning I drink lots of water with lemon. I don't sip. I gulp it. Water is the best fat burning agent on the planet!

I then switch to warm water with lemon and red tea with cordyceps. It resets my metabolism and alkalizes my body.

Don't start with coffee. Coffee is the third thing in my morning. And then I only drink healthy coffee, which is smoother and actually good for me. It contains ganoderma. This is one of the healthiest mushrooms on the planet. I could write pages and pages about ganoderma lucidum. I have been so impressed with this discovery! I've seen such a boost in my immune system since I switched from acidic coffee to healthy coffee. I can't even drink normal coffee anymore. It hurts my stomach!

Let me say something here. Did you know that your taste buds have a God-given ability to adapt to anything within a couple of weeks? That's why people in crazy circumstances can survive on foods that we find disgusting. If you are used to *your coffee* or *your foods*, then you will have to exercise *your will* in order to get your body to comply – at first.

But I promise you, within a couple of weeks, your taste buds will adapt to the changes in diet. It is amazing. I couldn't imagine drinking healthy coffee at first. But I knew that my body was acidic. And I knew that I had to make changes now, or deal with cancer or some other disease later. It was worth it to me to force my taste buds and my body to come into order! I knew I would pay for my health – either on the front end or the back end. Supplements and changes in diet and exercise are less taxing and less expensive than doctor visits and drugs later. Believe me!

Chapter
48   *...Limiting These and Adding These*

3) LIMITING THESE

I realize that this goes against the grain of most American diets. But these things are what are making us fat. I must admit, except for the first two, I still occasionally partake. The key is awareness and moderation. And when I was losing my weight, I considered these things my enemies. The biggest one for me was sodas. But now it has been at least thirteen years since I last drank a soft drink of any kind. I did not quit cold turkey. I weaned myself off of them. I accomplished this by adding water, not taking sodas away completely. The same goes for fast food. I just started adding the right things to my diet, and you can only eat so much in a day. By the way, if you truly want your health, these first two are non-negotiable!

- Smoking: Please stop! Make it the thing you attack this year. Treat it as a stronghold and walk through the steps to break addiction off of your life. Just like Connie, you can be free! Chew on straws. Just please quit. It is killing you!

- Artificial sweeteners: Please stop! These are completely toxic to your body!

Aspartame is a known carcinogen. Please get off of all diet soda! They are absolutely terrible for you! If you look up Aspartame online and do your own research, you will never pick up another packet of artificial sweetener or drink another diet soda. The rest of the items on this list are things you want to begin eliminating and replacing as soon as possible...

- Refined sugar: juices, sodas, cookies, candy, ice cream, sorbets, syrups, many condiments, sugary yogurts, etc.

- White flour: pastries, store-bought breads

- "Diet" foods: just about anything labeled light, low fat, no fat, fat free, sugar free

- Many cooking oils: corn oil, canola oil, soybean oil

- Packaged snack foods: chips, cheesy crackers, etc.

- Alcohol and caffeine: Okay, I told you, I love coffee. But as I already said, I drink non-acidic healthy coffee that I absolutely love. Go to my site and check it out. It tastes amazing! And I do occasionally drink alcohol. I love a glass of red wine every now and then. Everything in moderation.

- Dairy: Milk is really not good for us. So many are allergic to dairy and don't even know it. People that deal with sinus problems don't usually link it to dairy. Try to eliminate this from your diet for a couple of weeks – just for a detox period. Afterward, if your body feels good, you can start bringing a little dairy back. Again, moderation.

- Gluten (wheat products): Recently, in the news, you've probably heard about the potential health-damaging effects of gluten. But, wheat also spikes your blood sugar. Whole wheat is supposedly healthy for you, but the fact is that wheat contains an unusual type of carbohydrate not found in other foods called *Amylopectin-A*, which has been found in some tests to spike your blood sugar higher than even pure table sugar. In fact, Amylopectin-A raises your blood sugar more than almost any other carbohydrate. I apologize that this awful, fattening carbohydrate starts with my name... (Okay, that was supposed to be funny.) Just remember that when you want to eat wheat-based foods such as breads, bagels, cereals, muffins, etc. These often cause much higher blood sugar levels than most other carbohydrate sources. Amylopectin-A = fat.

Now, I realize that these may be all of your favorite things. So let me take you back to the beginning of the book when I talked about your body lining up under your soul and your soul lining up under your spirit. Remember? Alignment.

Think of it this way. The body *has to submit* to the soul (the mind, *will*, and emotions.) When your soul is healthy, then the body can safely submit. When the soul is submitted to your spirit, and your spirit is submitted to the Holy Spirit, you are in correct alignment!

When you are in correct alignment, the body has to come into order. It still takes discipline, but you can use your *will* to tell it what to do and what to eat. *Tell* your body it needs to exercise, etc. And it will obey.

That said, it is hard to give up all of the above, so my advice is to *add* some things instead. Don't look at it as a diet. Look for a lifestyle change, which brings me to my next point. Be prepared. Fix yourself little baggies of snacks, and eat all the time. Never allow yourself to get crazy hungry.

4) ADDING THESE: SNACK SEVERAL TIMES PER DAY

> I finally figured out how to keep fruit and vegetables from rotting in the bottom of my refrigerator. I eat them!

I grew up eating three meals a day. I now eat all day long. Think of a bear who eats a lot and stores it, as opposed to a horse who grazes all day. Now think about their bodies.

I finally figured out how to keep fruit and vegetables from rotting in the bottom of my refrigerator. I eat them! One of the best tips I could give is to buy a nice bowl or tray, fill it with fruit and vegetables, and sit it prominently on the top shelf. Only buy a few things at first. I would rather run out and have to make another trip to the store than to have overripe fruit and vegetables. Try to limit your fruit. Go for raw (mostly green) vegetables!

Find some you like. I eat bell peppers like they are apples. You will be surprised at how fast your body will take to these new additions! Soon you will start craving "live" foods. We'll talk about that more in detail later. One other tip regarding vegetables: buy the sacks of frozen vegetables. They have them in all varieties. I love those! You can opt out of a bowl of cereal. Throw some frozen veggies in a bowl, stick them in the microwave for two minutes, and you have a great snack! Just try it a few times. You will have to speak to your body at first and let it know that *you are the boss* ...not your cravings. But it is just like water. If you just force yourself to do it, your body will eventually catch up with your brain.

I also added nuts to my diet. I love almonds, pecans, cashews, and soy nuts. Preferably unsalted. These are great, because along with carrots, snap peas, broccoli, and beef jerky, you can put them in your purse or bag and take them with you. Which brings me to my next point.

The body is a living organism made of billions of living cells. The only thing that truly feeds these living cells is living food. I think this is one of the most important things we can learn about our body. The body needs live food, not dead, processed food. I had to learn to stay away from the center of the grocery store where all my favorite aisles were. Aisles of packaged and boxed food that were full of preservatives and had absolutely zero nutritional value. I started shopping around the perimeter of the grocery store where all of the fresh (preferably organic) food is.

> The body is a living organism made of billions of living cells. The only thing that truly feeds these living cells is living food.

All that said, while fresh foods are so much better for you than processed foods, even the fresh stuff can be nutrient deficient. Because these foods must have an abnormally long shelf life, they are pumped full of preservatives and are picked early before they get their enzymes. So, even fresh vegetables are usually lacking. That's why I am an advocate of supplements. However, snacking can be good for you and actually *help* weight-loss. Snacking between meals reduces your likelihood to over-eat during meals. It also keeps your metabolism revved up. The key is to snack with *the right foods*! Then you add extra nutrients, such as antioxidants, minerals, and vitamins with very few calories. These are great snack foods:

- Crunchy snacks: baby carrots, baked apple chips, celery, snap peas, cucumbers, edamame, rice cakes, bell peppers

- Salty snacks: popcorn, jerky, pickles, baked sweet potato fries, lightly-salted rice cakes, hummus, kale chips

- Sweet snacks: apple-cinnamon rice cakes, baby carrots, berries, yogurt, cherry tomatoes, fruit, snap peas

Chapter
49   ...Juicing, Green Smoothies, and Recipes

5) JUICING / GREEN SMOOTHIES

When Steve and I lived first moved to Australia, our apartment came with a juicer. I fell in love with it, and now it is part of my daily regimen. This has been such a great addition to my life! Because we are not just what we eat – we are what we *absorb*. And we've established that the body needs "live food" to build "live cells." I just mentioned eating fruits and vegetables. But juicing them is like having an IV of super energy-rich vitamins and minerals pumped immediately into the body, supplying all the quintessential nutrients you need for the day. Juicing removes the fiber from vegetables which normally slows and can sometimes inhibit nutrient absorption. By extracting the fiber, it only leaves the readily-assimilated vitamins and minerals. When you are looking to lose weight, improve your cardiovascular health, build more lean muscle or improve energy, juicing provides a straight shot of essential building blocks to your system.

There are lots of websites out there that show you how to juice. Look on www.amysever.com for links. Here are some basic juicing fruits and vegetables:

- Fruits: prunes, grapes, apples, oranges, grapefruit, pears pineapples, peaches, plums, apricots, cherries, and lemons.

- Vegetables/fruits: tomatoes, cucumbers

- Root vegetables: beets, carrots, onions, radishes, sweet potatoes,

- Vegetables: asparagus, peppers, Brussels sprouts, ginger, sprouts, broccoli, califlower

- Leafy vegetables: lettuce, kale, chard, collard greens, spinach, cabbage, parsley, cilantro, watercress

I've also learned to love green smoothies. If I'm hungrier, then I usually juice several things and throw that juice into the blender with some lettuce, kale, and/or spinach. If you have never done this, don't knock it until you try it! One of my favorite smoothies is juiced green apple, cucumber, and celery thrown in a blender with spinach and lettuce. Blend it with ice and it gives you an amazing burst of energy and your body will start craving it from the first sip.

On a recent trip back from Australia, Steve and I stayed with my parents for a while. The first thing I did was buy them a juicer. We dug their blender out from under the cabinet and went shopping in the vegetable aisle. We bought beets, cabbage, kale, cucumbers, green apples, ginger, celery and lemons. Every morning we got out the juicer and blender and I created all kinds of crazy concoctions. We had fun with it. Our bodies immediately responded. We raised our glasses and shouted "Here's to Life!" as we downed the green liquid.

I suggest you do the same thing. Become your own vegetable bartender. Create drinks that you like. You will be amazed at how fast you start craving it! Your body knows what it needs. And when it receives the right nutrients, it will reward your efforts.

Here are three of my favorite juice recipes and a dessert smoothie recipe. I got them from the links on my site. Again, please check them out and subscribe, just like I have. There are folks that know more about all this than I do!

- 1 cucumber, 3 celery, 1 lemon, lime, 1 inch ginger, coconut water

- Handful of parsley, 2 cloves of garlic, 4 carrots, ½ lemon

- 3 kale leaves, 2 leaves of collard greens, handful of parsley, cilantro, 1 cucumber, 2 celery, 1 green apple

- A chocolate lover's smoothie:

  2 cups spinach, 2 cups unsweetened almond milk, 2 cups cherries, (pitted; frozen is recommended), 2 bananas, 1 teaspoon cinnamon, 3 tablespoons cacao powder (or cocoa powder). Blend spinach and almond milk until smooth. Add the remaining ingredients and blend again.

Chapter 50 ...*Xylitol, Apple Cider Vinegar, and Coconut Oil*

6) Xylitol

One of the biggest changes I made early on was exchanging sugar for xylitol. I was at a health and wellness expo and listened to a speech on this incredible natural substance. Remember, I was addicted to sugar. I drank several sodas a day. I drank sweet tea. I ate candy bars. I always had a piece of candy in my mouth.

Here is what I learned at that expo that changed my life – I had a candida problem. I had yeast in my system that was causing me to crave sugar. Xylitol is a natural sugar that your body already makes. But, it tastes and looks just like table sugar. Your brain needs sugar to function. However, when you have too much candida in your system, the candida consume all the sugar, so you have cravings.

Here is the good news though. Candida doesn't like xylitol! So if you eat xylitol instead, it feeds the brain, but the yeast won't eat it. You will eventually starve off the yeast and your sugar cravings will go away!

One of the greatest things I did was to put xylitol and lemon in my water early on. If I wanted sugar, I got a strawberry and dipped it in xylitol and ate that instead. Sometimes I just put a spoonful under my tongue and let it melt. It was amazing how fast the yeast died off and I got rid of my sugar cravings! Try it. You will love it. You can get it at any grocery store.

Our bodies produce from 5 to 10 grams of good sugar every day from other food sources using established energy pathways. It is not a strange or artificial substance, but a natural, normal part of everyday metabolism. It is widely distributed throughout nature in small amounts, with some of the best sources being fruits, berries, mushrooms, lettuce, and corncobs.

Some health regimens require iron willpower, discipline, and commitment. But because it tastes so good, using xylitol becomes automatic. Even children love it. You can also cook with it.

Another huge benefit of xylitol is dental. I hate toothpaste with sugar and fluoride. Incidentally, fluoride is another accepted practice for most people. We think we are supposed to have fluoride for our dental health. We just accept what we have been told at face value without researching for ourselves. I could write a whole page on fluoride! It is terrible for you.

> With extended use, fluoride eventually begins to calcify the pineal gland in the brain. Remember the pineal gland?

I will be succinct. With extended use, fluoride eventually begins to calcify the pineal gland in the brain. Remember the pineal gland? It is the seat of the soul, the God organ. It serves to connect intellect with the spiritual dimension. I know it sounds crazy to relate xylitol to how you communicate with the Lord, but ask yourself, do you suffer from brain fog? Do you have trouble praying and hearing the voice of the Lord? Do you feel like you are just not connecting with the Holy Spirit? This is something very practical that you can change. I switched toothpaste. I quit using fluoride and started using ganoderma toothpaste with xylitol instead.

Remember, you get a whole new body every year. The body constantly regenerates itself, so the changes you begin to make today *will have a beneficial effect!* Take heart!

7) Apple Cider Vinegar

This is a recent discovery in my health regimen. The more I research, the more impressed I become. This is a type of vinegar that is made from the fermentation of apple cider. Fermentation involves a process in which sugars in food are broken down by bacteria and yeast. Apple cider vinegar has been noted as a health tonic that can be helpful for just about anything!

Apple cider vinegar has some amazing health benefits.

Because of its antibiotic properties, it has been researched for its ability to aid in combating bacterial infections in the stomach and gut. Adding 1 tablespoon of raw apple cider vinegar mixed in 4 ounces of water can help combat indigestion and heartburn. It will also help improve your digestion.

Apple cider vinegar can also aid in relieving sinus drainage.   I encourage people to take 2 tablespoons in warm water. This helps break up mucous and other toxins.

Exercise and even stress can cause buildup of lactic acid. Symptoms of lactic acid buildup include sore muscles and even fatigue. Amino acids in apple cider vinegar can help counteract lactic acid buildup. Apple cider vinegar also contains potassium and other enzymes that are responsible for relieving symptoms of fatigue and stress.

It is also a natural skin remedy. It gets rid of pimples and skin irritations. Raw apple cider vinegar may also help you with hiccups, stomach aches, and joint pain. Apple cider vinegar boosts your metabolism and breaks down fat in your bloodstream and body. There are also many studies on how apple cider vinegar can aid with diabetes and high cholesterol.

Diabetes benefits: A study conducted in 2007 showed that when subjects with Type 2 diabetes consumed two tablespoons of apple cider vinegar at night their glucose levels were lowered in the morning by at least 4-6%. (1)

High cholesterol benefits: Apple cider vinegar contains pectin. Pectin is a type of soluble fiber. Soluble fiber (also known as water soluble fiber) helps to lower LDL cholesterol levels by "grabbing" and essentially absorbing cholesterol and taking it out of the body. Apple cider vinegar also contains amino acids that help to neutralize LDL cholesterol. (2)

1.   White AM, Johnston CS. 2007. Vinegar ingestion at bedtime moderates waking glucose concentrations in adults with well-controlled type 2 diabetes. *Diabetes Care 11*: 2814-2815.

2.   http://www.ehow.com/how-does_4923648_apple-cider-vinegar-reduce-cholesterol.html

There are also many studies on the weight loss benefits of apple cider vinegar. A great way to consume apple cider vinegar is to add it to your green juices and smoothies.

Note: Apple cider vinegar is acidic, so it could damage the enamel in your teeth. Always dilute apple cider vinegar before drinking it.

8) Coconut Oil

Coconut oil is one super food that can be used in every room of your home.

90 percent of coconut oil is composed of medium chain fatty acids (or triglycerides) which are easily digested and sent right to the liver for energy production. By traveling directly to the liver, it is not stored as fat and actually can help boost your metabolism. These powerful acids actually help increase immunity and fight infections.

Coconut oil can be substituted 1-for-1 in most baking recipes that call for butter or oil. You can even cook eggs in coconut oil. Any coconut flavor is hardly noticeable. The slight flavor is great and I don't miss butter at all! Occasionally I even add 2 tablespoons of coconut oil to my green smoothies for a healthy fat boost.

The triglycerides in coconut oil also help keep skin smooth and moisturized by trapping escaping moisture. It's antifungal, antibacterial, antiviral, and antimicrobial. These properties make it ideal for a multitude of epidermal uses, including soothing sunburns.

Coconut oil has about 0.1 mg of Vitamin E in 100 grams, which definitely gives it skin-nourishing properties. Vitamin E is essential for healthy skin growth; it repairs

> We constantly put a known carcinogen right into the lymph glands under our arms every day!

weathered skin, keeps skin smooth, and protects against cracking. It prevents aging and wrinkling of skin. It is also great for eczema, psoriasis, and other skin irritations.

One of my favorite uses for coconut oil is to use it as a deodorant. Aluminum is another terrible ingredient just like fluoride, yet most deodorants have it. When you look at the explosion of breast cancer and compare it against the study of aluminum, there is definitely a correlation. We constantly put a known carcinogen right into the lymph glands under our arms every day!

While we are still in the bathroom instead of the kitchen, I will tell you that I use it as a facial moisturizer and eye cream. You can also use it as eye make-up remover.   Just make sure you are using high-quality coconut oil for your face. I use organic virgin unrefined cold pressed. Remember, a little goes a long way with coconut oil. At least once a month I soak the tips of my hair in coconut oil for a few hours. Then I brush it through and massage my scalp before I shower.

You can also coat your nasal passages with coconut oil to keep nose bleeds at bay.   Because we've lived in West Texas most of our marriage, Steve always struggled with his sinuses.   When we discovered coconut oil, his nose bleeds ceased.

There are endless uses for this amazing super food. Entire books are written about this wonderful substance! It is inexpensive, yet a necessity for every healthy home.

You can buy coconut oil practically everywhere now, but don't. A discount store is not the place to buy this super food. You want to use a brand that has high standards, uses organic products and makes quality coconut oil. If you plan on using it like I do, then buy the good stuff for a little more money.

There are many websites that can give you a list of uses for coconut oil. I encourage you to research it yourself. Like I said, the internet is an amazing source of health information if you are willing to just sit and read.

Notes and Reflections

Notes and Reflections

Chapter

51   ...*Probiotics, Enzymes, Detoxing,*

and Fasting

9) PROBIOTICS

When it comes to overall health maintenance, I can't leave out a section about probiotics and enzymes. Probiotics are live microorganisms that are similar to the beneficial microorganisms found in the human digestive tract. They are also called "friendly bacteria" or "good bacteria." The idea is that the "friendly bacteria" will help fight the good fight, to scare off pathogens, improve immune function, and aid in digestion.

They impact just about everything in the body. I've read how they clear up everything from a bloated stomach to a depressed mind to acne and psoriasis. They boost the immune system and improve your skin. They delay allergies in children and prevent urinary tract infections in women. The list is truly impressive. They are probably most known for their help with irritable bowel syndrome in adults and antibiotic-induced diarrhea in children.

The following foods provide that probiotic benefit: unpasteurized miso, live cultured pickles, tempeh, unsweetened kefir, and yogurt, as well as kombucha teas. Sauerkraut and blue algae are also a great sources of probiotics. The most common form of probiotics is found in yogurt. This is a quick, easy way to get a spoonful of healthy flora. However, I encourage you to check nutrition labels, to make sure they actually have live cultures and don't have too much sugar or fat. Some yogurts are ice cream in disguise.

10) ENZYMES

The enzymes in the stomach ensure that food is cut into tiny particles that can be converted into energy in the body. Wherever one substance needs to be transformed into another, nature uses enzymes to speed up the process.

Enzymes are the workhorses of the body. The process starts in the mouth where an enzyme called amylase attacks all incoming food particles. Like a well-trained team of engineers, different enzymes continue to break down the food all the way to the stomach and intestines.

The breakdown of food is an essential part of the conversion of food into energy. Undigested food is unable to pass on the energy stored within it. The enzymes involved in the digestion process carry out the final cutting of the food particles, so they can be easily converted into the essential energy needed by all parts of our body. Enzymes are catalysts. This means that they make biochemical reactions happen faster than they would otherwise. Have you ever eaten a really big meal and just feel awful afterward?

First of all, please avoid overeating. Remember to graze. Don't gorge. But when you do eat more, take some enzymes. You can buy them at the local health food store and keep them with you in your purse or your car. They look like a roll of mints. Amylase helps digest carbohydrates. Lipase helps digest fats, and protease helps digest proteins. So if you eat a big steak dinner with a baked potato and have dessert, the enzymes you take afterward will help you feel so much better!

11) DETOXING

I'm a firm believer in the statement *"We are not fat. We are toxic."* Toxins are everywhere. They are in the water we drink, as well as the water we shower in. They are in the air we breathe. They are in the chemicals we put on our skin. They are in our cleaning agents. I could go on and on. There are over 40,000 new chemical toxins every year!

The rise in chemical toxins directly relates to the astronomical rise in obesity. When we look at obesity in children and teens, it is safe to say that they are not growing up in the same environment the older generations have enjoyed. Granted, they *are* more sedentary, but that alone does not account for the diseases they are facing.

These new chemicals are not normal in the diet and our bodies are not used to them. If it can't remove them, the body has no choice but to surround and store them to keep them from harming the internal organs. Cellulite and fat are bi-products of stored toxins due to the environmental conditions we live in, as well as the foods we consume.

You may be thinking that your body removes a lot of these toxins naturally. Well, it does have natural detox methods. Your kidneys, liver, and lungs are the three organs the body uses to help clear the toxins. But if you are full of bad habits and those organs are busy dealing with

> So the body is forced to surround those toxins with fat and water in order to protect itself from harm.

dehydration, smoking, or other challenges, then toxin removal moves to the bottom of the "most critical list." So the body is forced to surround those toxins with fat and water in order to protect itself from harm.

Even with the body's self-preservation methods, diseases like cancer – along with all kinds of auto-immune diseases – are ravaging our society and affecting one out of every two families. Diseases like dementia, Alzheimer's and Parkinson's have seen a sharp increase in the last decade. These diseases have been linked to aluminum, mercury and lead in our systems. Let me ask you: Do you use deodorant? Do you have mercury fillings in your teeth? Are you ever around paint?

In addition, pesticides are a huge culprit for the rise in those diseases. We don't think about them, but they are everywhere. They are on our lawns, our crops and the weeds on the side of the road. They are even sprayed out of airplanes. They are virtually inescapable. But I want to distinguish pesticides on our food.

Did you know there are 42 pesticides on a non-organic apple? Just because it is a fruit or vegetable doesn't mean it's healthy. Just the other day Steve and I juiced some carrots. I washed them but didn't peel them. We are used to living in Australia. The food there is amazing. There are natural markets everywhere. No pesticides, preservatives, etc.

Anyway, we couldn't drink the carrot juice. It tasted terrible! It tasted like a chemical factory. Both of our mouths went numb. I immediately got a headache and a stomach ache. Isn't that crazy? Some fruits and vegetables are more susceptible to absorbing pesticides. You need to buy organic as much as possible. If not, at least buy a fruit and vegetable spray to wash them. I certainly learned my lesson!

Here are some foods that you need to buy organic if possible: apples, peaches, nectarines, blueberries, grapes, strawberries, cucumbers, bell peppers, lettuce, kale, potatoes, spinach, celery and green beans.

Foods low in pesticides: kiwi, watermelon, mangos, grapefruit, cantaloupe (or rock melon as it's called across the pond), corn, onions, sweet peas, sweet potatoes, eggplant, cabbage and asparagus.

Back to detoxing. There are a lot of different ways to effectively reset your body. I encourage you to do some research online. Put yourself through a detox cleanse every few months.

The goal of a cleanse is to reset the body and clean the slate. No matter how healthy we try to be, we are still ingesting toxins that overwhelm our systems. Pesticides, preservatives, hormones, chlorinated water, smog – some are out of our control and some aren't. Either way, our bodies are constantly dealing with foreign intruders. Some of the effects of these toxins on our body are:

- low energy
- excess weight
- brain fog
- caffeine addiction
- craving processed foods
- acne
- dull skin

If you are experiencing any of these symptoms, chances are your body is having a hard time keeping up with what you're ingesting. A daily green smoothie is a great habit to adopt into your lifestyle, but I've learned it's just the beginning.

If you regularly put yourself through a strong cleanse, you will be amazed at how the weight falls off! Not to mention how much better you feel!

There are certain nutrients you need to effectively detox. Some of my favorite detoxifying foods are: apples, avocado, beets, blueberries, broccoli, Brussels sprouts, cabbage, carrots, cilantro, dandelion greens, flaxseeds   (freshly ground), garlic (preferably raw), grapefruit, green tea, lemons, parsley, peppers, pineapple, spinach, and tomatoes. Again make sure they are organic, if possible, or at least washed thoroughly!

Biochemical reactions occur in your body with every type of food you eat on a daily basis. Some foods age you faster than your actual years, while other foods (the ones in the last paragraph) help to fight aging. If you eat the wrong foods regularly, you can look and feel 10 or more years older than your real age. If you eat the right foods however, over time you can start to look 5-10 years younger than your real age. Oxidative damage, acidity, and inflammation are very real and they are directly tied to our diet.

> If you eat the wrong foods regularly, you can look and feel 10 or more years older than your real age.

Again, because of cell regeneration we get a whole new body each year. A completely new body, bones, blood, organs, skin, everything! If you decide to make a commitment to give your body the nutrients it needs, this time next year you will be a healthier person. Guaranteed!

Unfortunately, if you continue to eat the bad foods on my "limit these" list, this time next year you will be more acidic and less healthy – with more toxic weight. Guaranteed!

12) FASTING

I'm a huge believer in the Daniel Fast for detoxing. Here is a quick Bible story. Daniel and three of his friends were taken captive into Babylon and were forced into the service of King

Nebuchadnezzar.   Daniel made an unusual request of the King's Chief Official...

> *The king assigned them a daily amount of food and wine from the king's table.   They were to be trained for three years, and after that they were to enter the king's service.*
> *~ Daniel 1:5*

> *But Daniel resolved not to defile himself with the royal food and wine, and he asked the chief official for permission not to defile himself this way. ~ Daniel 1:8*

> *Please test your servants for ten days: Give us nothing but vegetables to eat and water to drink. Then compare our appearance with that of the young men who eat the royal food, and treat your servants in accordance with what you see." So he agreed to this and tested them for ten days. At the end of the ten days they looked healthier and better nourished than the young men who ate the royal food. So the guard took away their choice food and wine they were to drink and gave them vegetables instead. ~ Daniel 1:12-16*

We should put ourselves on the Daniel Fast regularly. This is a great way to cleanse and reset. It would yield the same results as it did for Daniel.   And benefit us in the same way!

Fasting is also an exercise of alignment. Remember that I said you can command your body to "line up" under your soul? Your mind, will, and emotions can control your body.

By fasting, you are teaching your body that you will not bow to its whims. You can effectively quiet those loud annoying cravings for foods on the "limit these" list by fasting every now and then.

Chapter
52   ...Grounding and Exercise

13) GROUNDING

I don't know about you, but when I was a kid we always played in the sprinklers. Then my mom would make us lie on the sidewalk in the sun until we were dry. I don't blame her for not wanting wet kids running through the house and she didn't see the need in lots of wet towels laying around. We played outside all the time. We climbed trees. We rolled around in the grass. We played the game of tag in the yard ...and we were always barefoot.

Now, don't think I'm weird here. I'm really excited about this! There is a pseudo-science documenting how conductive contact with the earth is highly beneficial to your health, and completely safe.

This technique is known as "Grounding or Earthing." Grounding is simply walking around with bare feet – whether it is dirt, grass, sand, or concrete – especially when it's humid or wet.

When you ground to the electron-enriched earth, an improved balance of the sympathetic and parasympathetic nervous system occurs. Grounding appears to minimize the consequences of exposure to potentially disruptive fields, like electromagnetic pollution.

Research documents that your immune system functions optimally when your body has an adequate supply of electrons, which are easily and naturally obtained by barefoot contact with the earth. Electrons from the earth have incredible antioxidant effects that can protect your body from inflammation.

Think about it. Like I just mentioned, as kids we used to run around barefoot, climb trees, and roll in the grass in our front yards. As adults we walk on asphalt, wood floors, and carpet.

Modern medical science has thoroughly documented the connection between inflammation and all of the chronic diseases, including the diseases of aging and the aging process itself. Inflammation is a condition that can be reduced or prevented by grounding your body to the earth. Negative charges have always been available, thanks to the earth, to prevent the inflammatory process from damaging healthy tissues.

This sounds crazy, but it is what virtually all of your ancestors did for thousands of years. God created conductive systems within your body that deliver electrons *from your feet* to all parts of your body. This has been the natural arrangement throughout most of human history.

Traditionally, shoes have been made of leather, which actually continued to conduct electrons and therefore maintained a conductive contact between the earth and your feet. All of this changed, however, when we began to wear shoes with rubber and plastic soles. These modern shoes are electrical insulators and therefore block the beneficial flow of electrons from the earth to your body. Interesting, right? I find it fascinating.

The earth is a natural source of electrons and subtle electrical fields which are essential for proper functioning of immune systems, circulation, synchronization of biorhythms, and other physiological processes.

> Earthing could actually be one of the most important and overlooked factors for our health.

This may actually be the most effective, essential, least expensive, and easiest way to obtain antioxidants. When you are in direct contact with the ground (walking, sitting, or lying down on the earth's surface), the earth's electrons are conducted into your body, bringing it into synchronization with the earth.

Earthing could actually be one of the most important and overlooked factors for our health. Continued research has produced amazing results. When grounding is restored, people are reporting significant improvement in a wide range of ailments, including chronic fatigue. These changes are rapid and often occur within 30 minutes. Grounding also affects cortisol dynamics, sleep patterns, inflammation, autonomic nervous system balance, muscle tension, and reduces the effects of stress.

Recent research has shown that individuals, who had previously experienced inflammatory issues, have benefited from Earthing. This includes people with various severe auto-immune diseases.

Do you remember the scene in the movie "Pretty Woman" when Richard Gere walked around outside barefooted in the grass before deciding "to do life" differently? I love that scene! I suggest we do the same. Go outside for at least 10 minutes a day. Longer if you can. Sit on the ground. Walk around barefooted outside as much as possible. Breathe deep and thank God for everything you can think of. You'll be glad you did!

14) EXERCISE

I have spent a lot of time on the foods we eat and some new technologies and concepts. But the bottom line is that our bodies need exercise. If you really want to lose weight and improve your overall health, you have to find something you enjoy and do it several times per week.

I'm not going to get specific here. I could give you an exercise regimen, but the bottom line is that if you don't enjoy doing it, you won't. So find what suits you best. You may love swimming, or riding a bicycle, or running, or racquetball, or dancing.

For me it is kickboxing. I absolutely love it! It suits my tomboy nature. I find that beating a punching bag is very satisfying. Hitting things hard deals away my stress like nothing else. That may not be for you. You may need to go for a brisk walk instead. Just MOVE. If you can exercise 30-45 minutes 3-5 times per week, you will improve your life in ways that you can't even imagine!

The key is to get your heart rate up. You have a fat-burning zone depending on your age. There are ways to calculate it. I wear a heart rate monitor. Get educated on this. Find out your own target heart rate for your specific health goals. And if you are going to exercise, make sure it counts. Be strategic!

> Building muscle is the absolute *best way* to burn fat. If you do resistance training, you will actually *reshape* your body, rather than just shrink it.

I also added weight training. That's when I took my fitness to a whole new level. Building muscle is the absolute *best way* to burn fat. If you do resistance training, you will actually *reshape* your body, rather than just shrink it. The key to weight training is to find a good personal trainer to put you on a program at first. Don't just go into a gym and start picking up weights. Frankly, it's a good way to get hurt. Make sure you know how to properly do each exercise, so that you aren't putting your body in an unnecessary bind.

Once you get on a routine though, take that personal time and *truly invest it in yourself.* Get a small mp3 player, put your favorite playlist on, and escape the world for a few minutes. Be selfish. Tell yourself out loud that your personal time for exercise is your most favorite few minutes of your day. Eventually your *body* will believe your *will.* And your personal exercise will indeed become just that. You will come to cherish that time!

If you are lifting weights, push yourself. Go to failure. Keep doing reps until you just can't do another. That's when you force the muscles to get stronger. You will love the changes your body makes! Keep track of them in your food journal. Create a place for your "exercise journal" in the same book.

Take your measurements. Take your own "before" pictures. And keep track of everything! If you are doing this in addition to cardio, as well as changing your eating habits, you will see improvements right away! Tracking it is fun.

Just remember, there is no magic bullet for weight loss. As my friend and fitness coach Tad Tomaseski says, "Calories in, minus calories burned, equals calories stored." It's a simple equation.

Think about that. If you want to lose weight, there are really only two ways. You either restrict your calories, or you burn them.

If your body burns more calories than it takes in, it is forced to burn fat instead. As a matter of fact, did you know that just 15 more minutes of cardio exercise at your target heart rate will force your body to burn calories for up to two and a half more hours than it would have? The difference between 30 minutes and 45 minutes of cardio will produce dramatically different results over time!

I highly suggest that you do both simultaneously. Start your health journey with a detoxing cleanse to reset your metabolism and clean your liver. Those effects, coupled with a change in diet and exercise, will yield dramatic results!

Chapter 53 *... Chiropractic and Consistency*

15) CHIROPRACTIC / MASSAGE

Even though massage holds that single bad memory for me, I still believe in it wholeheartedly. Massage was my full-time career for six years.

I've worked with renowned sports massage therapists and world-class chiropractors. I've had numerous continuing education hours on understanding how the skeletal and muscular systems of the body work synergistically with the sympathetic and parasympathetic nervous systems. Believe me, *it is all connected.* The human body is an absolute miracle. God designed it perfectly. And when it all works together correctly, you are unstoppable!

Chiropractic is a big deal. The spine and the nerves flowing out of the spinal vertebra control every aspect of your life. The spinal cord is your life force.

Subluxation occurs when the vertebrae in the spine are misaligned. Subluxation affects the nerves that flow out of the spinal cord to all parts of the body.

When those nerves are pinched, it affects whatever those nerves control. For example, if I put a rubber band around my finger really tight and just left it there for years, my finger would turn purple from lack of blood supply and nerve intervention and eventually it would completely malfunction. Well, what about the nerves that supply your heart or your liver?

You see, if you have ever had a pinched nerve in your back, it usually manifests as muscle or skin pain. But the internal organs don't feel pain. If the nerve supply is cut off to your internal organs, they don't tell you through pain. They just eventually malfunction. I could go on and on about the importance of maintaining your spinal health.

Please educate yourself of the benefits of a chiropractic lifestyle. If you aren't incorporating it into your health regimen, find a good chiropractor and combine it with someone who knows the muscular system... and have regular work done on your body.

If you do go to a massage therapist, just make sure they know what they are doing and it isn't just a relaxation massage. Be strategic and have the therapist work with your chiropractor to complete your health regimen. Just do me a favor and promise me you will behave yourself! (Smile...)

16) CONSISTENCY

This is the last bit of practical advice. Consistency is truly where it all comes together. Words like consistency and perseverance are not usually synonymous with words like diet and exercise. But it is *the key* to your health. You have to look at your health as a continuous journey. You may ebb and flow with the particulars of the last several pages.

But if you just know that your body is the temple of the living God and you treat it as such, then you will stay consistent. I use this scripture to keep balanced. Even though it is referring to sexual sin, this passage reminds me that I only have one body. It was purchased at a great price. My body houses *The God of the Universe!* That knowledge sobers me and helps me persevere in my health journey.

> *Do you not know that your body is a temple of the Holy Spirit, who is in you, whom you have received from God? You are not your own; you were bought at a price. Therefore honor God with your body.* ~ 1 Corinthians 6:19-20

Consider this. If you know that your body is the temple of the Holy Spirit, then every day just pray and ask the Lord for wisdom on how to take care of His temple.

On Monday, He may ask you to simply start your day with hot green tea with lemon and to eat several live foods instead of a sack of chips. On Tuesday, He may ask you to go for a walk with Him or just sit in the grass and read for about 20 minutes. On Wednesday, He may ask you to juice a green smoothie instead of a large caramel macchiato and then go for a bike ride to watch the sunset.

You get the drift. Just be obedient, and be consistent with small choices each day. Just as with me, those small choices will begin to cluster together to create an emerging portrait of health and vitality. Simple decisions compounded over time will change the direction of your health. Believe me, I am living proof.

> God wants you to be healthy! He will *partner with you* on the health of your body and the health of your soul.

Eat some yogurt instead of ice cream. Drink lemon water (with xylitol if needed) instead of your daily soft drink. Move your body. Eat live foods. Walk around barefoot for a few minutes each day. Laugh often. Commit to the journey of a lifetime.

Because your life is in fact ... a journey. No matter where you are physically, you *can* change that. God wants you to be healthy! He will *partner with you* on the health of your body and the health of your soul.

As I wrap up this section I want to give you one more scripture. Hopefully it gives you as much comfort as it does me.

> *For you created my inmost being; you knit me together in my mother's womb. I praise you because I am fearfully and wonderfully made; your works are wonderful, I know that full well. My frame was not hidden from you when I was made in the secret place. When I was woven together in the depths of the earth, your eyes saw my unformed body. All the days ordained for me were written in your book before one of them came to be.* ~ Psalm 139:13-16

You see, each of us is a divine creation of the Most High. Before we were ever even in the womb God fashioned us in the secret place. He saw our unformed body, and He has ordained our days. He *knows* us. And He *loves* us. He also knows what our particular needs are, spiritually, emotionally *and* physically.

Trust your Creator to know what you need. Follow the impressions of the Holy Spirit as He leads you to information that could radically transform your health. He will guide you, I promise!

Our time together is winding down. I find myself a little sad by that. I feel like there is more that I need to say. I need to tell you that this book is *not about the devil*. It is about *the Blood of Jesus*. It *is* designed to expose the plans and schemes of your enemy and it was necessary to expand on some of those tactics.

But it is first and foremost about how Jesus died so that you could be free. He is the King of Kings and the Lord of Lords! *All things* are under His feet. At the name of Jesus every knee shall bow and every tongue confess that He is Lord!

And Jesus gave us the authority to take back the things the devil has stolen from us. You – through the power of the Lord – have the ability to change *every aspect* of your life!

Chapter 54

...Final Thoughts and a Request

I want to give you a couple more scriptures. They applied to the Prophet Jeremiah and they apply to you.

> *Before I formed you in the womb I knew you, before you were born I set you apart. I appointed you as a prophet to the nations. "Ah, Sovereign Lord," I said, "I do not know how to speak; I am only a child." But the Lord said to me, "Do not say, 'I am only a child'..."* ~ Jeremiah 1:4-7

Jeremiah knew from the earliest age that God had a plan for his life. And He has a plan for yours. Even when you were a child. God is no respecter of persons. God does not make mistakes. He created you in His image and He created you for a specific purpose! That purpose has been hard wired into your gift mix, your talents and your passions.

> *"For I know the plans I have for you," declares the Lord. "Plans to prosper you and not to harm you, plans to give you hope and a future. Then you will call upon me and come and pray to me, and I will listen to you. You will seek me and find me when you seek me with all your heart. I will be found by you," declares the Lord...* ~Jeremiah 29:11-14

As for me, I was not able to pursue my passion and purpose because I was so bound by issues of my soul. But as my soul rested under the protection of my spirit and I was systematically set free from the bondage, I watched my body begin to respond immediately and I regained my health.

My purpose is still unfolding. But my goal is to make every day count for His glory. After my fitness career began to wind down, I took the same drive and determination and went into entrepreneurial business. I have enjoyed success in that arena for the last ten years.

Over the last decade I have occasionally missed the mark. I am not immune to sin. And I am the first to admit that since gaining my freedom all those years ago, I have blown it several times, although not at the same levels.

I have had to use this information to again renew my spirit and restore my soul. The keys herein are invaluable and I will use them the rest of my life.

At times over the past decade I have felt I disqualified myself from the mantle of heralding this message. Who am I to be an ambassador for the Lord and His life-giving freedom and abundance? Remember, the devil is still real and he is still the accuser!

> At times over the past decade I have felt I disqualified myself from the mantle of heralding this message. Who am I to be an ambassador for the Lord...?

Even so, as I stated earlier, the message of *The Three Rs* has continued to beat a steady rhythm in my heart. I finally realized that my passion for business is second to my passion for helping to unlock doors of bondage for my friends. I needed to re-engage in the fight. I needed to finish the work. I needed to sequester and write. I needed to give this life-saving message back to the Lord and let Him use it as He sees fit. It was time.

So please understand; *YOU* are my friend.

I hope that the journey you and I have taken together has enriched your life. I need to ask a couple of favors of you. Please share this book with those around you. I know that this message is edgy and raw, and could be considered controversial. But if the information has benefited you, please find someone else who is hurting, grab these keys, and start unlocking prison doors.

Also, please feel free to get copies of the book and give them as gifts to those around you who need this information. I would be honored if you use it as a "spiritual tool" for your friends and family.

We need to raise up an army of believers that are walking in freedom, health, power, and authority. People who are not afraid to walk in authentic truth. People with unveiled faces who aren't afraid to "*do greater things than Jesus did.*"

The days of deception *are coming*. And we need to be able to hear the voice of the Lord, discern it, and follow instructions with instant obedience. I have more to say about this at a later date.

Be ready...

I am looking for a team of people that would like to join me in The Three Rs message and ministry. I'm asking you to pray. God is raising up a group of people in this generation, from all over the world who are unashamed to be authentic. People who are willing to, without judgment, help others out of bondage and into freedom. I need people to help with the seminars that take place as God directs. If that is you, then please contact me on www.amysever.com I would love to hear your story!

Notes and Reflections

Notes and Reflections

Chapter 55

...My Prayer For You

Please allow me to pray for you one more time before we part.

Dear Heavenly Father,

Thank you for allowing me the opportunity to spend some time with my friend as they have traveled through the words of this book. I pray that their lives have been touched in some way. Lord, thank you for sending the Holy Spirit to continue to guide us into all truth. I thank you that He is the Comforter and the Counselor. I pray that my friend has been comforted by you. Counseled by you.

I pray that they are using the keys in this book to gain their own personal freedom. Lord, I pray that as they work through this knowledge and gain health in their body, soul, and spirit, that they would take the keys and continue to share them. I pray they would find their own purpose and passion, and that you would use them mightily in the weeks, months, and years ahead.

Thank you that you watch over your Word to perform it. I thank you that you promised that your Word never returns void, but will always accomplish your plans and purposes. I thank you that all things work together for the good of those who love you and are called according to your purpose.

Whatever circumstances my friend is facing right now, I ask that you would work all things together for their good. I pray that they would completely walk through the message of The Three Rs and would experience total health, freedom, joy, and abundance in every area of their lives. I pray that you would do exceedingly above all they could ever ask or think according to your power that is at work in them.

And now for you, my dear friend...

May God himself, the God of peace, sanctify you through and through. May your whole spirit, soul and body be kept blameless at the coming of our Lord Jesus Christ. The one who calls you is faithful and he will do it.
~ 1 Thessalonians 5:23-24

In the matchless name of Jesus I pray, Amen...

Epilogue

Thank you for reading all the way to the Epilogue. Time is the most precious commodity you have, so the fact that you have invested it with me through these pages is truly an honor. I am humbled by that.

Many times throughout the last several weeks I have become really scared. I have had days when I couldn't write. I just stared at my computer screen and wondered what in the world was I thinking? I must be crazy! Why did I start pouring out all that was inside my heart? Because now I feel responsible for the information you have just received. It is a sobering thought, and I have wrestled with it repeatedly through this whole process.

If you accept The Premises in the beginning of the book, then you know that the scriptures contained within these pages are Truth. But sometimes the truth hurts. I know that full well. Sometimes the journey to freedom is difficult. It is arduous and it takes work. I don't know your story. What I do know, however, is that after reading the entire book, yet again, there are three categories of readers.

The first category is that you are well along in your spiritual journey with Jesus Christ, as not only your Savior, but also your Lord. You have an intimate relationship with God. You are growing and maturing in your walk with the Lord.

You have a working knowledge of the fact that God sent His one and only Son to die for the sins of mankind. You know that Jesus came, was born of a virgin, lived a sinless life, was crucified for the sins of the world, and was resurrected on the third day. You know because of His resurrection, death has been defeated and Jesus made a way for us to live eternally with our Father in Heaven. You know that Jesus offers that same gift for all mankind. He is the only way to the Father. You know that when Jesus ascended back to the Father,

He sent the Holy Spirit to guide you and comfort you. And you have accepted all of this as Truth and have invited Jesus Christ into your life.

You understand spiritual warfare. You also understand that your walk with the Lord is a beautiful journey and that you constantly have to strive to maintain freedom from sin and continually nurture your relationship with the Lord. You have invited the Holy Spirit to come on you in power and authority and you are moving in the gifts of the Spirit. You are developing your passion and your gift mix and are following the Lord on His path for your life. You are walking it out in joy and freedom. And you are experiencing the abundance promised to us as our inheritance.

If that is you, then this book makes sense. Hopefully, you have experienced some new revelation on how it all ties together and you know people that would benefit from the information.

The second category is that you believe all of the above, you have accepted Christ as your Savior, and you know for a fact you are saved. You are going to Heaven. But you are *not* experiencing the joy, freedom and abundance that we are entitled to as sons and daughters of the Most High.

You are like I was. Or so many of the other examples in this book. You know you have areas of bondage that you need to deal with. As you have worked through these pages, the Holy Spirit has been gently speaking to you about areas in your life that need the touch of the Master's Hand. You know that your soul has taken some hits and the Lord is dealing with you about gaining freedom from strongholds. You know you need to break chains of bondage off of your life.

If you are in that category, then pray. Ask the Lord what your next step should be. For some it is just that you make lists of words, soul ties, areas of strongholds, and those you need to forgive. You need to inventory your life in depth. Spend quality time with the Lord, and let the Holy Spirit guide you. Work through the steps outlined in the chapters. It doesn't have to be a long, drawn-out process.

You can "recover yourself" from the snares of the devil. You can just work through it and repent, renounce, break it off, and use specific scriptures from the Word of God to speak blessing into those areas of your life.

I still do this when I miss the mark. I just stop and turn around. I have an intimate relationship with the Lord, and when I sin I immediately feel the conviction of the Holy Spirit. I never want to grieve the Lord, so I repent quickly and close any doors that I may have opened in the process of my sin. It is an ongoing relationship of intimacy and fulfillment. I am constantly working to renew my spirit.

You may also be in that second category, but you know that you are dealing with things you can't handle on your own. My life was a great example of that. I had to have help from Steve and several others. If you have had any kind of physical, emotional, psychological, or spiritual trauma, then you may need help working through deliverance from the bondage that trauma created.

This book may have stirred up a hornet's nest. It may have created a deep anger. I know that I was angry the night of "Forgiveness." I hated the guy in the front of the room! It was as if a sleeping python in the pit of my stomach woke up and began to uncoil. It proceeded to try and choke the life out of me. And I didn't even know it was there! I thought I *had* forgiven. So I know full well this information may have caused things that have been lying dormant to wake up and uncoil inside the recesses of your soul.

So many are dealing with demonic interference and have just lived with it. Just like me, you may not have known what it was or that you could be free from the torment. This book may have exposed the plans of the enemy in your life. You are now aware of the devil's schemes. Please, if that's you, find help. There are very effective deliverance ministries available. I believe those most effective are found in non-denominational or inter-denominational churches. The basis for these types of ministries must be Jesus ...not church doctrine. These churches will understand demonic deliverance.

Some have ministries that specifically deal with freedom from bondage. Here is what I know. If the Lord has led you this far, He absolutely will lead you to the next step toward your freedom.

I feel compelled to tell you though, that if you aren't ready to take the *whole trip* of restoration of the soul, please don't start the journey yet. Think what would have happened with me if I had not walked *completely through* forgiveness that night. Once I got the information on soul ties, the bondage reacted. Once you wake it all up, you definitely need to get rid of it. What if I had left Leah in the state she was in that last day of class? Or Deborah and Braden in marital turmoil without working through everything and breaking it off and casting out the spirits that were tormenting them? What if I had left Elaine alone to deal with the shadows of her home? All of these people were in need of finishing the work they started – once they got the information.

The freedom they experience today is *so* worth the work it took to get there. My freedom is *so* worth it. But you have to count the cost yourself. There most certainly is a price to pay. You may need to just hide the information in your heart and pray for wisdom on the right timing. You may have a spouse that isn't ready or willing to walk through it with you. Just use wisdom. Because the devil *will* throw all kinds of things at you to keep you from walking it out. He did that to me. My ruptured cyst on the night of soul ties is a prime example. So please pray for that wisdom. It is so necessary!

If you *do* decide to wrestle for your freedom, just make sure that you finish what you start. Do not stop until you know you've won the victory! Believe me, you *will* know it. You will immediately feel the release. Sometimes demons try to make a dramatic exit. Again, please seek counsel and wisdom from people involved in a deliverance ministry. Make sure you have people interceding for you. I salute you for working through it. You will be so glad you did!

Now for the third category of reader. After reading this book you know you have never accepted Christ as your personal Savior. As you read the first category in this epilogue, the Holy Spirit was convicting you that *you need that relationship.* You have a spiritual void in your life.

You may be a very spiritual person, but you don't have an intimate relationship with the ONE who created the spiritual realm. You may have been on a spiritual journey and just like Elaine, you may have entertained spirits, but not the *Holy Spirit.* Or like Steve, you may have grown up in a church and just never came to a saving knowledge of Jesus Christ.

I want to speak directly to your heart right now. Because if that is you, then you can change that. It only takes a willing heart. Jesus Christ is *the only true answer* for every question, every problem, every sickness of your body, every problem of your soul, and the emptiness of your spirit. If you know you want to accept the Lord as your Savior and also receive the baptism of the Holy Spirit, then please pray this prayer with me:

Dear Heavenly Father,

Thank you for sending your Son, Jesus. I come to you in His Name. Your Word says that "everyone who calls on the name of the Lord will be saved." (Acts 2:21)

So I call on You now. I know that I am a sinner, and my sins have separated me from you. I realize that you sent your Son to die for my sins, so I could be reconciled back to you. So I pray and ask Jesus to come into my heart and be my Lord and Savior. According to Romans 10:9-10:

If I confess with my mouth Jesus is Lord, and believe in my heart that God raised Him from the dead, I will be saved. For it is with my heart that I believe and am justified, and it is with my mouth that I confess and am saved.

I do that now. I confess that Jesus is Lord and I believe that God raised Him from the dead. Thank you for saving me! Thank you that I am now a child of God!

Now, according to your Word that says in Luke 11:19, "If you then, though you are evil, know how to give good gifts to your children, how much more will your Father in Heaven give the Holy Spirit to those who ask him!" So I am asking you, Father, for the Gift of the Holy Spirit. Holy Spirit, please come on me now. Fill me with power. In Jesus' Name, Amen!

If you just prayed that prayer, then *Praise God!* You are saved! You can now begin your walk with the Lord. You are already so far ahead of most Christians because you have just spent time working through all the ways the enemy can trip you up. So you know the pitfalls. As a matter of fact, you now need to enter directly into category two. Go back and read all that again, because it now applies to you. You can be saved, spirit-filled, and set free all in a short amount of time. I know that is what the Lord desires. He wants to collapse time frames for you.

The whole purpose of this book is just that: For the Lord to use my journey to help others take months, years, and decades out of the equation. He wants to start collapsing time frames for the body of Christ. God wants to take you from bondage to freedom in a few days or a couple of weeks at most. To move you gently but quickly through the process of deliverance and inner healing so you can finally put the trauma of the past under your feet. So that the wounds can become scars and you can walk in the abundance of your inheritance. I pray that is your story!

But I must also caution you. Please do not attempt to gain freedom from demonic strongholds without first being saved. If you have not prayed the prayer above and are considering working through your strongholds, please read this scripture. It is sobering. Let it sink in...

When an evil spirit comes out of a man, it goes through arid places seeking rest and does not find it. Then it says, "I will return to the house I left." When it arrives, it finds the house unoccupied, swept clean and put in order. Then it goes and takes with it seven other spirits more wicked than itself, and they go in and live there. And the final condition of that man is worse than the first. ~ Matthew 12:43-45

These are the words of Jesus. Please heed them. Remember what I explained about the difference between possession and oppression? If you have a wicked spirit *possessing* you and you cast it out but don't fill your spirit with the Spirit of Christ, then you *will* be visited again. I have seen this happen. Please do not let it happen to you! Make sure the Spirit of the Lord is there instead.

So again, if you are going to take the journey, make sure you take the *whole trip* and are committed to finish the work. And I also say again, *it is so worth it!*

Here is what I promise. God will walk with you every step of the way. He knows you at the deepest level. He created your inmost being. He understands your pain. He holds every tear you have ever cried. He loves you so much! And He wants you to be free! Full of health, joy, and vitality. He wants you to be walking out your passion for life. And He is willing to go to the ends of the earth with you. No matter where you are at this moment in your life, He will find you. And He will sustain you.

> *Where can I go from your Spirit? Where can I flee from your presence? If I go up to the Heavens, You are there; if I make my bed in the depths, You are there. If I rise on the wings of the dawn, if I settle on the far side of the sea, even there Your Hand will guide me, Your Right Hand will hold me fast.* ~ Psalm 139:7-10

I want to leave you with two more scriptures and a promise that I am constantly praying for those of you that are receiving the information on these pages! May God bless you on your journey!

> *What, then, shall we say in response to this? If God is for us, who can be against us? He who did not spare His own Son, but gave Him up for us all – how will He not also, along with Him, graciously give us all things? Who will bring any charge against those whom God has chosen? ...Christ Jesus, who died - more than that, who was raised to life – is at the right hand of God and is also interceding for us. Who shall*

separate us from the love of Christ? Shall trouble or hardship or persecution or famine or nakedness or danger or sword...? No, in all things we are more than conquerors through Him who loved us. For I am convinced that neither death nor life, neither angels nor demons, neither the present nor the future, nor any powers, neither height nor depth, nor anything else in all creation, will be able to separate us from the love of God that is in Christ Jesus our Lord. ~ Romans 8:31-37

I thank God every time I remember you. In all my prayers for all of you, I always pray with joy because of your partnership in the gospel from the first day until now, being confident of this, that He who began a good work in you will be faithful to complete it until the day of Christ Jesus. ~ Philippians 1:3-6

~ Amy Sever

Notes and Reflections

Notes and Reflections

Notes and Reflections

Notes and Reflections

About the Author

After finding the freedom that Amy Sever writes about in this book, at 5'2" and 170 lbs, she made the decision to lose her weight. One year later she became involved in the fitness industry. Within three years she won 1st Place in the North American Nova Championship and 2nd Place in the World Galaxy Competition.

Today, because of her demanding schedule, Amy travels extensively, having business in the United States and abroad. But she will tell you that her heart is for this message and ministry. It takes precedence, because the journey to freedom found in these pages is what has made her other successes possible.

To find out more, or contact Amy, go to www.AmySever.com.